Executive

EXECUTIVE

Harry Levinson

with the assistance of Cynthia Lang

Harvard University Press
Cambridge, Massachusetts
and London, England

Library of Congress Cataloging in Publication Data

Levinson, Harry.
  Executive.

  Original ed. published in 1968 under title: The
exceptional executive.
  Includes bibliographical references and index.
  1. Executives.   2. Leadership.   I. Lang,
Cynthia.   II. Title.
HF5500.2.L375 1981   658.4'2   80-26107
ISBN 0-674-27395-8 (cloth)
ISBN 0-674-27396-6 (paper)

To those dedicated teachers
who made the most difference

Sarah Haney Zeh

Isabelle M. DeWolfe

Edward W. Geldreich

M. Wesley Roper

George R. R. Pflaum

David Rapaport

John W. Chotlos

Karl A. Menninger

William C. Menninger

Gertrude R. Ticho

Preface

Since the 1960s the business environment has changed radically, forcing executives to learn how to deal with new problems and situations. Top management is now deeply involved in pollution control, complying with health and safety standards, product liability, and affirmative action. Tension has grown between middle and top managers, owing in part to the pressures of inflation. And women and minority-group members are taking positions of managerial responsibility formerly reserved for white, middle-class males.

Today the business leader's fundamental function is to perpetuate the organization. In order to survive the cycles of individual industries, organizations frequently need to diversify. They grow—both in size and complexity—by accretion, acquisition, internal expansion, and agglomeration. Despite the heavy emphasis on MBO (management by objective) programs and on pleasing security analysts, it is clear that the reason for such growth is to ensure the company's survival. Organizations can no longer operate for the short run without considerable cost to themselves, to their geographical localities, and to the nation as a whole, as the predicaments of Lockheed and Chrysler have shown.

Executives who do not build adaptive capacity in their followers or subordinates do their organizations and their employees a disservice. If an executive is to be concerned with perpetuation, then his or her role as a teacher becomes central: this point, made in the original edition of this book (*The Exceptional Executive*, 1968) has been borne out in the years since its publication. Because in 1968 so few executives practiced the role of teacher, I labeled the teaching executive the "exceptional" executive. But the function is now commonplace. Management training at various levels has proliferated, with an increase in M.B.A. candidates, the development of in-house company institutes that frequently rival business schools, and the establishment of other kinds of training institutions. Adult educational opportunities are available in a wide range of community institutions. Not only is learning a life-long process, but a fundamental task of the executive is to teach people how to adapt more effectively, both on their own behalf and on behalf of the organization. For this reason, the title of this revised work is no longer *The Exceptional Executive*, but merely *Executive*.

Since the 1960s almost all managers have become more aware of the importance of psychological issues in management and leadership. This does not necessarily mean that these issues are better understood. People still want quick and immediate answers to complex problems, and much of the new-found "knowledge" about matters psychological is in the form of clichés, gimmicks, slogans, and techniques. Since everyone is human, each presumably is an expert on what motivates humans. This book, while taking into account the complexity of psychological dynamics, attempts to describe them in a straightforward way.

It has also become clear that business leaders must deal with multiple constituencies. Over the years higher management has become increasingly involved with all levels of government; a large company's affairs may even be adjudicated by the Supreme Court. When years ago I described the executive as a social engineer, the need to interact with multiple constituencies was on the horizon. Now it is in full view, and examples of such interaction have been included here.

Another change in the nature of the organization concerns middle management. Fifteen years ago, it was simply assumed that middle management would go along with whatever higher management dictated. Now many middle managers feel that the illusions held out by profit-sharing, stock options, bonuses, and other forms of supplementary compensation have turned out to be just that: illusions. Few believe that they have had an opportunity to build an estate, after having sacrificed for many years as their superiors demanded, to attain and sustain the profitability of their organizations. This dissatisfaction and alienation, too, will be examined in the pages that follow.

What about the people who *are* the organization? There is a growing need for executives who have the capacity to abstract at higher levels, to discern complexity and live with ambiguity. This is partly a product of the increasing size of organizations, partly a product of geopolitical and highly complex socioeconomic issues. In turn, expectations have risen regarding the level of competence of executives and the people who follow them. This means that executives must become leaders who will teach their followers to be more effective. Executives who cannot do so tend to withdraw into paralysis and let their organizations drift—to the dismay of their employees and the loss of their stockholders.

As requirements for leadership have become more sharply defined, new actors have entered the arena. The presence of women and minority-group members has engendered both conflict and vitality, and an important task of this book on leadership is to address some of the ramifications of their energy in the world of management.

Things have changed in other ways. The information explosion is now an old story. Organizations must move ever more rapidly. Competition is keen as new discoveries are quickly turned into products and as the costs of advertising and promotion rise astronomically. Organizations that seek to perpetuate themselves must act with aggressive agility, but many have acted too hastily. Decentralization has been effected, often without adequate coordination and communication, and without psychological help for those who must accept, accommodate to, or effect the changes. The cry for greater productivity has become shrill, but most of the widely heralded efforts that have been implemented lack solid psychological foundations and shrivel quickly into obscurity.

As Harvard professor George Lodge has pointed out, our society has become increasingly communitarian. We recognize the interaction of all kinds of forces and their effects on people, particularly those set in motion by business organizations (such as efforts to improve the quality of working life) and those resulting from the social growth of mutual-help and support groups. But neither businesses, communities, nor social groups can accomplish anything without effective leadership. Leaders must be prepared to understand their contemporary role and to act accordingly. This book is designed to foster such understanding—to help senior executives learn more about their role from a psychological point of view and to help them meet the expectations of their organization and the public.

Although a great deal of research has been conducted on various aspects of leadership, much of it is still in an early stage of development and is not yet sufficiently refined and integrated to form a firm base for a theory about the leadership role. Readers therefore should view much of what I offer here as conceptual and not experimental. The test should be whether what I have written fits their experiences or helps them better understand and respond to the problems they face as executives. The addition of case studies—a major new element in this revised edition—will help define the links between theory and practice and should enable the reader to work with the ideas more concretely. These case studies, along with other situational examples used in the book, have been adapted from problems presented to me by executives over the years. The names of the persons involved have been altered.

Finally, I wish to recognize the contributions of Cynthia Lang, whose perceptive insights and editorial contributions helped shape this book.

H.L.

CONTENTS

 **PART 1**

Management is, all things considered, the most creative of all arts. It is the art of arts. Because it is the organizer of talent.
—Jean-Jacques Servan-Schreiber

Defining
the Problem

The essence of management is indeed the organization of talent, as Servan-Schreiber says. But what sort of talent? The answers to this question are as numerous as the problems faced by an executive during a lifetime of work. The art of executive management, as it has been developing, is just able to keep pace with the changes presented by the larger world. Its greatest source of strength lies not in computer modeling or the use of econometric forecasts, helpful though these tools clearly are, but in the best use of human resources. The leader is the one who can use these resources, but in order to use them well he or she must understand them.

The human landscape is made up of geography and atmosphere, personal psychology and social cross-currents, changing patterns and lasting perspectives. Part One examines some of the complex interactions of power relationships, personality theory, social change, and assumptions about motivation. It draws on some classic conceptual outlines and augments them with events and discoveries currently taking place in the fields of medicine, management, psychology, and marketing—in fact, in any of the fields that contribute to an understanding of the way in which people operate and of the problems they encounter in the context of achieving personal and organizational goals.

Rate of change is one of the most conspicuous aspects of

organizational life. The problem is not so much that we cannot be sure what tomorrow will bring, but that each executive must decide how best to marshal the abilities and talents of the people with whom he or she works and to focus them on the tasks at hand and—at the same time—on the task of inventing the future.

ONE Tomorrow's Executive

I'd just mastered the game, and then they changed the rules" is a complaint heard often in the last quarter of a century, which has seen more changes than any other in the history of man. The changing rules and the changing nature of the game are features of life in family structures, political strategy, personal life stories, and cultural trends. They are a major feature of the construct we call "the organization" and the character part we call "the executive." We speak frequently of "the organization" as if it were a clearly defined concept. Yet the definition in the sense of "a body of persons organized for some specific purpose" is so diffuse that it could be applied, without criticism, to a bridge club or the United States Congress. Many of the difficulties encountered by organizations and their members derive from this lack of understanding, or, more probably, from a misunderstanding: we think we know what is meant, but on closer examination it turns out that we do not.

Specifying that in a given context "organization" means a private business, and not the bridge club or Congress, trims away some of the ambiguity but not nearly enough. The problem, of course, is not to rewrite definitions of the organization for use in upcoming editions of Webster's—a job for the lexicographer—but to surmount the difficulties inherent in managing an organization when misunderstanding exists about its boundaries, purpose, and responsibilities. And managing the organization *is* the job for executives. ·

The corporation, as has been obvious for years, is not a feudal empire run at one person's pleasure for arbitrary reasons. It survives at the pleasure and discretion of the public, which purchases its goods and services; when the public no longer wants these goods, the corporation's days are numbered. But the links between the organization and the consumer public go beyond this level of quid pro quo. What is less obvious is that the corporation is a public trust and not simply an economic instrument. The corporation has an impact on all sides of society, exerting power that is social as well as economic. A corporation, not to mention an entire industry, can manipulate prices, influence housing and employment patterns by opening and closing plants, make changes in governmental and legislative practices through lobbying, and affect the natural environment through pollution or conservation. When businesses were owned and managed by the same people, as family-owned businesses still are, the double investment of ownership plus management served to integrate them socially and economically with the community. The divorce of ownership from management has had a ripple effect: corporate managers are less sensitive to the social implications of their actions. Being transient, they are not as personally involved in the community as they would be if they had always lived there and always would. Power, with some exceptions, is no longer the feudal issue that it used to be.

Ambiguity about the nature of the organization contributes to uncertainty about the role of executives. The definition of an executive as "someone capable of carrying out duties and functions" still begs the question, and leaves unanswered the crucial one: What are those duties and functions, and who is to decide which are the most important?

One problem with being an executive these days is that a person can no longer be an executive in the classical sense. Traditional ways of wielding managerial power have become obsolete. The historical conception of the executive, whether company president, admiral, secretary of state, or bishop, is that he directs and commands. (And in the historical view, of course, the executive is a man.) He plans, decides, assigns, and controls. True, he may have assistants with varying responsibilities, but in such a conception it is he who *does*. If the business year has been a successful one, he has made it so. If the war is won, he has won it. He may be magnanimous enough to share his glory with his subordinates or democratic enough to share his decision-making with some of them, but there is no question that when he does so, *he shares.*

Characteristically, the executive has an image of himself as combination coach, quarterback, linebacker, and end. He designs the plays and calls the signals. He evolves strategy and manages tactics. He tackles the competition head-on, or makes brilliant broken-field marketing runs, or throws surprise product passes over the heads of the competition, or punts the economic ball safely out of danger by merger, cost-cutting, or some other emergency device. And he does it every season.

Such an image is largely fantasy. No executive can run an organization this way any more than a football coach can both execute strategy and play on the team. The contemporary business scene is vastly different from that of a century ago. With less outright power to face greater responsibility, the executive can no longer function effectively by control and command. The Imperial German General Staff Plan—the most commonly used organization chart, with its underlying assumption of control from the top—is obsolete, for the more rigidly an organization is controlled the less its adaptibility. The executive role has changed, too. Current executive practice is as radically different from nineteenth-century procedure as is driving a stagecoach from piloting a supersonic airliner. Often, however, executives are trapped by the organizational structure and reward-punishment concept of management that keeps them from being able to act as freely as they would like. It is the conflict between this expectation of themselves and the realities of organizational life that causes much of the pain of leadership.

These realities are a function of the distribution of power. Power exists only in relation to other people who also have certain kinds of power. These people have expectations of the way in which leadership power should be used. Unless they can be coerced into doing what the leader wishes them to do, they will use their power against him. Therefore, the task of the executive in dealing with these realities is not to pit his or her power against other sources of power, although sometimes this may be necessary. Rather it is to meet the expectations of the other powerholders so that they willingly lend their power to further the interests of the organization.

There are essentially five sources of power related to organizations. Each has its own expectations. These facets of power can be illustrated by the experience of a small businessman. A man or woman who goes into business to earn a livelihood may have acquired a skill or invented a product, rented a shop or bought a truck. Sometimes the business grows because the owner is very capable, or perhaps innovative, or sometimes just lucky. Whatever the case, as soon as the business begins to expand, it is no longer merely a means of earning a livelihood. It becomes a locus of power, and the owner begins to create both expectations of and responsibility for himself.[1]

First, the owner creates a dual relationship with the public: he incurs both the obligation to serve and the obligation not to harm. Football fans, the clientele of a government bureau, and the customers of a department store all have one thing in common: they require services or goods and they demand that certain needs be met. The more they demand of a given vendor or entrepreneur, the more powerful they make him—that is, the larger and more successful he becomes. This success has two consequences: the more powerful the owner becomes the more he has a vested interest in maintaining and protecting that power, and the greater is his potential power to hurt those who avail themselves of his goods or services. Leaders of such an enterprise lose their power when the fans no longer come to watch the game, the clientele disappears, or the customers turn to other products. They therefore must continuously generate special publics if they are to retain power.

The executive creates an obligation to serve when his company offers goods or services; indeed, an organization must continue to exist if it is to serve. When it becomes apparent that people are injured by what the owner does or sells, the owner's obligations to the customer are increased in number and complexity. Government controls were established to counteract the increasing power of the entrepreneur to hurt others, however unintentionally. Every corner drive-in needs half a dozen licenses. Every pharmaceutical manufacturer must conform to the requirements of the Food and Drug Administration before marketing a new drug. If a mail-order book club fails to live up to its promises, a purchaser can use the strength of the United States Postal Service to obtain redress. The entrepreneur as an executive thus incurs both public responsibility and public obligation.

Second, when an owner's business grows, he or she creates a financial obligation. A fundamental problem of every small business is the fact that the owner rarely has sufficient capital for growth needs. Sooner or later the entrepreneur must "go public" with a stock-offering or obtain long-term credit from banks, in either case incurring an obligation to those who invest in the business, an obligation backed by law and assorted regulatory bodies. Once this step is taken, others have an interest in the survival of the business beyond the owner's lifetime.

This, too, is a power relationship in which owners must maintain their own strength while at the same time drawing on the strength of others. The executive must cope with the broad, uncrystallized power of mass ownership—stockholders, alumni, constituents, or (if leading a trade association, professional organization, or union) various kinds of publics such as grocers, teachers, and bricklayers. From this source of power owners must draw and maintain support without harming. They must prevent the inherent power in the mass from being fragmented and destroying the group, as in a proxy fight, and must keep the power from being used against themselves if they want to maintain their leadership position. They must capitalize on the resources inherent in the mass to further the organization and to return value to the investors.

Third, the owner must contend with the concentrated distillation of the power of the mass in the form of a board of directors or its equivalent. This means that owners have to deal with others who are, as they experience it, intruders into the business. Furthermore, in many organizations the government shares control with the corporation's board (antitrust, the Federal Trade Commission, the National Labor Relations Board, and so on) to minimize harm to the public.

Fourth, owners enter their power into competition with the power of others when they begin competing for the same public. Much of the time they compete under tournament rules: codes of ethics, trade association policies, informal norms, industry self-policing, and accrediting bodies. In addition, they often have the protection of governmental practices such as tariffs, rate controls, inspections, and quotas. These controlling and protecting devices become instruments for the survival of the organization beyond the individual. The license to operate a television station, a farmer's wheat allotment quota, and a

commuter airline's subsidy all have commercial value and ensure the continued function of that production or service unit.

*Fifth, owners incur obligations to the people to whom they give di-
rect leadership—employees, subordinates, colleagues.* This is the facet
of power with which the modern executive has the most difficulty and the greatest pain. Just how much pain is reflected in
a common issue in labor relations, "management's right to
manage," and in the widespread phenomenon called "management by guilt."[2]

The social importance of the executive's power in relation
to employees is evident in the process of hiring and firing. A
firm with only a few employees would create little stir if it
went out of business or discharged long-term employees. But
a larger firm which does the same is resented by the community at large for being irresponsible. Both employees and community regard such action as unfair. The employer's obligation to employees is reinforced by court decisions holding that
a person has a vested interest in his or her job. Workers cannot be deprived of this interest as a result of a merger or of ca-
pricious relocation of the firm.[3] Economic obligations to employees are now fixed by tradition and union contract.

Think again of the executive's expectation of himself. People's expectations of themselves and of the way in which they
should use power have many origins—in the personalities of
the individuals who seek positions of power, in the traditional
conceptions of the way in which power is to be used, in the
modes by which power is acquired, and in the multiple
sources of power already discussed. Power accretes like fat on
a middle-aged man. Before a man realizes it, he has girth. Even
when he becomes aware of his girth, it does not seem nearly as
large to him as it is in reality and as it appears to others. Similarly, often before he realizes it, a man has power—power that
seems greater to others than it does to him.

The head of an organization unwittingly assumes the responsibility of being all things to all employees who work for
the organization. Chief executives must revere the past, predict and succeed in the future, make a profit, carry the burdens
of people and operations no longer efficient, and enjoy themselves besides. Their whims become magnified into other people's law, try as they may to make it clear that a whim is not
the same as a law.

If an executive demands that the people produce, he is exploitative. If he treats them with beneficence, he is paternalistic. If he is unconcerned about their worries, he is rejecting. If he opposes what he believes to be irrational, he is hostile. If he gives in, he is weak. Unlike his predecessors, he does not always know which way to turn.

In addition to more complex responsibilities within the organization itself, contemporary executives are the pivots for vast technological and social changes. They are expected to assume a major responsibility for training and employing the disadvantaged members of society—drop-outs, the handicapped, the aging, and minority groups. They also are expected to arrange matters so that as technical efficiency increases, those whose skills have become obsolete will not be discharged. Furthermore, they are expected to assume a leadership role in their industry and community. Indeed, they expect themselves to fulfill these responsibilities. They are frequently conscience-driven.

These people suffer the same internal turmoil that every other person must live with and, in some respects, a little more. The leader must never admit to being frightened or ignorant, for the leader's doubts become the subordinates' panic. Yet leaders are perennially vulnerable, sometimes like blind people who must operate by echoes and soundings. They can never know all that they need to know to make wise decisions. Counselors advise, often for their own purposes. A trusted secretary is no less manipulative than a lieutenant, not because they both are dishonest but because each sees the world in his or her own way and wants to go that way.

Rivalry is also a problem. To achieve the pinnacle, leaders must pass others by, some older, some seemingly more capable. They may have arrived at the top by dethroning a less successful predecessor. If they came from humble origins, each advancing step was also a step further away from the family. For some, these experiences produce feelings of guilt and the anxiety of adapting to successively higher social roles. Additional anxiety results from knowing that others are competing for the top spot. Ultimately leaders will have to give up their position, and the higher they rise, the more painful will be the fall if they fail.

In one direction, then, executives must grasp the realities

of the distribution of power. In another direction they must recognize that the environment is changing continuously and must react to the changes rapidly, creatively, and productively.

Responding to the Environment

The organization exists as part of the community, depending for its market on the interest and goodwill of the consumers in the community. It exerts social power by manipulating prices, opening and closing plants, polluting and cleaning up the atmosphere, lobbying to affect legislation. In turn, it incurs social obligations. If it fails to meet these, it may find that its ability to operate in the community is curtailed. The organization cannot view itself only as a profit center and expect to last.

In countless ways, then, the success of the organization depends on the ability of its executives to assess what is happening in the community—to test the waters, read accurately the present state of affairs, and make and adjust plans accordingly. Writing about modes of management, Leslie Dawson describes a bit of graffiti written on a New York sidewalk. "Marvin can't relate to his environment," said the words in cement, and, as Dawson points out, they form a potential epitaph for any organizational executive.[4]

The need to relate to the environment is clear. How to go about it is another matter. One metaphor to consider, in thinking about the best way to proceed, comes from the space industry. Early on, spacecraft were designed and launched with finely calibrated directional instructions, so that from the moment of lift-off the entire journey, with all of the subtle shifts and changes necessary for the craft to proceed through its orbit, was already programmed, in a kind of spatial predestination. Later, however, as technical capabilities increased and a track record of successes and failures in space launchings accumulated, a different approach was preferred. The craft was launched, not carelessly, to be sure, but with less finely calibrated adjustments; all of the fine tuning necessary to keep it in the best flight pattern was then carried out in progress, to accommodate to the actual rather than the projected realities of the journey.

One difficulty with long-range planning is that it calls for a particular kind of abstract thinking, and in the top-level corporate talent market the kind of person who can make major, high-level decisions is not always easy to find.[5] Another difficulty is that nearly all long-range planning is based on present data, extended into the future without taking into account the degree to which these data will bend as the future inches into the present. Robert Heilbroner has pointed out that economists failed to predict the five major economic trends since 1945: strong growth in the industrial world, chronic inflation, the weakening of the United States' position in the international economic arena, the rise of the multinational corporation as the main instrument of international economic relations in the capitalist world, and the advent of environmental constraints as a major economic problem.[6] Even econometrics forecasting, which uses elaborate computer models to make economic predictions, is based almost entirely on past history and often does not take into account fundamental changes in economic conditions.[7]

The present direction of economic changes has been apparent for some time: slowed growth in the industrial nations, a shortage of capital investment, scarcity of resources, and uncertainty about future growth. Overall, it can be seen in the slowed rate of increase in productivity in the manufacturing sector in all industrial nations; in some major industrial groups, it shows up as an actual decline in worker output.[8] Other influences, such as the gradual aging of the population, alter the nature of the business scene. The post–World War II baby boom is moving through the population curve like a goat through a boa constrictor. Today's economy reflects the interests of a youthful market, but as the population ages, configurations of products, services, and sales can be expected to change. Patterns in the clothing, recreation, travel, and entertainment industries will shift. In the United States there is likely to be increased demand on the health-care community and a drop in the home-building industry.[9]

Economic, demographic, and social trends can interact to produce uncertainty and confusion in the general population. A business does not need to be directly involved in energy, for instance, to feel keenly the impact of energy shortages. Boredom, alienation, and stress among workers have been reported, both by the workers themselves and by their supervisors. In a recent interview, first-level foremen in a gas company mentioned that the newly recruited young people they supervised were quickly bored with their routine work. The supervisors felt that they should be doing something to stimulate the recruits because they were going to be doing the same routine work for the next thirty years! Executives recognize that this malaise is not restricted to line workers. Restlessness exists in middle-management as well, because with slowed growth there are fewer opportunities for moving up. Ambitious managers, stalled at an intermediate rung, are frustrated. In the lush times of the mid-sixties they could have moved to another organization if they felt blocked, but now there are few open slots available.

From the point of view of executives, responsible for the perpetuation of an organization, what kinds of solutions exist to these problems? One of the most common proposals is to reorganize. Reorganization usually means a broad-scale, radical restructuring of the group: existing managers change chairs, some people—deadwood or controversial—are removed, and new people are brought in. Reorganization often takes place in response to a crisis, or in a last-ditch effort to head off an impending catastrophe. It has all the appearance of solving a problem.

There is another approach to meeting the changes of the environment—an approach that permits flexibility and does not depend on radical, crisis-situation responses to be effective. It consists of a systematic use of the best people for a given job, under the conditions that prevail at the time. A good way to understand the approach is to compare it to football. The coach, as the executive of the team, assesses the situation at any given moment and, taking into account the particular strengths of the players on his defensive and offensive teams, plugs them into situations where their skills are needed. This requires more than a knowledge of each player's abilities: the coach has to size up all the conditions (prevailing wind, state of the ground, knowledge of opposing players) and then decide who is the best player for a particular play—this time. He must be able to interchange players year after year without losing the vitality of the team, and therefore must constantly be developing men. His plays must fit the changing skills of new men, the yearly changes in rules, and the varying characteristics of different playing fields and opponents. Plays that work brilliantly in the sunny, early fall may fail miserably in bitter cold and mud. Technical innovation, such as the introduction of the forward pass, requires drastic reorganization of tactics and demands new player skills. A team that does not have weight in a given year must have speed and plays that call for speed. A team that has neither weight nor speed must have determination. As the players have become more educated, coaches have found it wise to let them make more decisions on the field. Some football coaches have even turned to computers to analyze the myriad data that affect performance.

Organizations, too, can operate on the assumptions at work in a football game. Organizations need both offensive and defensive teams and need people in reserve—"substitute players" who can be placed in temporary roles. This creates greater flexibility and responsiveness in the face of changes in the marketplace, the supply of materials, and government regulation. The approach requires a number of things. First, one must believe that the football model is the best one. Second, behavioral job descriptions are needed to enable the organization to meet the demands of a varied environment. An organization has to switch tactics quickly when the game changes, which means that roles may stay but different people will be shifted in and out of them. Managers will need help in evaluating their own strengths, weaknesses, and behavioral styles, and this will require serious attention to the selection and assignment of people in managerial roles. Third, the approach calls for continuing education—a program that will pick up the people presently in reserve and sharpen their competencies and skills, perhaps sending some people back to school. It means creating a psychological climate in which employees are not made unnecessarily anxious by being asked to change roles from month to month. Fourth, when workers do become obsolete, help is needed in arranging financial packages, transitional activities, or outplacement services. Fifth, counseling by psychologists or psychiatrists would be desirable, to help people adapt to the anxiety resulting from frequent role changes.

This model poses some problems. "Matrix management," one method of moving people in and out of roles, is designed to give people more flexibility and involvement in their work, and is supposed to cure all kinds of managerial ills. But too often people in matrix organizations do not know what they own, whether it is a job, an accomplishment, or the satisfaction of seeing the effect of their work. If they are called in to handle a piece of a project, they may never see the whole. People in matrixes suffer when they are team players without clearly designated positions. Their anxiety level increases because they are often not sure what is expected of them. The emotional climate is turbulent, and the rate of turnover soars.

An executive—like a coach—can help foster group feeling. People need to understand their places in their projects. When people are committed to performing their tasks in a flexible, cooperative, and often ambiguous atmosphere, matrix management can work. A top executive must assess the strengths of the players and use them to the greatest advantage. A major part of the task is to develop skills in both new and seasoned players. A deliberate program to develop skills presents a double advantage: it offers people a chance for growth and change and it makes the most of the organization's best resource—the people that work in it. Developing skills in subordinates is always possible, and the game not only permits it, but requires it in order to perpetuate the organization.

The Teaching Role of the Executive

Fletcher Byrom of Koppers Company says, "Our theory is that the best motivated person is a five-foot ten-inch nonswimmer in six feet of water. If you're doing this as well as you should be, everyone's head ought to be a little bit under water all the time. People perform best under conditions of moderate tension."[10] Swiss psychologist Jean Piaget distinguishes three stages—assimilation (taking in a new experience), accommodation (recognizing where it conforms with and where it deviates from old knowledge), and equilibration (creating balance between the new experience and old knowledge)—a conception that provides a theoretical basis for the view that Byrom and many other executives subscribe to.[11] But this view does not automatically assume that letting subordinates sink or swim is the best procedure. On the contrary: to facilitate the learning process and development of management skills, the executive needs to acknowledge that one of his major responsibilities is to be a teacher.

To fulfill this role, the executive must develop a greater understanding of psychological dynamics and the role of unconscious motivation—greater than is generally present in organization life. This is not to say that organizations have ignored the human-awareness techniques that have surfaced throughout the rest of the culture over the past twenty years. Many organizations have embraced psychological techniques that promise to accomplish quick changes, but most of these techniques have been abandoned in disillusionment. Communications consultants, for instance, have been able in some cases to teach managers to talk more easily with one another, but although words are exchanged more freely, original conflicts often remain unresolved. People still do not talk about what is really bothering them. Meanwhile, top management continues to press for profits. The greater the downward pressure from the chief executive, the more impossible it is for people to admit their concerns without appearing weak, and the less time there is for listening. Increased stress is the result. People deny their feelings not only to others but to themselves. They are unwilling to sit with one another long enough to confront their feelings and to mobilize the support of their peers and superiors. Managers may think everything is going well because their subordinates grin and bear it and talk superficially about their problems, but the subordinates who have been "organizationally diagnosed" and still feel in conflict are likely to feel exploited and increasingly angry with the organization.

This backlash from techniques that promise but fail to provide simple answers to complex problems can be a destructive force in a group. Sensitivity training, behavior modification, transactional analysis, and encounter groups can bring about some changes, to be sure. There is always the chance that a particular individual's needs will be met, in part, by one of these approaches. But executives who want to understand more about themselves and those they supervise must recognize the limitations of these methods. Speaking against one technique (but the criticism applies to others), Abraham Zaleznik and Manfred Kets de Vries say that what is wrong with sensitivity training is that it completely disregards the need to understand the origin and the pressures of unconscious motivation.[12]

Executives can better understand their subordinates—their motivations, behaviors, and expectations—by being more reflective and realistic about their own. That is the major focus of this book. Ancient explorers spent centuries searching for the illusory Fountain of Youth, which supposedly could ensure their survival. Modern day executives have something of the same task, but theirs is more easily accomplished. If organizations are to survive their founders and if executives are to survive in their positions, they must build into their organizations the capacity for perpetual life. Robots make good workers, in the appropriate place. They can weld automobiles, deliver mail and meals in offices, check radioactivity in nuclear power plants, and do without pensions and pay raises. Robots in industry could grow to be a $3 billion annual business by 1990.[13] But in spite of their fine circuitry and silicone chips, there is a good deal they will never be able to do. Perpetual organizational life can only be achieved by making it possible for people within the organization to fulfill their responsibilities innovatively and responsibly.

TWO The Reinvestment of Human Drives

A particular organization may look like an ongoing concern, with an illuminating history, a solid future, and defined activities and goals. Observed casually in this way, from the outside many organizations seem to exist as if functioning under a Latin motto that translates as "I am, therefore I will be tomorrow."

The fact that an organization is here today, of course, is no guarantee that it will be here tomorrow. Just as individuals flourish in large part because they have figured out how to be adaptive, businesses, too, flourish only if they learn how to adapt—to channel present energy and ideas in order to meet the changing future. If organizations are to survive their founders, and if executives are to survive in their positions, the capacity for perpetuation must be built into the organizations.

The organizational structure and its personal dynamics must permit the people within the organization to act creatively and responsibly. Behavior results from a combination of drives, needs, expectations, and external demands, and the capacities of people to deal with these forces. Any program for survival and perpetuation must be based on these sources of motivation.

For present purposes, we shall consider two sources of needs and expectations: those forces within the personality that give it its basic direction and those external and cultural forces that, interacting with internal forces, mold and shape

17

attitudes toward power. Let us look now at the internal forces.

When an executive comes to work, he or she brings—besides a briefcase—an assortment of drives, needs, and expectations shaped by the essential personality, interacting with the history of life events encountered up to that moment. These drives will be reinvested in the organization.

The future of the organization depends on the innovation and determination of the people within it and on the decisions that they make. In turn, these depend on human drives. Business decisions are not as rational as executives like to think. "Intuition disguised as status, seniority, and rank is the underlying normative mode of all business decision," notes Bruce D. Henderson of the Boston Consulting Group. It could not be otherwise.

> Too many choices must be made too often. Data is expensive to collect, often of uncertain quality or relevance. Analysis is laborious and often far too expensive even though imprecise or superficial. All rigorous analysis . . . starts with an intuitive choice and ends with an intuitive decision. The first definition of the problem is inescapably intuitive. It must be in order to be recognized as a problem at all. The final decision is intuitive. It must be or there is no choice and therefore no need for a decision.[1]

It is precisely this fact that makes it so important to have a fundamental body of knowledge about psychological matters. An intuitive choice is one that relies on unconscious processes. But these processes cannot be turned to advantage without an established frame of reference. What can we know about the nature of the human personality?

Theories of Personality and Development

Psychoanalytic theory as formulated by Freud, historically the first comprehensive theory of individual motivation, conceives of three systems or structures within the personality and attributes to each one certain functions and energies.[2] One of these structures is called the *id*, within which, it is hypothesized, are two constantly operating drives: a *constructive* drive (derived from the sexual forces within the person) leading to love, growth, expansion of the personality, and integration of the personality with the surrounding world; and a *destructive* drive (derived from the aggressive forces within the personality) leading to feelings of hate, contraction and constriction of the personality, alienation from the surrounding world, and death. One of the major tasks of the personality is to fuse these drives so that the constructive drive is dominant. Also the site of repressed memories and experiences and of primitive wishes and impulses, the id comprises the uncivilized core of man that continually struggles for expression.

The job of the *ego*, considered to be the executive part of the personality, is to control, guide, and direct the pressures from the id. The ego is made up of the five senses, together with the abilities to concentrate, judge, attend, form concepts, think reflectively, recall, learn, and act. The ego is in touch with the outside world and takes it into account when dealing with the id. It seeks to master the outside world so that the person can survive.

The third structure is the *superego* or, more colloquially, the conscience—an internal self-governing agent with four functions. First, as part of the process of growth, children identify with their parents and other important figures in their environment. In doing so, they assimilate many of their parents' rules for living—rules about expressing aggressive impulses and about giving and receiving love. Second, by the same process of identification, children adopt and evolve certain values which become the bases for their attitudes about important aspects of living. These values range from such firmly and universally established ideals as the sanctity of human life to more specific ones which are part of a professional discipline, such as the values of privacy and confidentiality that govern the practice of medicine. Third, the conscience spurs people on to attain an ego ideal, an internalized image of oneself at one's future best. This image is constructed from expectations held by parents and others, from aspirations children develop for themselves out of recognition of their capacities and abilities, and from identification with important figures in their environment. Mark Twain said, "It may be called the Master Passion, the hunger for self-approval."[3] Concepts of "self-fulfillment" and "self-actualization" in part refer to a person's efforts to attain his ego ideal. However, the ego ideal, like a distant mountain peak, is beyond one's capacities so that it continues to serve as a goal toward which one is constantly striving. Various social models ranging from presidents, artists, scholars, and saints on the one hand, to con men and drug dealers on the other—depending upon the cultural milieu from which the child comes—serve as the raw material for the ego ideal, and their function as models is reinforced by history, literature, religion, myth, and folklore. The fourth part of the conscience, and the most evident, is the one that polices and makes judgments. Everyone has experienced pangs of conscience or twinges of guilt after having violated the rules or values by which he lives or when he has not met the demands of the ego ideal.

Theorists speculate on the nature of the human personality, devising different models to explain it. Freud also described stages of development of the child based on the evolving refinement of the nervous system and the growing capacity of the brain to think abstractly. This he called the theory of psychosexual development, because of the gratification the child derived from different parts of the body as the developing nervous system sensitized them into zones of pleasure.

Erik Erikson, following Freud, outlined a psychosocial conception of the stages of personality development.[4] The earliest of his eight stages complement Freud's, but his subsequent stages go beyond the development of the nervous system to give more attention to the growth possibilities for adults. During the years of early adulthood, when people are faced with the conflicting alternatives of intimacy and isolation, they demonstrate their capacity (or their inability or unwillingness) to form close bonds. Once intimacy has become real, adults can proceed to show care and concern for the next generation. If they fail to establish intimacy, they may indulge themselves as if they were their own children. In late life, individuals either integrate their ideal images with the reality of what they have become, or face the danger of succumbing to despair. At each stage of life, people face three tasks: to rework issues left unresolved from the previous stages, to handle well the dominant theme of the present stage, and to prepare for the next stage.

In the process of development, according to Erikson, people must deal with others in their environment who are more powerful than they—parents and other dominant figures. Early in life people are completely dependent on parents, then gradually become more independent, in itself a struggle, for there are many gratifications in being cared for. It is the critical struggle of adolescence. Freeing oneself from dependence on parents is not enough to form the adult personality. People must decide who they are. They must consolidate and organize the myriad experiences of their young lifetimes into a consistent, coherent pattern in keeping with the demands and expectations of their ego ideals. Accepting certain values and rejecting others, each person adopts favored ways of behaving that are consonant with some picture of the self as an adult. In a society that does not specifically define a person's social role based on his position or that of his parents in the society, a person chooses his own vocation. This task of self-crystallization is part of the problem of identity formation.

Other theorists have postulated slightly different constructs to explain the development of personality. Harry Stack Sullivan, for instance, formulated the Interpersonal Theory of Psychiatry.[5] Sullivan agreed with much of what Freud said, but felt that it was important to look at development not simply in terms of psychosexual stages, but also from the social context in which people form relationships with others. He viewed this context as being made up of *social determinators.* Sullivan delineated six stages of development, and was careful to consider them in relation to Western European culture, not, as other theorists often did, as universal in nature. These stages were infancy, childhood, the juvenile period, preadolescence, early adolescence, and late adolescence. Sullivan believed that personality changes as new personal relationships are begun and as older ones are resolved and cast away. Carl Jung, too, emphasized that as adults, one's life is in a state of constant development, never ceasing, always yearning for expansion.[6] For Jung, midlife was an especially important time: during this period people often try to change the way they view themselves, to discover new insights, and to become more aware of their capabilities and powers.

In addition to individual differences, group characteristics affect the way in which people behave. Members of minority groups, for instance, may find themselves at a disadvantage because they lack adequate models and a social permission that can "frank" their efforts. These factors, along with a lack of previous experience that can be applied to new roles in management, create obstacles. One important group that has encountered such obstacles in recent years consists of women.

Women's traditional place in the work force, and especially in management, can be partly explained by favored ways of adapting that the group as a whole (with individual exceptions, naturally) accepted until about a decade ago. To this day, the numbers of women in management remain small: in 1977 women made up 39 percent of the labor force but accounted for less than 5 percent of those earning more than $10,000 a year in the census category of Officials, Managers, and Proprietors.[7] It is beyond dispute that cultural biases on the part of those already in management positions (reflecting the biases of American life in general) have played a strong part in keeping women out of roles of power. There is a strong attachment to stereotypical sex roles. In a study that asked 72 personnel directors in private and public businesses to evaluate extensive résumés, the qualifications on many of the résumés were identical; only the sex of the applicant varied. Although the personnel directors felt they were being quite fair in their judgments, the results showed considerable favoritism. Men were preferred, despite identical qualifications, for such jobs as automobile salespeople or hardware clerks, whereas women applicants were favored for so-called feminine jobs such as telephone operators or office receptionists.[8]

In the past decade it has become clear that women themselves have been inadvertent collaborators in the perpetuation of this stereotype. Feminine self-concepts and perceptions from early childhood persist into adulthood. Eleanor Maccoby and Carol Nagy Jacklin have described the differences in self-concepts that can be inferred from the way in which boys and girls perform on psychological tests and in everyday life. Boys score higher than girls on "lie" and "defensiveness" scales (intended to measure the degree to which children can see themselves in a good light and can preserve self-esteem). Boys see themselves as responsible agents in their own successful actions more than do girls, who, as classic externalizers, credit luck or other people with good things that come their way.[9]

Matina Horner's benchmark study of college women underlines the conflict that women perceive between femininity and successful achievement.[10] Margaret Hennig and Anne Jardim looked at twenty-five women who "made it," scrutinizing their childhoods, family dynamics, patterns of continuity and change, and associations with peers and mentors in an attempt to discern what factors make a difference.[11] Lois Ann Koff and Joseph H. Handlon summarized a six-year study of 1,775 women, ranging in age from twenty to fifty-five and employed in various business and industrial organizations, in an effort to find out what contributes to success.[12] Among women they classified as upwardly mobile, they found three groups. "Pioneers" are the innovators and initiators, primarily self-motivators and not afraid to take risks. If they don't find adequate opportunity in one company, they will simply find another. "Climate sensitive" women are strongly motivated toward achievement, but rely on positive company climate to develop their self-confidence. They don't need pampering, but they do need approval and recognition from their superiors. "Support seekers" are the ones who require a lot of hand-holding and reassurance. They will take on managerial responsibilities only if they are sure the situation is safe; once they become skilled, they can be counted on to remain loyal to the company. The women who don't make it are hindered by various fears—of conflict with tradition, of disloyalty to a peer group, of failure, or of new social status. Koff and Handlon's study gives an idea of the variety of managerial problems that will be encountered by companies trying to develop women. Women bring to their jobs a full range of motivations and needs, just as men do. They cannot be treated effectively as a single group.

It remains to be seen what the long-range effect of these changes will be. The presence of large numbers of women in the work force has already produced a shift in the economy. Their higher income level has created a demand for more consumer products, and some economists maintain that future economic growth depends on their continued participation. Eli Ginzberg calls the impact of women in the work force the "single most outstanding phenomenon of our century."[13] The fact that women are now stretching their traditional limits and aspiring to roles in management has had another direct effect: it has helped increase everyone's awareness of the importance of personal psychology in work life.

The Meaning of Work

The conception of personality developed by psychoanalytic theory has two implicit assumptions. It assumes that personality is a genetic phenomenon, evolving continuously from a changing physical matrix and shaped by experience. Earlier experiences, as in childhood, have considerably more impact on the shaping of personality than later experiences because people are more malleable earlier in life. This conception assumes, further, that personality is a dynamic phenomenon—that it is a result of many different forces and seeks to maintain its equilibrium.

These assumptions about personality underlie two propositions. First, people bring to their jobs attitudes, expectations, and modes of behavior that have evolved from their life experiences. Second, as they work, they are continually trying to maintain their personality equilibrium. But what, in psychological terms, is work?

Although mankind has been preoccupied with work for thousands of years, no one has yet proposed a satisfactory definition of the word. To understand its paradoxical meaning is no simple task. Work is simultaneously a curse and a blessing. People cannot free themselves from work, nor would they do so if they could. People work when they are hungry; it is equally obvious that they still labor when they are so satiated with material goods that they cannot even use what they have. One person's work is another's play; some make work out of play, and some make play out of work. A few people spend their adult years trying to escape work; more escape into it. Some sing of working to pass away the time, and some sing of being oppressed by barges and bales. Working adults devote nearly half of their waking hours to their jobs. One may with good reason ask someone, "Do you work to live or live to work?"

When Morse and Weiss asked a national sample of 401 employed men whether they would continue to work if they inherited enough money to live comfortably, 80 percent said they would. The researchers were particularly impressed with the vividness of the responses: "It was almost as if they had never consciously thought what working meant to them but now that they were presented with the imaginary removal of it, they would see for themselves and verbalize to another person the feelings which had really been there implicitly all the time."[14]

Occupation is universal to mankind; in the West, it is synonymous with work. With this conception, the occupational millennium that automation promises is not freedom from work, but freedom from being a substitute for a machine.

Most people need to provide financially for themselves, to protect themselves against possible emergencies and to prepare for old age. Work, then, as a medium for survival, has a fundamental economic meaning. Bare subsistence rarely satisfies anyone. The need for money is a basic reason for working but not the only one. When a person is able to earn enough to meet fundamental financial needs, other reasons for working become proportionately more important. Thus, many people prefer white-collar jobs at which they earn less than they might as skilled technicians, or prefer to work in a more elite downtown business district than in a factory area.

For the majority of women, as for men, work is a means to earn money. By and large, the labor force is not peopled by women who, in the words of one social critic, "were especially susceptible to the postwar feeling of expansiveness and possibility, and the urgent faith in the flowering of self."[15] At the same time it is true that for many women—who previously would have filled traditional occupational roles as pivotal figures in the family, caring for children, providing a comfortable home and diverting social life for their husbands, and finding creative or community outlets for personal talents or concerns—the symbolic significance of paid employment in "meaningful" jobs has become an irresistible magnet. Apart from the inducement of money, women are responding to other benefits that accrue from working, such as autonomy and independence. More and more women are working as welders, auto mechanics, fork-lift operators, plumbers, ship-fitters, and laborers, and for the same reasons that men do—for a sense of personal satisfaction, for a sense of identity, and for the money. Studying these patterns of employment, sociologist Mary Walshok concludes that women have taken on nontraditional work because they needed greater autonomy and challenge than they could find in traditional jobs.[16]

Not everyone, however, agrees that the significance will have staying power. Diana Trilling expresses the view that the majority of present-day, middle-class female students will return to their traditional role as subservient to men. Though they profess concern for the poor, for blacks, for women's rights, they will—once returned to their communities—begin to revert to middle-class mores, including abdicating any claim to economic power except through their marriages or own inheritances.[17]

This may turn out to be true. But money is an important incentive to both men and women, not for its own sake, but because it represents power, achievement, success, safety, and public recognition; to many women it means independence for the first time in their lives. In recent years, studies of motivation to work have frequently emphasized the importance of factors other than money, leading some managers to think that money was of little importance. This has had unfortunate consequences.[18] Many businesses today suffer from inadequate leadership largely because they have allowed people of initiative to be lured away by higher financial rewards.

A study of executive views of management compensation reported that the higher the level of management, the less satisfied executives were with the amount of their pay, regardless of the amount they were receiving.[19] Unskilled workers, on the other hand, have few sources of gratification in their work other than the money they earn, since their lack of skill deprives them both of esteem from superiors and of a sense of accomplishment from the skill itself.

Work also has many social meanings. When people work they have a contributing place in society and earn the right to be the partner of others. The fact that someone will pay for their work is an indication that what they do is needed by others, and therefore that they are a necessary part of the social fabric. To have a skill, trade, or occupation is to be a "who" and "what." People are identified in their own mind and to others by what they do. Their work defines the nature of their partnership with others and the value of that partnership.

In Western societies, work has traditionally been of especial importance to men because it is associated with a specific definition of manliness: the head of the family. Most men take this role for granted and most can do so until they have no work. Then the importance of work in their lives becomes painfully clear. As more women become heads of households, the same obligations and expectations accrue to them.

During the extended depression of the 1930s a number of

studies of the unemployed showed how a man's work was tied to his place as head of the household. One classic study was conducted by Eli Ginzberg.[20] Ginzberg and other researchers found that when a man lost his job and went on relief, often his whole family's picture of him changed. He was regarded as less of a man both by his family and by society at large.

Most people are guided by a personal governor and guide: the superego or conscience. Much of a person's behavior is an effort to appease or alleviate the pressures of the conscience. The traditions of being "fair and square," of doing the "right" thing, of being our "brother's keeper" are strong in American culture. Among these traditions is the generally unspoken belief that a person must earn the right to be alive.

Philosophers and theologians have debated for centuries about the purpose of man's existence. Ordinary people do not usually debate such questions in so many words, but they do make certain assumptions about their purposes in life and act accordingly. A man who reads meters for an electric utility company whose basic function is service and who devotes every spare moment to Boy Scout work assumes, among other things, that a fundamental reason for living is to render service, to give something of himself to others. A chemistry teacher who also makes furniture assumes that, in addition to communicating knowledge about science, it is important to use a part of her life to create enduring items that increase comfort. A landscape gardener tacitly assumes that it is important to create beauty and thereby to enrich life.

People often justify themselves by their aspirations. A woman may aspire to a certain position in life, to "arrive," to provide a better social and economic springboard for her children, to protect herself from adversity, or even to make the world better. Sometimes a man justifies his life through his desire to be loved, which he assuages by seeking popular acclaim or prestige. A man may be uneasy because he does not have a justification. This leaves him dissatisfied with himself because none of his achievements provides any lasting internal satisfaction. Work goals and achievements can become both temporary and enduring justifications.

Work helps people live with their consciences by enabling them to achieve personal goals and live up to private aspirations. They feel inadequate when they are not doing as well as they think they can or should. Even though they may not yet have fulfilled their aspirations, so long as they are working toward them people tend to feel more comfortable with themselves.

In the course of one experimental study, conducted at the General Electric Company, some hourly workers were made to feel that they were overpaid and others that they were being paid fairly. Those who felt that they were being overpaid increased their productivity to justify to themselves their higher wages.[21] Work provides a means of reinforcing the conscience. Usually a person has to be at the job regularly at a given time, and produce goods or services of a certain quality. The task demands a level of performance, stimulating and reinforcing internal desires to do well. Artists or commission salesmen who have no externally imposed schedules or demands often have a difficult time motivating themselves to produce; those who become successful usually have had to discipline themselves to work consistently so that it seems as if the work itself is making demands on them. An interesting sidelight to this phenomenon is that people who are unemployed seem to lose a sense of time. It is as if work, work schedules, and work demands become measures of time. Time is irreplaceable. When people devote significant amounts of time to anything, implicitly they are assuming that it is important to do so.

The need to justify oneself is so strong that many people have difficulty accepting welfare, charity, social security, or hot lunches in public schools. Yet all these forms of assistance are intended to help people resist family disintegration. If the purpose of the work is not worth living for, it does not meet the implicit assumptions of the workers. If it does not make reasonable demands of people, then it should be no surprise if employees are apathetic and need constantly to be bought off with higher wages and fringe benefits. Trends in business and industry toward participative management and toward improving the quality of work life are one step toward increasing the responsibility of employees. Responsibility for the success of the business helps many people meet the demands and expectations of their consciences.

Freud once said that in order to be mentally healthy, a person must be able to love and to work. Work, he pointed out, was a consistent and fundamental way of staying in touch with the world and of mastering it.

Almost everyone has had the experience of being sick in bed. Before long, patients begin to lose touch with life beyond what they can see from their window. People whom they ordinarily saw every day at work, they now see only occasionally. The longer they are sick, the longer they are isolated. Sick people are desperate to *do something*. In the museum of the Menninger Foundation there is a large ball of string, perhaps two feet in diameter. It was made by a state hospital patient out of bits and pieces of string over a period of years—because he had nothing else to do. It is painfully eloquent testimony to a sick man's need to master some part of his environment.

In addition to being a fundamental medium by which an adult adapts effectively to the world, work is also a medium for mastering oneself. Each person has the continuous psychological task of controlling, fusing, and channeling the twin unconscious drives of love and hate. Work is a central device for this task. The carpenter who hammers nails is not only discharging his aggressions but also building a shelter. The salesperson who persuades a customer to buy a product also provides employment for the manufacturer.

Work helps individuals master themselves in another way. People frequently say, "I'd go nuts if I didn't work." By this they usually mean that two things would happen: they would become increasingly tense and restless, and they would have many fantasies ("I would think and worry too much"). In the Morse and Weiss study, one third of the men interviewed gave such reasons for wanting to continue working, even if they could afford not to. By concentrating on their tasks, people push out of consciousness many thoughts and ideas they would rather forget.

Work, then, is a way of being "on top." To work is to be in control of oneself and of a part of the surrounding world, to have some idea of what the future holds and to be prepared for it. It is also to be in touch with the changing world, and to grow more competent and secure in it. The motivation to work is strengthened as the employee is given greater opportunity to master and control his work in keeping with the task to be done.

Many people find in their jobs a means of socialization. A shared work activity requires interaction and communication. It is not unusual to find people who live lonely lives after working hours, particularly those who do not make friends easily. In the rehabilitation of the once mentally ill, often the most difficult problem to be surmounted is not quality of performance but the loneliness of the after-work hours.

Work has other social implications. It is a psychological truism that people tend to recapitulate their early family experiences in their subsequent activities. In fact, people often speak of their work group as being a "family." There are relationships to people who, like parents, are authority figures. Hiring and firing is psychologically similar to the parent's giving or withholding of love: to be hired is to be valued and to be discharged is to be rejected. Fellow employees can have greater, equal, or lesser power, depending on their seniority, experience, and skill; thus, a person's relationships with them may be similar to relationships with brothers and sisters.

As people have become more interested in the ways in which family dynamics are replayed within organizational settings, research has begun to confirm the existence of these behavioral patterns. Anyone who has had a subordinate who acted as if his immediate superior did not exist will be interested in Walter Toman's observation that the fatherless boy behaves toward these father-like persons as if they did not exist; above all, he will not let them tell him anything. "Fatherless" in this case refers to the loss of a father early on, not only through death but through divorce or other forms of separation.[22] A woman executive who is strong, approving, and nurturant may be a great success with subordinates who are men, but may discover that women subordinates resent the same behavior. The reason, according to one study, is that these women may not have had much approval or nurturing from their mothers. There is growing evidence that girls are more likely to want to achieve if their mothers were not particularly warm, or even a little hostile. Boys need a great deal of maternal affection and nurturing in order to achieve, but achievement-oriented girls (as Hennig and Jardim also discovered) seem to need praise not from their mothers but from their fathers.[23]

One of the deepest conflicts of married life results from people's lasting loyalty to their original family. A recent psychiatric study maintains that each person while growing up keeps a private ledger of credits and debits corresponding to the justices and injustices meted out by the family.[24] Over the years the person attempts to "balance the books," or make up for his or her deprivations. At times this may interfere with marriage, which in most cases gradually replaces the original loyalty with a tie to the newly emerging family group. For instance, a woman may be bitter about her own early deprivations and envious of her husband's comparatively happier childhood. This may prevent her from fully enjoying the gratifications presently available.

If people's sense of primary injustice is repressed and becomes unconscious, they may commit "crimes" against the outside world instead of blaming their parents. In this way they actually preserve their original loyalty ties. Student rebellions against universities reflect such deflected anger, and it may be that some part of the attack on the integrity of organizations has similar roots.

As the family fosters social activities among its members, so does the company. Coffee breaks, group lunches, and evening entertainment in coworkers' homes all encourage social relationships among people whose basic tie is that they all work together. Golf, fishing, hunting, and other group activities often stem from work associations. It is not uncommon for men to head for a bar as they leave the plant, to have a few beers together and to discuss jobs and sports. Women in the work force speak with pleasure of meeting friends or coworkers for a sandwich during their lunch break, contrasting it to the isolation from adults that often occurs when women are at home all day.

To understand the meaning that work has for employees, executives would do well to know the kinds of families from which their employees come. If the work process can recapitulate the style of family relationships typical of the employees, so much the better. If it is radically different, executives are likely to have difficulty keeping their people. Conversely, they would be wise to select people whose family experiences fit the particular work process. A highly mechanized work process in which people cannot talk to each other because of the noise level or the distance between them will hardly meet the needs of people who are accustomed to close family relationships.

The person who finds gratification in work has attained a harmonious coordination of experience, interests, capacities, skills, drives, and conscience. Work is essential to achieve and maintain psychological balance. It should be no surprise, therefore, that one of the indications of emotional disturbance is a person's inability to find gratification in work. For some men and women this means an inability to hold a job. Others seem unable to be happy no matter how much they change jobs. Still others are never able to find themselves or to realize their potential. A few will manage to fail no matter what opportunities are presented.

The Value of Case Histories

In the chapters that follow, particular problem situations will be used to illustrate themes under discussion. Readers will undoubtedly catch echoes of familiar controversies among subordinates they know, or gain some insight into the "why" behind a recalcitrant personality problem with a particular supervisor. For the most part, however, the ideas are deliberately presented in general terms in order to reflect the variety of human nature and experience.

The case histories provide a useful opportunity for the reader to examine the way in which these dynamics work in particular instances. Against the background of the ideas outlined in each chapter, a situation will be described in detail to show more specifically the way in which individual motivations affect organization life. The situations and their analysis are designed to show how the principles presented here can be applied, in practical and constructive ways, to situations encountered in the course of day-to-day work. The cases have been adapted from problems presented to the Levinson Institute by executives over the years. Identities of the persons involved have been disguised.

When executives are in a turmoil about some problem—whether with a subordinate, a superior, or a peer—and are not clear why, there are several important questions to ask. "Why do I have pain about this? Am I angry? Am I guilty? Do I have rescue fantasies that this person is not letting me fulfill? Just what is it that is turning me upside down?"

For instance, executives who feel that they are being put on the spot by subordinates, however inadvertently, may ask the question, "Why me?" Often subordinates unwittingly blame their superiors for denying promotion or for unfair treatment by others, when in fact the superiors had nothing to do with these problems and are unable to do anything about them. Frequently this happens in such a subtle fashion that the superiors do not know they are being used and merely feel responsible for whatever is happening to the subordinate. This is why it is important also to ask, "Whose problem is this? Who owns the problem? To what extent am I being used as a receptacle for somebody else's problem?" It is surprising how often executives discover that they have been put in the middle. The reverse is an old story—the pattern of superiors displacing their problems onto their subordinates. But displacement upward is not always so clearly seen.

The case analysis approach focuses on four primary psychological realities—a fruitful way to find out the actual (as opposed to the apparent) shape of the problem and to consider what might be done about it. These realities are (1) the dimensions of a person's ego ideal and the degree to which he feels he has lived up to this ideal; (2) the way in which he handles affection; (3) the way in which he deals with feelings of aggression; and (4) the way in which he reacts to dependency. The analysis of each case is broken down to acknowledge these aspects. In identifying a problem and looking for a solution, they are always factors. They operate continuously in everyone, but, like nerves in a tooth, they only become apparent when something is wrong.

CASE HISTORY 1   "There are four people on my level in our company—a family-owned business—but I am the only woman. I have been in my present position three years, and my boss, who is in a middle-mangement position, about ten years. My problem is with him. For years Ralph has operated following an undeviating plan. He parcels out assignments to those under him, without explaining the overall issues or how he sees the long-term goals, but with detailed instructions as to how to proceed in the specific task. He is a rather stiff, solitary person and does not encourage on-the-job interaction among his subordinates, although my peers are a friendly lot. I feel he lacks imagination and is very set in his ways. Since I have been there, I have been able to confirm what my predecessors had told me—that is, if the outcome of their assignments was inconclusive, they were criticized, but if successful, they never received credit.

"I have many ideas about how to do my work, and would like to have a free hand to pursue them, to be of greater value to the company. The one time I went against Ralph, I got a lot of smoke from him. In fact, he became angry almost to the point of violence. Afterwards, he was very embarrassed and apologetic, and suggested I might like to go to a training course. My work is always in the nature of a project, and Ralph responds negatively to my being involved in something of a more ongoing, less piecemeal nature.

"My performance appraisals from Ralph have been good. He has put in for the maximum raise for me, but would not really let me thank him. Nevertheless, I feel I am being stifled.

"There is another aspect to my problem. Management is making a special effort to comply with EEO requirements, and I would like to take advantage of this. In my opinion, three years in my present job is about the limit, and I would like to move up. Ralph has turned aside any attempts to discuss my career path. Ralph never invites me to meetings, has not put me on any committees, and thus further limits my contact with my peers. Nor do I have opportunities for access to those higher up. I want assignments of a broader nature that would permit me more visibility. Ralph says I am not ready—but I wonder what his real motives are. To what extent does my being a woman affect the situation, or is he being threatened by my competence and desire to try out new approaches?

"I don't know what to do in order to (1) expand the assignment horizon to prove my competence, and (2) get exposure so as to place myself in a better position for advancement.

Analysis

Where Is the Pain?   The narrator is aware of considerable pain, while her superior, Ralph, is only troubled after a confrontation.

When Did It Begin?   The problem started three years ago when the narrator took her present position.

Ego Ideal   Ralph is a rigid, uncompromising person who doesn't like change. He needs to have things done his way to feel secure. His self-esteem is lowered by his outbursts of anger. The narrator is ambitious, but would receive more gratification if her work were more challenging and if she were able to put more of herself into it.

Affection   Ralph is reserved with everybody. He cannot receive affection even in the form of thanks when it is due.

Aggression   Not being able to handle his anger very well means that Ralph must pay a heavy price for it. It makes him vulnerable.

Dependency   Ralph does not understand dependency relationships, and thus denies his need. He keeps people at arm's length, and would like to prevent his subordinates from interchange. His set approach to work is what he leans on.

Is It Solvable?   The problem is not solvable through Ralph.

How?   The narrator should proceed with caution. She cannot change Ralph's basic nature or his long-term pattern of managing, but there are ways in which she can ease the situation. Ralph has recognized the narrator's value to him and her competence. Therefore, the narrator could be a support to him. Confronting Ralph would probably make the situation worse, and might raise Ralph's anger again. Because the narrator's peers are friendly, she can get to know them on a social basis. However, if she does indeed want to move up and time is running out, she will either have to go to higher management or get a job elsewhere. It is unlikely that she can do anything to get exposure higher up without intensifying Ralph's feelings of insecurity.

THREE

The Purposes Served by Organizations

ork has become an important social device for resolving three major psychological problems: unconscious pressures, dependency, and identity. As
an individual reinvests personal drives in an organization,
both the organization itself and the leadership that represents
its power become important aspects of the person's environment. They define the modes within the organizational structure through which aggressions may be expressed and affection obtained or given by promotion, demotion, transfer, reward, assignment, job definition, and other methods of control. The organization and its leadership have an important
bearing on how people perceive themselves as adults—
whether they fulfill the aspirations of the ego ideal, are held in
esteem, or judge themselves to be a failure.

People choose occupations that fit their psychological
needs. For example, Raymond Hill of the University of Michigan, using beginning M.B.A. students as subjects, found those
opting for accounting and systems analysis preferred less active interpersonal relations than did subjects opting for marketing, manufacturing, or personnel, whereas people in these
three fields needed vigorous and friendly interpersonal contacts.[1] Another example can be seen in a former paratroop
captain, an excellent manager, who had extreme difficulty
coping with a department store role that entailed making style
decisions. Neither those who promoted the manager, nor the

manager himself, acknowledged how radically he would have had to change in order to perform the new role. The more rigid people's self-control, the less they are likely to sense subtle nuances of line, color, and human feelings or to be able to deal with the ambiguity inherent in a new situation. Efforts to impose order usually lead to overcontrol; intense overcontrol results from trying to repress feelings. The greater the control or repression, the less people can entertain their own fantasies—a prerequisite for creative thought.

Although young M.B.A. students typically insist that they have made a clean break with the past and are starting out absolutely fresh, their childhood experiences still exert a strong influence on their choices. This is the primary reason that no single managerial technique will apply across the board.

What goes on in the process of reinvesting human drives? In a study of the Kansas Power and Light Company, my colleagues and I observed transference phenomena (that is, borrowing attitudes from one period of life and applying them to experiences in another) and people's efforts to fulfill various psychological needs in their relationship with a company.[2] It was apparent that in large measure the relationship arose out of efforts to fulfill expectations, only partly conscious, of both the people and the organization. This process of fulfilling mutual expectations and satisfying mutual needs in the relationship between people and their work organization was conceptualized as a process of *reciprocation:* carrying out a psychological contract between the people and their company or any other institution where people work.[3] It is a complementary process in which the individual and the organization seem to become a part of each other. The person feels like a part of the corporation or institution and, concurrently, like a symbol personifying the whole organization. The public image of the organization is displaced onto the person and vice versa.

For example, a middle-management man in a medium-sized company said, "After all, in this locale I *am* the company. Anything I say reflects back on the company." Another man at the same level in the same company observed, "You can't divorce your position from yourself. Various social groups catalogue you." He then recounted all of the community activities, and specific jobs within those activities, which he had been asked to assume because he was a manager in his particular company. This same phenomenon can occur at any level in the organization. A foreman in the company said, "In your neighborhood, you are [the company]. The neighbors think if you weren't the right sort of a fellow, you wouldn't be with them. Most people think our salaries are above average, so you have to keep your place looking halfway decent and your kids in shoes."

The psychological importance of the organization to the individual who works in it has increased in the last two generations. Radical changes in contemporary Western industrialized society have altered many of the ways in which people satisfy their economic, social, and psychological needs. These changes have forced people to find new ways of obtaining job security; new social devices for protection against injury, sickness, and death; modes of developing new skills, new forms of recreation, and new sources of support. Increasingly, people have found new devices for dealing with their problems through employment in organizations.

In an average American town, between 40 and 60 percent of the population leaves every ten years, a figure that has remained relatively constant for one hundred fifty years. It used to be that poor people moved when they couldn't make it any more. Now the middle and upper classes are the most mobile and their lives are being taken to represent society as a whole.[4] Greater mobility, both social and geographic, has made it more difficult for people to establish enduring friendships. Many who anticipate further moves from one area to another are reluctant to involve themselves deeply in friendships in order to avoid the later pain of separation.

The extended family unit is less likely to be found living in a single geographic area where family members can turn readily to each other for social activities and mutual aid. Family elders in many cases are too far away from their grandchildren to become models for identification and sources of psychological support, which means fewer sources of support and less sense of family continuity. People who turn to professionals for help in dealing with some form of stress frequently speak of being without support: "I have nobody to turn to." Children, seeing other children's experiences with grandparents, express regret because they have none or theirs are far away. The rise of cooperative ventures—food cooperatives, for ex-

ample, or nursery schools directed and staffed by parents—
can be explained as much by a need for affiliation in an age of
transiency as by a need for economy in an era of inflation. The
need for affiliation also helps account for the rise in volun-
teerism, which has increased by 30 percent in the past ten
years.[5]

Even in the workplace, some sources of gratification are
being lost. Rapid technical changes have altered the composition of work groups and work tasks. Occupational and status
achievements are tenuous when skills can readily be made
obsolete or when their social value can depreciate rapidly, as
occurs with technical changes and new industrial developments. Many of the services formerly performed by small entrepreneurs are now carried out by larger units of production
and marketing. For those who are members of work groups,
these changes contribute to the loss of a sense of group purpose about work and a loss of group solidarity. When skills
become obsolete, they not only cease to be instruments of economic security but of psychological security as well, for a man
thus loses an important method of mastering a part of his
world. Movement from a small business to a larger enterprise
usually means some curtailment of personal freedom. Affiliation with an organization seems to have become a major device for solving the problems resulting from these economic,
social, and psychological changes.

Organizations have recognized and fostered the intention
of people to seek financial security in the organization by
means of long service, even though college recruiters may be
impatient with young college graduates who ask about company retirement provisions. Seniority advantages in union
contracts, vested rights in pension funds, and the tendency to
promote insiders (rather than urging people to move upward
by going from one business to another) have encouraged
long-term affiliation with one organization.

Instead of geographic orientation, many men and women
now have corporate orientation. They identify themselves
with an organization—whether a company, church, university,
or government department. When people move from one
neighborhood or community to another, the work organization is their thread of continuity and may become a psychological anchor for them.

Frequently, as already noted, social friendships arise from work associations. Old navy men have long had a ready bond of friendship, and two strangers who work for IBM are likely to have much in common. In the course of our research, my colleagues and I encountered a number of men who had moved from one electric generating station to another in the same company. On their days off, these men frequently would drive long distances to visit their old work buddies in the plants from which they had moved. They did not mention visiting friends in their old communities.

It is not unusual for the company, both by means of its staff services and the personal interest of an employee's associates and superiors, to come to the assistance of the person in emergency circumstances. The "kitty" for emergencies is a ubiquitous phenomenon in organizations, whether raised by contributions or by profits from coin machines. Fellow workers mobilize for blood transfusions as well as cash, and in some instances the organization continues employees' salaries beyond sick leave provisions until they can return to work. When colleagues mobilize to help, people see this support as personal giving by friends because of their common interest as organizational members.

Custom reflects another aspect of the psychological meaning of affiliation with the work organization (and affiliation means as much to executives, it seems, as to people on hourly wages: a far larger number of graduates of business schools go into companies than start their own businesses). At one time a man was introduced to others by his name or by identifying him with his trade. Now a person is more likely to identify his or her place in society in terms of organizational affiliation—identified to others not merely as Joan Smith, for instance, but Joan Smith, manager in the Midland Utilities Company, or more simply as being "with Midland Utilities." This, together with the movement from small businesses to large organizations, means less recognition of people as individuals and more as part of an organization. It gives added importance to the relationship between people and their work organization as a way for them to gain social power.

Within this relationship, however, the people seek support from their organization to gain increased individual recognition, consideration, and responsibility. Among what Daniel

Yankelovich describes as the "New Breed" of men and women, the urge to be recognized as an individual is more important than the need for interesting and nonroutine work. The traditional equation of identity with work role chafes on these workers, who say in effect, "I am more than my role. I am myself."[6]

More Than a Social Matrix

Apart from the purely social role played by organizations, Elliot Jaques has observed, they are used by their members to reinforce individual defenses against unconscious anxiety.[7] In this he follows the conception of Melanie Klein, the late British psychoanalyst, who believed that infants respond to early frustration by experiencing the outside world as hostile and potentially harmful.[8] Jaques suggests that as people mature, they are on guard against recurrence of these anxieties and use social institutions to ward them off. For example, the phenomenon of dividing people into those who are "good" and those who are "bad" is commonly observed in clinical practice, as one way of handling paranoid anxiety. The "bad" impulses of people in an organization may thereupon be projected onto a "bad" figure or figures. Jaques calls attention to the way in which the first officer of a ship is commonly regarded by the crew as the source of all trouble, permitting the men to idealize the captain and identify themselves with him. There is often a similar polarity in the army between the executive officer and the commanding officer or "old man." In high schools, it is the vice-principal who is given the responsibility for maintaining discipline and dealing with offenders, leaving the principal's image untarnished by negative associations in the minds of students and putting him in a better position, presumably, to deal with them in an open, friendly, and helpful way. Executives will recognize another phenomenon of the same order: the tendency of people to see those in other divisions of a company, or certain key figures in their own, as the "bad" ones who cause all the problems.

In everyday life, transference phenomena occur subtly with great frequency. When people are close to each other for a long time, their continued closeness creates conditions in which reality tends to merge with fantasies of the past. It is not unusual, for example, for a wife to call her husband's attention to the fact that she is not his mother, or for someone to say, "He is like a brother to me." When such feelings are strong, they tend to obscure real identity and thereby distort judgment. To avoid such problems, physicians do not treat their own families and lawyers do not take theirs as clients.

Transference occurs with respect to organizations and institutions just as it occurs with individuals. People project upon organizations human qualities and relate to organizations as if they were human. From their feelings about people in the organization who are important to them, they generalize to the organization as a whole, as well as extrapolate from the attitudes they bring to the organization. This phenomenon makes it possible to use a hospital as a therapeutic device because patients believe it to have therapeutic powers.

Philip Selznick, a sociologist, argues that organizations quickly become invested with psychological meaning by their members.[9] In fact, he makes the point that organizations cannot endure for very long unless this does happen. Norman Reider, carrying this one step further, reports that patients in a psychiatric outpatient clinic maintain ties to the clinic rather than to the therapists who treat them. "As soon as a medical institution achieves a reputation," Reider says, "it is a sign that an idealization and condensation of the magical power and the benevolent greatness of parental figures have been posited in the institution . . . The phenomenon is widespread and *touches upon every type of institution which has any characteristics of benevolence.*"[10] Reider sees such transference as a way of gaining power to deal with reality by participating in a great organization.

Another psychiatrist, H. A. Wilmer, notes that an institution can stand as a symbolic parental surrogate, and that a person's positive or negative attitudes toward the institution may well be, at least in part, transference reactions.[11] This phenomenon is well known in relationships with other institutions. In this country even today, some men seek to enroll their newborn sons in their alma mater. In England there is a similar attitude toward some clubs. In both countries some men look upon the army as others would upon their college or club. Then Wilmer adds a critical element: "It is in *affiliation*— to take a son—that the whole phenomenon of transference to a center takes on new meaning and new members."

The contemporary organization can have benevolent characteristics as well. An organization today is a medium for recouping psychological losses in a rapidly changing society. In an organization the actions of individual people are viewed by them, by the objects of the action, and by observers as actions of the organization. For example, if a local manager of Midland Utilities cuts off someone's service for nonpayment, it is *the company* that is perceived as cutting off the service. There are many reasons for this. The organization is legally, morally, and financially responsible for the actions of its members as organizational agents. The organization has policies that promote similar behavior by agents of the organization at different points in time and in different geographic locations. These policies are supplemented by precedents, traditions, and informal norms as guides to behavior. In many instances the action of an agent—for example, a personnel officer—is a role performance that will have common characteristics throughout the organization regardless of who carries it out. In addition, selection processes in an organization tend to result in the clustering of people whose personality structures have much in common and who therefore tend to act along some personality dimensions in the same general way. These factors result in what is sometimes referred to as a "corporate personality." People also tend to have a shared perception of a given person as a result of discussions with each other about the person and his or her actions. This is particularly true if there are systematic and periodic appraisal and decision processes in the organization.

As a legal and group entity, the organization has power independent of that of its agents. Often it also has financial and other resources that can be used on behalf of people. The organization's capacity for aggressive and benevolent power can be perceived by its members, particularly when it is used either against people or to support them in emergency situations. Furthermore, it is often difficult for a person to know who in the organization has done what to him. There is much talk of an undifferentiated "they" who make decisions and take actions. Vague organizational policy permits people to form and express such thoughts.

And finally, those who act within the power structure can often act out transference feelings that are well rationalized. The executive who complains that his subordinates are too

dependent may be treating them as children, using the product of his behavior as a rationale for continuing it. Another
might justify her sadistic behavior with the time-worn ration-
alizations of parents: "It hurts me more than it hurts you," or
"It has to be done."

Understanding Employees' Needs

Those who act on behalf of the institution or organization
have power and use it in the manner of parental surrogates,
according to the folkways of the organization. For example,
the management of a major heavy manufacturing industry believes that employees should want nothing from their jobs but
their salaries. Management complains that although it pays its
people relatively well, they do not understand that the stockholders need a return on their money and they keep demanding more wages. "Look at all that we give them in fringe benefits," the management says. "Look how good we are to them.
Why don't they understand our point of view and not keep
demanding more money?" The parallel between this attitude
and that of many parents is obvious. The industrial culture is
replete with such examples.

Since the major concern of most top managements is not
today's profitability (though that is important) but the long-
term survival of the organization, the employee's relationship
to the company is of primary importance to contemporary
business organizations. With larger capital investments which
must be amortized over longer periods of time and with an
emphasis on organizational growth and creative innovation as
a means of adapting in a competitive economy, corporate
managements encourage personnel to remain in the company.
Permanent employees presumably will be more loyal, productive, and willing to assume increasing responsibility. Their
psychological investment in the organization will be likely to
stimulate creativity. Legal decisions relating to retirement,
workmen's compensation, and labor relations, pressures from
labor unions, and concern about the company's public image
all tend to foster company interest in the individual, tran-
scending the interest of any given management group.

The employer-employee relationship is not simply a two-
party arrangement. It is not without good psychological reason

that one speaks of paternalism in industry and that some companies are referred to by their employees as "Mother [name of company]." It is an important psychological fact that companies that are called "Mother" by their employees are benign and kindly and have either no union or a relatively nonmilitant union. In fact, some of the kindliness is an effort to head off unionization.

This defines one psychological meaning of the union—namely, its mothering function. When the union plays its mothering function well, it enhances the employees' relationship to the organization. When the union does not fulfill this function well, it either inadequately replaces the organization or deprives workers of significant psychological ties to their work. Some of the major industrial unions are examples of the first problem. They are highly militant, define the company as an exploitative enemy, and, with unwitting cooperation from a too aggressive management, encourage workers to identify with them. Even under the best of circumstances, the union cannot provide workers with the gratification that ideally they could and should be getting from their work because the union does not manage productive processes.[12]

In some industries the employment pattern is a temporary one. Employers hire workers from among those who gather daily at the union hiring halls. The workers' basic loyalty is to the union. As a result, they may be deprived of significant psychological ties to their work because, without a consistent relationship to any single producing organization, most of them work primarily for immediate monetary return. They are criticized for featherbedding, for failing to use their skills to produce high-quality work, and for their seemingly exorbitant wage demands. They do not seem to have much interest in their work. This is not to be construed as an argument against unions. Rather, it illuminates some of the psychological meaning of the union and the ways in which union-management relations can affect person-organization relationships.

The person-organization relationship is vital, then, because it meets certain needs of the organization. In addition, people use the organization to replace certain psychological losses, to reinforce their psychological defenses, and to serve as a major object of transference. Those who go to work in organizations have two tasks. Presumably, they are always working on the organizational task, whether it is to produce goods or render services. Invariably, they are also working on personal psychological tasks. In addition to its other social functions, the work organization is an arena for the resolution of psychological problems.

As the preceding chapter describes, individuals expect to meet certain important needs by working in an organization. Yet in working out its own perpetuation and future, the organization must adapt to the changing environment, and in the process may no longer offer the kind of work setting that particular individuals want and need. Conflicts arise. Depending on the degree of flexibility on both sides and the communication skills used, the conflicts may be resolved to everyone's satisfaction—or they may not. The case below is an example of the importance of the right match between a person and an organization.

"I am a senior vice-president for an organization that is old in years, but has always kept pace with the changing world. I have been with the company for twenty-three years now. My problem is with Jason, a general manager of one of the divisions for which I am responsible. Jason has been with the organization for nearly twenty years. He is one of our best managers and an excellent go-getter, but tries never to concern himself with anything that is not directly related to his own job.

"If you want a job done, you have only to ask Jason— he's willing to try any managerial technique, but only if it's going to be profitable on the bottom line.

"He reminds me a little of the old robber barons in that he sees everything in terms of profit. Not that he's oblivious to other concerns, but his first and foremost concept about the business is to "make money." What's more, he always does.

"Jason is forty-seven, married, with three children, all in college. Although he doesn't talk much about his family or his past, I do know that he graduated from a small midwestern college, served in Korea as a ninety-day wonder, and then entered his uncle's business where he was quite successful. Conflicts arose later between his uncle and him over the way the business was going to be run, and when Jason felt they couldn't be resolved, he came to us. We quickly hired him, and in most ways we have never had cause to regret bringing him into the organization.

"The problem is that his entrepreneurial style is now outdated for our organization. We are trying to reorganize on a team-management basis, and Jason will not or cannot—I don't know which—adjust to it. He typically likes to relate to his subordinates on a one-to-one basis, and aims for short-range achievements. We are now looking for long-range planning. His style is appreciated by his subordinates but the younger, brighter people are often held back because he won't give them opportunities to carry out their jobs, or to offer long-range solutions to any problems. He says that it's 'OK' for them to do that kind of thinking 'on their own time.' His style over the years has created an entire group of individualistic managers—all of whom, like Jason, work with their people on a one-to-one basis.

"We want to change this approach. My boss does not see Jason as contributing to our future growth, but I think that because of his track record in the profits category, he deserves our continued attention and support. Is there anything we can do to help him learn to participate in team management without losing his special profit-making skills? Is there any way to make him realize that the corporation's larger concerns should also be a part of his concerns?"

Analysis

Where Is the Pain?   The pain is being felt by the senior vice-president. Apparently Jason has no pain.

When Did It Begin?   Apparently Jason has always been this way, since the narrator describes his style as now outdated.

Ego Ideal   Jason's measure of success has historically been profitability. The chances are the profit line also was the dominant theme in the corporation, and may even be so now. His ego ideal includes his being successful at whatever he is asked to do in profit terms.

Affection   Jason is able to relate to his subordinates individually in such a way that they appreciate it. They must like his individual attention and be pleased with the results of his concentration on the bottom line. Obviously Jason invests himself in his company and in his work and has taught his subordinates to do the same.

Aggression   For the most part his aggression seems to be fused with his affection into task accomplishments, support for individuals, mastery of immediate problems. He maintains tight control over the situations in which he is involved. Those, in turn, are very circumscribed. He seems not to be able to tackle a range of problems simultaneously and a range of people simultaneously.

Dependency   He handles dependency by his very structured way of going about things, by his concentration on the simple bottom-line orientation, and his close relationships with other people.

Is It Solvable?   Probably not. For practical purposes the organization has outgrown Jason. He is unlikely to respond to training or counseling because of his long, consistent behavior pattern, and because he knows the organization wants his profits. The alternatives are to tolerate him as long as he can be tolerated or to move him off to the side in roles where his one-to-one methods can continue to be helpful, but where he does not hamper newer and younger people. Sometimes such men are placed in other parts of the organization or in older plants where their style of management fits declining profitability but where they can have control over the operation and the people who work within it. It may well be that although the corporation says it wants more long-range thinking and group processes, it still also leans heavily on the bottom line, which sends people like Jason conflicting messages. In addition, they know that if there are hard times and the chips are down, the company will always fall back on the bottom line and will not rid itself of people who get and maintain high profits.

Reflections of the Culture

losely related to personal psychological factors—
and equally important for the purposes of this
book—are the social and historical forces that create the context for individual behavior. National attitudes, cultural ways of doing things, and community points of view all
have an effect on people. They are translated into the ways in
which each person behaves within an organization.

Even quite local environments send messages that can
have an impact. Summarizing studies on the effect of environments on people's behavior, Paul M. Insel and Rudolf H.
Moos of Stanford University point out that environments
clearly have "personalities" to which different people react
differently.[1] In general, settings that encourage cohesion and
interdependence have positive effects on job growth and recovery time from illness. Those that threaten people's self-
esteem through status differentiation, overcontrol, or constant
work overload are likely to increase illness.

It is not difficult to find examples of a local environment
influencing the people in it. A major company recently moved
into a new high-rise and found that separation by floors
greatly increased status conflicts. Another organization moved
into a building with open, floating partitions and staggered
floor levels and immediately found that people needed more
privacy to function effectively. When a third corporation
opened its company headquarters in Boston, employees were

invited to tour the beautifully appointed building. Instead of being proud to see the interior beauty of the upper floors of the building, lower-level employees contrasted this luxury with their own facilities and cafeteria, and some came away dismayed at what they interpreted as executive grandiosity.

Consider the implications for leadership of individual attitudes and expectations toward power. As a result of extended experiences with people who have wielded power over them when they were children, adults have expectations about how they should relate to others who have power and how they should behave in return. Each person has a posture toward authority, derived from relationships with the only authority figures known as a child—parents and parent surrogates. These attitudes are somewhat modified as a consequence of experiences with teachers, ministers, scout leaders, and other authority figures, but fundamental attitudes toward power are derived from the earliest and most intense experiences with authority figures. Experiences vary from family to family.

In spite of individual differences, however, these experiences reflect a strong common element in any given culture. As a result, there are generalized expectations about how authority is to be wielded, how the more powerful people should act toward the weaker, and what kinds of behavior the latter might expect from the former. It is expected that one will use social strength according to culturally established norms. Therefore, when acquiring control over others, one also incurs the effects of these expectations about power figures. In short, in a particular culture, a person who becomes authoritative in direct relationships to others is expected to act in much the same way as a parent acts in the family. This does not mean that a man is expected to be a father or is consciously recognized as such. It means only that as people develop their expectations of power and attitudes toward it, based on their earliest experiences with it, they will tend to work from these attitudes in every encounter. A superior who fails to conform to these expectations will be seen as an inadequate, unfair, or unjust leader.

National Attitudes

Management practices vary according to the more obvious aspects of the family structure in a particular culture or subculture. For example, Germans speak of Germany as "the Fatherland." The father's role in that country is authoritarian and directive. The style of business management is also authoritarian and directive. Robert Weiss points out that the German emphasis on role-taking as an element in superior-subordinate relationships, in contrast to the American emphasis on role-taking as a way of pitching in, is reflected in the fact that German organizations place much more emphasis on lines of authority and much less emphasis on informal communication. He gives the following example of the way in which national attitudes are played out in the work setting.

> A German student of industrial psychology and I discussed the way group decision might work out in the American factory and in the German factory. We took the problem of deciding on a vacation time. In the American factory there would be give and take, probably ending with a vote, and the agreement that the majority should rule. In the German factory the first suggestion could be that the foreman decide. If the foreman said, "No, you men decide," the men would individually state the period best for them: "May," "Early August," and so on. If the foreman then said, "We can't shut down the plant all that time; you have to decide on one time," they would say, "All right. You decide on one time. We have told you our preferences." Further insistence by the foreman on group decision would be met by increased opposition among the men. The difference is that Americans are able to see themselves as forming a group, aside from their working relationships. The Germans are a group only as they are led by their foreman.[2]

Britain, in contrast, is referred to as "the Motherland," and historically its queens are more widely known by name than its kings. British boys, compared with American boys, have relatively less contact with their fathers.[3] Lower-class fathers until recently did not help care for the children. Upper-class boys traditionally went off to public school as soon as they left their mother's knee. Britannia, who rules the waves, is a royal feminine figure. American executives allege that their British counterparts prefer the economic comfort of protective arrangements to open competition.[4]

For Greeks, an "ingroup" of people personally concerned with one's life is the basis of social survival. Thus, Greeks develop virtues associated with interdependence—patience, cooperation, sharing, and responsibility for others. In a group, they can accept only a leader who belongs to their ingroup, and they expect him to set the goals for the group. They relate to each other through him. Once they reach an initial understanding, they are open with one another and mutually responsive to subtle nuances of feeling. Although they will express anger very freely outside the ingroup, they do not do so within for fear of being cast out of the group. Consensus is supremely important to Greeks.[5]

Russians speak of Russia not as "the Motherland" or "the Fatherland" but as "the Homeland"; alternatively they refer to "Mother Earth." Here there would appear to be little identification of the state as the surrogate of the family, despite its all-encompassing qualities; it is as if only the land is important. For the Russians, who have always had to struggle to fulfill the most primitive needs, the land takes on an especially poignant meaning. With land one always has something to eat, a place to hide, and a space to be buried. Professional management in the American sense is very poorly developed in Russia.

Further corroboration for the influence of national attitudes comes from a study of business organizations in Turkey.[6] There, employees tend to be evaluated in terms of loyalty to the manager rather than on the basis of objective criteria of job performance. Authority within the business organization is highly centralized and even routine decisions are referred upward for approval. "The relation of superiors and subordinates is highly particularistic and mirrors in many respects that of father and son in the Turkish family," writes Norman Bradburn, the social psychologist who conducted the study. Patterns of relationship with in the business organization parallel those in the Turkish family, which is characterized by close family ties, strong emphasis on family loyalty, and the dominance of the father. Luigi Barzini describes the same phenomenon in Italy, and John Fischer reports that in Japan the role of the ancient clan has been taken over by business and other organizations.[7]

Furthermore, explains Takeo Doi, a Japanese-born, American-trained psychoanalyst, the Japanese place high value on a passive kind of love based on the early mother-child relationship. They call it *amae*, which means "to make up to with confidence," much the way a dog does when it nuzzles to be petted. With people in their inner circle of friends, the Japanese expect to be able to indulge themselves, or presume on each other, even as adults. Americans often think they are being rude. To the Japanese, maintaining a place in such a circle is far more important than achieving independence. As a result, they become skilled in accomplishing things in groups. In business, although they may be intensely competitive as organized groups, they will rarely go out on a limb as individuals. A Japanese entrepreneur is a rarity. With people just outside their inner circle, the Japanese must limit their desire for self-indulgence. Restraint is a burden, and may lead them to feel contemptuous toward those who impose it. This is why they sometimes seem to behave differently with insiders and with outsiders, and why they are moved to "buy" indulgence by apologizing to a degree that seems excessive to Westerners.[8]

In the United States, the parental image is less forceful: children have considerable freedom, and parents may even act like the subordinates. The American concept of governmental power is a benign Uncle Sam who may from time to time "want you," as recruiting posters have indicated. More often his task is to help his wards better themselves. The American tradition is one of being free and equal. Government should do only those things that people cannot do themselves or that they must do in concert. Its powers are derived from the sovereign states and from the people at large. It is not presumed to be, like the crown in Britain, the source of power which it then delegates to others. With such a tradition it is not surprising that concepts of human relations in business and industry have spread more widely in the United States than elsewhere. This cultural conception of power is reflected in a little-known character in the Horatio Alger myth: an older, kindly, wealthy, helping person who boosts Horatio along.

That there are similar expectations of the executive is verified repeatedly in American morale and motivation studies.[9] These show that a skillful superior gives recognition to his subordinates, helps them grow in the job, represents their interests to higher management, looks out for their interests, corrects them justly and in private, and does not exploit them for his own gain. In this country the major objective of parents is to help their children grow to independent responsibility. Implicitly the executive is expected to do the same in the course of fulfilling the objectives and goals of the organization.

Thus, business leaders come to have an important psychological role for their subordinates. Although analogies must not be taken too literally, it is important to recognize these often unconscious expectations as realities with which each leader must deal and from which there is no escape so long as one holds power.

American tradition affects work attitudes as well as leadership expectations. Since the United States is an amalgam of ethnic backgrounds—and since ethnic revivalism has kept alive subtle cultural differences—it is not surprising that there is less homogeneity in American work attitudes than there is, say, in those of Germany or Japan. Nonetheless, a distinctive constellation of attitudes and expectations color work life in the United States and affect the way executives, their superiors, and their subordinates relate to one other.

Political Freedom

Americans have a strong egalitarian tradition which has its roots in the concept of freedom. Probably the most deeply embedded and cherished American traditions, aspirations, and values are those related to the concept of freedom. No other nation in recent history has grown from so many diverse groups of people, each seeking freedom of conscience or freedom of opportunity. For nearly a century and a half, mobility was the concrete embodiment of the concept of freedom. The open frontier is still a vivid image in the minds of the grandchildren of those who trekked westward. People moved freely as need and opportunity motivated them. Even now, one out of five American families moves each year, many for greater economic opportunity or greater personal freedom. Mobility—social, economic, and geographic—is considered a very "American" characteristic, especially in contrast to more tradition-bound European countries.

The legend has been so dearly held, that the attack on it that has come over the past fifteen years has put many Americans on the defensive. We have wanted to believe that anyone could become president (and have continued to say so, in the face of evidence that showed no presidents who were female, black, Jewish, or—until 1961—Catholic). The advent of Kennedy's presidency coincided closely with a wave of civil rights activity mounted not only because blacks could not reach the White House, but because many of them could not even sit in a public bus and only a few of them could find more than subsistence jobs.

As had happened at the turn of the century, a civil rights movement focusing on perceived injustices to blacks was shortly followed by a second wave of activity on behalf of women. Succeeding waves of protest have focused on the rights of Mexican-Americans, Indians, the handicapped, and the gay.

The events of the past fifteen years have focused largely on basic necessities for large numbers of people—food, housing, schooling, and jobs—and have been only tangentially concerned with ethnic minorities on the boards of large corporations. But the impact has been felt throughout all levels of organizations, as it has been throughout the country. The Bakke case, accusations of "tokenism," and the tangle of affirmative action requirements all testify to the difficulties inherent in trying to reconcile present realities with historical rhetoric.

Few today have the naïve expectations of opportunity and mobility that characterized national attitudes in the past, but many believe that the concept of "freedom," overworked and underrealized though it may be, is being reformulated into a newer, tougher, less idealistic construct that may have meaning for larger numbers of people—at least in the middle class—and in greater numbers of situations. As clear-cut markers of hierarchy and authority have eroded, another American concept—leadership by consent—has gained strength.

Leadership as Consent

Kenneth Boulding has pointed out that the fundamental political problem is that of power and its distribution, sources, and use.[10]

American citizens are political adults. They are, in the full political sense of the term "free citizens" as no other people before them have been. They delegate power to those they permit to lead them. They also take this power away. Their leaders must perforce listen to them. This fact is as valid for industry as it is for government and the church.

The idea of poltical equality has a significant influence on the meaning of leadership in this country. People are not automatically leaders because they are born to it, or because of wealth or position. They may temporarily hold leadership positions because they inherit ownership of a corporation or because they are scions of prominent families. If, however, they do not operate their corporation as others expect they should or if they do not exercise responsible community leadership, they will lose their power. They can be dethroned in many ways. Business executives may be rejected because people will not work for them on their terms. Leaders also may be unseated if others who have financial ownership distrust their leadership. Leaders who abuse leadership may be shorn of their holdings and power by government action. Holding companies that controlled American railroads and public utility companies were broken up by antitrust actions because they abused their power. Railroads and public utilities are still regulated by government commissions in order to prevent recurrence of such abuse. More recently Watergate, for all the shabby ambiguities of its justice, demonstrated that there is a limit to which a leader—even the number one political leader—can abuse leadership and survive. Consent by followers constitutes much of the power of leaders. They lead so long as they have followers. They have followers so long as they lead their group effectively. Consent is thus temporary. Leaders must continue to earn their position; if they do not, they will lose it.

Currently in American political life, there is a disturbing gap between the constitutional ideal of participation and the exercise of consent as it is practiced. Curtis Gans, director of the Committee for the Study of the American Electorate, writes, "The crucial difference between democracy and other forms of government, it is said, is that in a democracy the leadership of the nation derives its legitimacy and support from the consent of the governed. Perhaps the principal problem facing the United States today is the degree to which that consent is being withdrawn—the degree to which fewer and fewer

Americans believe it necessary, important, or even worth their while to cast their ballots." He underlines the point with statistics like these: during the last decade more than 15 million eligible Americans, many of whom were regular voters, have stopped voting altogether; the level of participation in America, he adds, although never as high as in some European democracies, is lower today than in any democracy in the world except Botswana.[11] Just as citizens can withdraw their support from political leadership, so can workers in an organization withhold their consent.

Consent is limited in much of American business and industry, and executive power is correspondingly curtailed. In manufacturing, for example, rates of production in many cases are lower than necessary because of informal agreements among the employees to limit productivity. The employees do not consent to produce at the rate at which the leaders wish—they deny their leaders the power to require such production, even when their failure to grant that authority is against their own long-term self-interest.[12] Executive power is also constrained by the fact that public ownership of business is becoming more widespread. Leadership must constantly take stockholder relations into account, and this consideration limits arbitrary use of power.

American egalitarian traditions have fostered the growth of different forms of leadership, each based on varied group needs. A corporate president may be a company grade officer in the military during wartime. His commanding general could be his own chief accountant. The political ward leader may be looked upon with disdain by some of his more sophisticated constituents, but they could not fill his leadership shoes. Various kinds of leaders are required at different times. It has been said, for example, that the Catholic Church alternates between religious popes and political popes—first an "inside man" and then an "outside man."[13]

In the electric utility business, after the decline of the holding companies the first generation of presidents were generally engineers. For the most part, today's presidents are attorneys. Early leaders of electric utilities had to deal with constructing generating and transmission services. The present leadership has had to concentrate attention on governmental regulatory bodies and financial institutions. The next generation of leaders will have to contend with radical changes in engineering conceptions—for example, nuclear energy generators and consequent relationships among utilities. Political skills will be in demand. Varying circumstances demand different leadership capabilities and qualities at different times. Such flexibility is possible because leadership in this country increasingly means leadership by consent. Without voluntary consent, leaders can remain in power only if they can coerce consent by rigid organizational control. This is becoming less and less possible.

One result of rising prosperity has been a jump in what marketing people call "me" products. Arthur Shapiro, vice-president of the social research firm Yankelovich, Skelly, and White, says, "Once the family and self were one. We denied ourselves for our families."[14] Now, there is a growing distinction between "we" products (traditional household purchases such as washers, dryers, and barbecue sets) and "me" products (single-serving frozen dinners, small hair dryers, and vacations without the children).

"Me" products are only one symptom of what some describe as the "me generation." And money is not the only source of the change in attitudes reflected in these marketing trends. The boom in self-help books and therapy organizations and the widespread "focus on self" (as the Yankelovich firm calls it) have been attributed to various causes. Some social critics trace this attitude change to the younger generation's rejection of traditional values in the late sixties. Others, like Boston University sociologist Joseph Helfgot, see the self-awareness phenomenon as partly a result of the failure of the student movement to achieve the social and political restructuring it sought in the 1960s: having failed to muster the long-term, sustained effort needed to make the changes they were calling for, he argues, young protesters turned inward to find answers.[15]

If the economics of plenty have contributed to the "me generation," so have the economics of "living their dreams today." This term was coined by Hershel Sabin, president of Travel and Tourisms Consultants International, who says, "There's an awareness on the economic side that over the years inflation has stolen the future for a lot of people and there's a strong inducement to live for today."[16]

Not all social critics agree that the "new" narcissism is really new. David Riesman, for one, says that people have always behaved in a narcissistic or egocentric way, except that in earlier times they sought to conceal it by saying that it was for society's greater good.[17] Other observers believe that a timely self-assertion, rather than pure narcissism, may motivate many people, especially in the workplace. Workers themselves define their own best interests, and these increasingly include involvement in decisions about the work itself, as well as more tangible measures of job satisfaction such as hours or fringe benefits. In one study that measured the relative importance of five selected job characteristics, among the 1973–74 sample more than 50 percent ranked *meaning* as most important; less than 20 percent ranked other job attributes—promotion, income, security, or hours—as most important.[18]

Workers may rank meaning in their jobs as most important, but they do not necessarily achieve it, and many workers are not engaged psychologically in the jobs they fill. Daniel Yankelovich describes the alienation that employees experience: "Today, millions who do hold paid jobs find the present incentive system so unappealing that they are no longer motivated to work hard. As a consequence, not only do they withdraw emotional involvement from the job, they also insist upon steady increases in pay and fringe benefits to compensate for the job's lack of appeal. The less they give to the job, the more they seem to demand—a process that cannot continue for long without breaking down. A deep flaw in the incentive system, signified by the failure of the old incentives to catch up with the new motivations, leads inexorably to deterioration in the workplace, threatening the position of the United States as the world's foremost industrial nation."[19]

Within a given organization or industry, then, employees are less ready to be pressured into submission as a condition for obtaining goods and services. Executives operate without the consent of rank-and-file employees because the workers have withdrawn their commitment to the workplace and the work.

The trade or professional organization that spans an industry is also a device for countering possible coercion by the organizational leader. The job of such an association is to inform, to protect, and to serve as a vested interest. In addition to professional and trade organizations, today there are formally organized associations for almost every division and job in a work organization: for purchasers, institutional housekeepers, personnel people, training directors, safety engineers, finance officers, and sales people. In some respects, associations serve the same psychological purposes as adolescent peer groups.[20] An adolescent joins a group of fellow adolescents as one way of breaking away from parents, asserting independence, and warding off parental strictures. Association with peers provides acceptance, amusement with those who share common interests, opportunities for greater sophistication, and the leverage of group mores as pressure on parents. Adolescents establish certain standards for their parents' behavior and their own behavior, derived from the ingroup pressures of peers, and demand that their parents behave in these ways.

Trade or professional associations serve the same purposes for members, who can keep abreast of what other organizations are doing in the field and demand that their own organization do likewise, whether the concern is for a safety, a nursing, or a personnel program. Members may set up inspection and accrediting services, or establish criteria for effective functioning in their given fields. The association may give awards or other recognition for meeting its standards. Members use the association to exert leverage on the work organization. The effectiveness of such maneuvers is readily apparent. For example, a mental hospital superintendent or a state director of mental health may make little progress with the local governor and legislature. But allied with colleagues in a professional organization, they can establish standards and present them to a governor or to a legislature. United, they carry official weight and are in a better position to tell the powers-that-be how to behave. The same phenomenon is seen in diverse forms. Adolescents use their peer groups to discharge hostility: a girl may complain to her peers about her parents; the group may go to a football game where it takes sides and expresses its hostility to the other team by cheering for their own or deprecating the competence of the other; the group may become delinquent and express its hostility directly and destructively to the embarrassment of the parents. Much the same kind of thing goes on in a professional or trade association. Here people often talk about how bad things are in their own companies or what terrible bosses they have. For many people, the association meeting is an opportunity to criticize their organization safely.

In a peer group, furthermore, adolescents become more "cosmopolitan," developing loyalties and values that may be different from those of their parents.[21] This sometimes creates conflicts, because adolescents want to be approved by both. The same kind of phenomenon occurs in professional and trade associations. Those who are members of these associations and simultaneously of business organizations must balance the values of both. The safety engineer wants to be identified with his own organization, but at the same time he would like his organization to maintain safety standards like those his professional colleagues champion. He is more sophisticated about these standards as a result of having taken part in meetings where there was exchange of opinions, ideas, and factual information. The professional association serves to make him more "cosmopolitan" and less "parochial."

Like the adolescent peer group, the professional or trade association provides an avenue toward power. Just as one can become a "wheel" in an adolescent group by being president of the class or a star athlete, so a person becomes a "wheel" when he or she assumes official responsibilities in a professional organization or trade association (though status in the work organization may be low) and may even become more important in the work organization as a result. The trade or professional association, like the adolescent peer group, offers an association of peers and encourages people in their work, however unimportant this work may seem to their superiors and however little encouragement they give. In addition to its apparent functions, the professional or trade body serves to counter the possibility of coercion by the leader. Often its power is so great that an organization must be on good terms with the association if it is to recruit competent personnel or otherwise carry on its activities.

The Expanding Middle Class and Rising Expectations

For many people in the United States the concept of freedom has been largely academic because of their limited education and economic resources. But from generation to generation, more people have been attaining economic security and higher levels of education. More have joined the middle class. Between 1954 and 1974, the proportion of all families with incomes of $15,000 or more rose from 10 percent to 40 percent.[22] Today there are more white-collar workers than blue-collar workers. Comparing the occupations of employed persons in the years 1960 and 1975, one sees an increase in professional, technical, and clerical jobs, a slight decrease in managers, officials, and proprietors, and a decrease in operatives.[23]

Freedom and its accompanying power become real when they become functional. Some years ago, one subtle but important indication of the growing middle class was the recommendation of the American Medical Association's Council on Drugs that pharmacists, in order to protect patients, put the name of the prescription on the label. This reflected a higher general level of education and awareness on the part of the public. Patients expected that their illness would be explained to them and that they would be told about the proposed treatment and what to expect from it.[24] More recent AMA legislation on generic drug labeling reflects a further step in this direction: to an even greater degree, patients are seen as responsible agents, guarding their own health and making educated choices.

One outcome of having a large middle class is that more people have stronger feelings about their ability to manage their own lives. Eli Ginzberg, long noted for his studies of manpower, comments, "This is the first time in the history of the world that the masses have options, somewhat similar to those previously known only to the wealthy, about the kind of life they want to lead. They can decide whether they want to throw the major part of their efforts and energies into the job or into activities unconnected with the job."[25]

The expansion of the middle class has several important implications for leadership. The more education people acquire, the higher are their expectations about job responsibility, authority, and income. The longer people are in an educational environment which emphasizes individual initiative and participation, the greater the possibility they will carry these values into the working situation. Furthermore, as sociologist Daniel Bell pointed out, middle-class and white-collar people have greater expectations of job security than do blue-collar people.[26] The blue-collar worker expects to be laid off from time to time, the first to become unemployed or displaced by new equipment. White-collar people prefer to believe that they have and should have security because they are middle class and white collar. In mergers, acquisitions, and recent recessions white-collar workers, too, have been laid off in substantial numbers; nevertheless, traditional arrangements— career counseling, termination pay, and outplacement activities—work better for them.

Another aspect of middle-class orientation is the greater effort devoted to self-control, particularly to control of aggression. Middle-class people establish elaborate forms of self-control, manners being one of them. They are far less direct in their expression of aggression than are lower-class people. The larger the organization, the more control people must exert over their feelings, the more they must abide by formal and informal codes of conduct, the more middle-class values govern.

People who rise to the middle class are more conservative than those who are born to it, which is why suburbs of large cities tend to be more Republican than Democratic. They are also the group in society with the most emotionally intensive drive for success. As a result, they have greater identification with management and management values and with the organization in which they work. However, emulation alone is insufficient to satisfy their aspirations. One consequence of the concept of freedom and equality is that people do not feel free unless they also feel equal. Those who seek to fulfill their aspirations naturally want to be partners with others who have already attained leadership.

Middle-class, white-collar people, technicians, and middle management are therefore likely to be concerned about their relationships with top management. They also tend to have more intense expectations in their relationships with their leaders than lower-class, blue-collar people. Lower-class people have long since been alienated from the executive echelon or top management. They have withdrawn much of their consent from top management and have given some of it to labor unions to exercise power on their behalf in dealings with managerial leadership.

All of these phenomena compose a revolution of rising ex-

pectations. Unfortunately, the country's economy cannot fulfill all of these expectations. A comprehensive report issued by
the United States Commission on Civil Rights shows that the
gap between white males on the one hand and women and minorities on the other actually increased from 1960 to 1976 in
such areas as high-school attendance, job mobility, and unemployment, while income differences failed to narrow. The
study did find several instances of substantial improvement,
but in none of twenty-one different categories did it find minorities equal with whites, and "occupational segregation" has
increased substantially among women and minorities since
1970.[27] Even if we had continued in a period of rapid growth,
it is unlikely that the economy could have supported the aspirations of so many individuals and groups who saw an opportunity for changes in their expectations and for advances in
their work, their socioeconomic status, and the educational attainments of their children. But as the economy has slowed
down, competition has become fiercer than ever. Ironically,
those most affected, apart from the chronically unskilled and
unemployed, are the people in the middle. The profile of work
skills looks "increasingly like a champagne glass": still room
at the top for leaders and the highly technically skilled and
room at the bottom for blue-collar, support, and clerical workers, but less and less need for people in the middle.[28] This reality of the American economy, and the disappointment and
anger that it engenders, is one of the most significant culture
factors affecting work today.

Business Obligations and Society's Conscience

One of the most subtle yet most compelling changes in organizational life over the past ten years has been in the public's view of organizational obligation. A constellation of social
and political events, coupled with an altered view of where responsibility lies—and for what—have placed organizations in
the somewhat unfamiliar position of being held accountable
for actions that would once have been regarded as the normal
way of doing business. These tides of expectations and opinion are not confined to business organizations; indeed, the
dust stirred up by Watergate—trouble in a government organization, compounded by links to business interest—unques-

tionably contributed to new sensitivities about the appropriate behavior of organizations.

An expanded sense of organizational obligation has touched many areas, from protecting human rights to preserving the environment. General Motors Corporation, sometimes criticized for its lack of involvement in the towns and cities where it has offices and plants, has been acquiring title to some one hundred thirty rundown houses near its headquarters in Detroit. GM plans to renovate the homes and then offer them for sale to their former owners at the price GM paid before the renovation. The corporation may also put in some miniparks and try to interest retailers in building in the area.[29] Irving Shapiro, chairman of the board of E. I. DuPont de Nemours, estimates that 30 to 40 percent of his week is spent on activities outside DuPont. When asked why he is involved in dealing with attacks on the way United States companies are managed, with seeking an objective assessment of the dangers of fluorocarbons, with helping inner-city youths find jobs, he says, "I think we're a means to an end, and while producing goods and providing jobs is our primary function, we can't live successfully in a society if the hearts of its cities are decaying and its people can't support their families. We've got to help make the whole system work, and that involves more than just having a safe workplace and providing jobs for the number of people we can hire. It means that just as you want libraries, and you want schools, and you want fire departments, and police departments, you also want businesses to help do something about unsolved social problems."[30]

Overseas, new questions are raised about the degree to which American money and American power should be brought to bear on local politics of individual countries, as in the case of ITT involvement in Chilean affairs. American organizations, traditionally, have done in Rome as the Romans do, and everyone has winked. But in a Middle Eastern country, for instance, where the customary way of doing business involves large payments to middlemen capable of exerting influence on local powers on the Americans' behalf, international executives can now expect a good deal more scrutiny both from government officials and from their stockholders than they had received before. American stockholders and employees have shown that they are prepared to use their influence to alter company policies that are not to their liking. The South African situation has aroused particularly strong feelings. Under considerable pressure from American black employees, Polaroid went to some lengths to make adjustments in its corporate presence in that country (where Polaroid-made film was used to construct the passes that black South Africans must carry with them at all times) and ultimately withdrew as an official presence in South Africa. IBM stockholder reports for some years carried a resolution by a large stockholder to force IBM to account in a special report for its activities in South Africa. The issue of human rights has intruded on the practices of American organizations.

Nestlé has been taken to task for expanding its infant formula market into developing countries. INFACT, the Infant Formula Action Coalition, opposing the expansion because third-world mothers do not adequately understand bottled formulas and unwittingly harm their children by overdiluting the formula or by allowing the formula to spoil, is taking the position that Nestlé, rather than the unwary customers, must shoulder the responsibility.

Waves of concern for equal opportunities are felt in the United States, too. Because it is often difficult to translate good intentions into workable practices, and because a significant amount of paralysis among managerial ranks has been produced by the continuous sense of threat from government regulatory agencies, many people are afraid that any move they make will damn them. For example, if ten blacks have been hired at the entry level, the Organization for Economic Opportunity may ask, "Why haven't you promoted them?"—even though their education, skills, and training levels disqualify them as candidates for promotion.

Occupational safety and health are increasingly seen as the responsibility of the employer, and not only of the employee. One study of occupational safety and health, sponsored by the Ford Foundation, concludes that the problem of industrial safety is more widespread than almost anyone had thought and that the federal government cannot handle it alone. Nicholas A. Ashford of MIT contends that a significant proportion of heart disease, cancer, and respiratory disease may stem from the industrial process and that the task of redesigning technology and jobs is monumental.[31] We are getting closer, in Ashford's work, to defining the relationship of the occupational environment to problems of health, and this will increase the pressure for organizational responsibility. In France, executives now may be jailed for industrial accidents.[32] The trend toward holding executives responsible for on-the-job accidents is spreading to Great Britain, where a new health and safety act now gives inspectors the power to bring accused managers into court. We can expect similar pressures in this country—pressures to accept responsibility for psychological as well as physical damage. As soon as research studies begin to show a clear relationship between managerial style and psychological symptoms, it will become impossible for executives to deny the reality of psychological forces. Managements should begin to prepare now for a serious understanding of these issues.

If people's physical health—even their emotional well-being—has become an issue of organizational obligation, this raises the question of how the individual conscience fares in the context of organizational practices. Just as the questionable ethical behavior of one executive can skew the policy of a department, people suffer when asked to behave in ways that violate their personal values and rules of behavior. Their first reaction is guilt; then they become angry with themselves and their organizations. People frequently complain about such violations. Advertising people write books criticizing their own profession, teachers complain about school, and former CIA agents reveal the activities of their agency. Some people have exposed the dishonesty of their company's actions; others have reported that they have fudged figures.

Almost two-thirds of the 238 respondents to a survey conducted by Archie Carroll, a Georgia State University management professor, agreed with the statement: "Managers today feel under pressure to compromise personal standards to achieve company goals."[33] Lower- and middle-management employees agreed overwhelmingly with this statement, while top managers were evenly split. They responded the same way to the statement: "The illegal business campaign contributions of the last year or so are realistic examples of the ethics in business today." Sixty percent of the respondents agreed that "the junior members of Nixon's reelection committee who confessed that they went along with their bosses to show their loyalty did just what young managers would have done in business." Here again, top managers were in almost total agreement. The only way to maintain morality in business, Carroll concluded, is for schools, governments, and public groups to demand it.

More important to top management, however, is the need to have internal discussions about issues of morality, in order to clarify company position and expectations. The public image of business is already at a low point. Public-relations efforts will not raise it. Serious internal effort is the only point at which to begin.

American culture—not for the first time—appears to be at some kind of ethical crossroads: the old values no longer adequately cover the situation, and the new ones are not yet clear. Various scholars postulate fresh interpretations. George Cabot Lodge of Harvard, for example, thinks that the definition of right and wrong has changed radically and is still in the process of changing. He identifies our traditional ideology as "the Lockean Five": (1) individualism; (2) the sanctity of property rights; (3) competition and consumer desire—the open market; (4) the limited state; and (5) scientific specialization and fragmentation.[34] These have now been replaced, says Lodge, with the new communitarianism (not communism). Individualism is being subverted for the good of the community. The right to survive has become more important than the right to own property: the looters in blacked-out New York in 1977 were not shot. An active, planning state instead of limited government becomes the arbiter of community need. Instead of fragmentation and specialization, there is greater emphasis upon interdependence.

Lodge thinks that the most appalling ethical problems we face are those associated with this new ideology. We can only protect, preserve, and cherish our traditional ideologies by being ever conscious of what is happening around us. The manager who would be ethical, Lodge contends, must be realistic about both the situation and the roles and functions of business, government, and other institutions. He must keep in mind the long-term interest of the people and communities that his decisions affect. He must have the courage to place these interests above his own short-term preoccupations.

Because the ethical guidelines in American culture are not

entirely clear, it is not surprising that American organizations reflect them in contradictory ways. Nevertheless, society's conscience is an influential theme in national cultural life, and the ways in which it is manifested in organizations suggest an increasingly far-reaching and exacting set of obligations.

CASE HISTORY 3

This case reflects the manner in which the styles of leadership in different cultures are affected by the style of a family operation in a given culture. Hernando, in this case, is acting as he thinks an American parent would act. His subordinates expect him to act as a Mexican parent would act.

"I am the president of the international division of a multinational corporation. I have been with this company for eleven years and in this particular role for the past five. My problem is with one of ten regional managers who report to me: Hernando, who is in Mexico City. Hernando is about my own age and has had fifteen years of business experience. He has been in his present position for only a year. He is a person of considerable education for his culture and for the work he's doing because he has both a college background and an MBA from a major American business school.

"Hernando is determined to demonstrate to me and to others that Mexicans can be good executives, and he is particularly concerned that the people who report to him live up to his perception of how the American model of the good executive should be implemented in Mexico. He himself has a good performance record and his unit has done reasonably well. We can't complain about the profit margins or rate of return, nor can we complain about the manner in which he himself tries to represent us.

"Hernando responds well to suggestions. He has no hesitation about interacting with me, providing whatever information I ask, listening carefully to whatever thoughts and ideas I may raise. He is not hypersensitive to my criticism or defensive about and in our relationship. However, he has a problem with his managerial style. He is all business. He finds it hard to relax with the people who report to him. He demands no-nonsense adherence to the rules.

He is highly critical of those who report to him if they do not live up to his standard of how a good executive and a good manager ought to behave. As a consequence, some of his subordinates feel that he is too harsh and too critical with them and they feel that they are being unfairly treated. They contend that he fired them because of complaints from customers that they tried to unload goods on the customers and were too hard-sell in their relationship with the retail outlets through which we distribute our product.

"Some of the customers had apparently complained to Hernando that his men had taken too much privilege on themselves, because they pushed for shelf space and rearranged their own products on the shelves to the disadvantage of their competitors. They had also made demands on the customers for special discounts and other kinds of privileges that made the customers feel that they were both pretentious and exploitative. On the one hand Hernando wants his people to sell, to push the product, to get the best display space, to compete effectively with others; but on the other hand he also wants them to be polite gentlemen in their relationship with the customers. Sometimes this creates conflicts, particularly when competitors take advantage of their gentlemanliness. Hernando doesn't talk these things over with his people and try to help them bridge these two demands, nor does he lend a sympathetic ear to the problems they face in meeting his apparently conflicting demands. There is a greater morale problem in his area than in any other area. This is one thing he doesn't talk over with me. Of course, being the regional manager, he has a lot of leeway, but the manner in which he operates is just not the way this company would like to have its managers operate.

"Hernando has a good deal of self-regard for his effectiveness and for his achievements so far. He knows he does his job in a very practical and effective way and he knows his results are better than those of the average of his peers. He does run a tight ship. He feels that he has earned the right to do so, that he is objective, and that he will 'take no nonsense' about keeping his position. He has a great deal of self-confidence because after all he has been successful so far and has the conviction that hard-nosed treatment is the way to maintain high standards. To do otherwise is to coddle people and to condone behavior which is not in keeping with either our standards or the way business should be done. He believes that this is particularly true in his own country, where there is not yet a wide range of managers trained in the American way who can serve as models. He thinks that these standards have to be firmly established and even imprinted on his managers, and that these standards will lead to greater achievement and more effective business. He is not one to be concerned about pleasing others, particularly subordinates. He clearly has a great deal of personal pride—justifiably so— in his performance record.

"These episodes of 'corrective action' have increased. He seems unable to establish rapport between himself and his subordinates. Since he himself doesn't raise these issues, and I get echoes when I have occasion to talk to his subordinates, I have to raise them. He then resents the fact that I do so and resists my counseling in this area. This problem was not conspicuous before, or we might have had some reservation about putting him in this role. It's hard for me to understand the intensity with which he pursues this way of managing.

"How can I soften his heavy-handed approach and show him the need for a more humanistic attitude toward his subordinates?"

Analysis

Where Is the Pain?   The narrator is feeling considerable pain and is concerned about Hernando's methods of dealing with his subordinates. Hernando is feeling some pain and frustration at the complaints of his subordinates and the fact that his boss now has to take him to task for what he believes is a good job.

When Did It Begin?   Apparently the problem began only when Hernando took on his present job.

Ego Ideal   Hernando likes to see himself as tough and decisive. He set himself the task of "making it" in a difficult Anglo world. Because he is so visible, he is under extraordinary pressure to succeed—not only for his own sake, but also as a representative of his nationality. This magnifies the effect of anything he might perceive as failure. Given his background, he assumes everyone has to be especially tough to make it according to American managerial standards.

Affection Hernando denies his affection needs with respect to his subordinates. Apparently he does want the approval of his boss and wants to earn it by good performance.

Aggression Feeling that one has to meet the standards of another nationality or another culture inevitably means that one has, by comparison, a lower self-image than is comfortable. This leads to self-criticism as well as to efforts to cope with this low self-image by pushing oneself and one's people while denying the underlying resentment toward the more dominant culture. In such a role a person will tend to overcorrect himself and those around him and to be hostile to those of his own people who do not live up to his Americanized standards (because, after all, they represent him as well as an American company). His subordinates are always interacting publicly with their customers. They are always visible and he, too, is conspicuous. All this makes him demand greater perfection of himself, and this spills over onto his subordinates.

Dependency Hernando   appears   super   self-confident, which is a denial of dependency needs. He acts as if he doesn't need anybody, except his boss, and does not feel that he can rely on his subordinates.

Is It solvable? Probably.

How? Like any other manager, Hernando needs to develop managerial skills. The narrator should encourage Hernando to talk about what he's up against, what his particular kinds of pressures are—try to get him to open up. If the narrator can recognize that Hernando has special vulnerabilities because of his effort to live up to the standards of another culture, then he can then help Hernando focus on modifying his reactions and behavior. The narrator should lay out clearly how the company expects Hernando to deal with people—not just the rules, but the most acceptable way of handling them in practice. The narrator should point out that this isn't coddling people, it's really a way of helping them perform better by guiding and leading. The narrator should also help Hernando recognize a behavioral style of his own nationality, to make allowances for this, to recognize that he doesn't have to apologize for it, and to understand that one can reach American standards without having to be harsh and rigid.

FIVE What the Executive Doesn't See

There is an old Eastern proverb that says, "The fish is the last to know the water." In the West, as well, people are often the last to notice important dimensions of their world. They make assumptions about the conditions of their lives, often without realizing that they make these assumptions. Whenever there has been significant social improvement—as in the case of workers, women, and minority groups—it has been partly because here and there people broke through to a new consciousness and were able to give it a voice before any groundswell of public support existed for the ideas they proposed. Change must be preceded by realization—a willingness to take notice of the dimensions of one's life, to encounter new insights that can illuminate by presenting fresh perspectives for thinking about the surround, and to acknowledge the truth of what one sees.

Executives, too, constitute a special-interest group that makes certain assumptions. In general, they are better paid, more powerful, and hold more prestigious positions in our society than the majority of the members of the special-interest groups mentioned above (though individual executives may be women, may belong to a minority group, or may have begun as workers and risen through the ranks). Nevertheless, as part of the group that developed the game and the rules over a long enough time to impart to them an aura of inevitability, the typical executive, too, suffers from selective blindness. Executives take for granted the rules of the managerial game, even though the game may be changing around them. They make assumptions without realizing that they are making them. Because these assumptions go largely unrecognized, their implications for leadership and for the survival of innovative and flexible business organizations are never clearly examined. A whole range of data crucial to the survival of organizations never comes into consideration. For example, even today there is almost no mention in the management literature of unconscious motivation in conceptions of motivation, in incentive plans, in the way work groups are organized, in the way leadership functions.[1]

In an effort to better understand the total nature of organizational life, let us take a look at two realities that executives often do not recognize: the meaning of power and the psychological meaning of the work organization to the people in it.

The meaning of power. Many newly promoted managers ask, "Why do my subordinates resent my position? I haven't changed anything, but they've seemed suspicious ever since I joined the unit." People are always ambivalent about those who have power over them. They worry about how this power will be used. In Morris L. West's novel about the first Russian pope, *The Shoes of the Fisherman,* a fictional cardinal expresses sentiments that many subordinates feel: "We elected him in the name of God, and now suddenly we're afraid of him. He has made no threat, he has changed no appointment, he has asked nothing but what we profess to offer. Yet here we sit, weighing him like conspirators and making ready to fight him. What has he done to us?"[2] More recently, events in real life reiterated the observations of West's fictional cleric: Philadelphia's John Cardinal Kroll, recalling the election of Pope John Paul II, said that as the cardinals walked up the center aisle to vote, Karol Cardinal Wojtyla of Krakow appeared "all alone—as terribly alone as man is when he dies," and that the separateness became more distinct and traditional as Wojtyla became pope. In Kroll's words, a distance opened between Wojtyla and the cardinals—a distance felt by all and regretted, but inevitable.[3]

Moreover, there is little recognition among leaders in American business and industry that expectations of how power will be used are derived from a person's early experiences with authority. It follows that leaders often do not realize that these expectations must be met if leadership is to function effectively. The typical American executive seeks personal power and fears relinquishing any part of it. The concept of leadership by consent is dimly perceived. The concept of "father figure" is rarely understood; the words alone frequently are used in a negative sense. As a result, leaders seldom acknowledge their psychological obligation to their followers.

The boss who guides careers, sets salaries, and makes assignments wields considerable power over people and can change the way things are done. Subordinates, no matter what they or their bosses may think, are therefore in the *psychological* position of children, dependent on the parental boss to take care of them and watch out for their interests. Some will deny this observation; but one has only to observe what happens when executives are fired to see how powerful such underlying feelings are. And with good reason. We all started out in life totally helpless and therefore afraid. A playful adult might unintentionally have hurt us, our parents might suddenly have rejected "babyish" behavior, a teacher might have given us a bad grade. Even when we trusted adults, they controlled situations and we did not. Internally we remember being small and helpless, and we do not like being reminded of it.

The psychological meaning of the work organization. Although some companies have been concerned about the welfare of their employees to the point where they are described as maternalistic or paternalistic, these concerns tend to be material. Such provisions, beyond good wages, hours, and working conditions, are fringe benefits. They include support in emergencies, medical insurance, recreation facilities, and educational opportunities. They are *off-the-job* rewards in payment for loyalty, reliability, and time spent in the organization. What is the assumption about motivation that the executive makes here? It is that good employees will do as they are told; if they do, they will find a pot of gold at the end of the occupational rainbow. Some rainbows have a short arc—the recreation program after work. Other rainbows have a much larger arc—a pension at sixty-two, sixty-five, or seventy.

There is a perfectly sound historical reason for this quid pro quo, but it is no longer operative in the way it used to be.

When companies were family-owned businesses, those in charge had a sense of noblesse oblige: they could undertake responsibility for the employees, could in special cases make the choice to keep someone on for a while at company expense, and could generally provide a paternal kind of care. But when companies shifted to public ownership, executives were no longer free to undertake these kinds of responsibilities. An individual executive might have wanted to, but he was no longer in charge of his own resources. Rather, he was the custodian of resources belonging to the owner. He, too, had become a hired hand.

In the shift from family businesses to professional management, the old gestures of noblesse oblige were replaced by fringe benefits. From the employees' point of view, they did have the advantage of being guaranteed in a contract, rather than dispensed (or withheld) at the whim of a boss. But the change had another effect, unforeseen at the time: employees no longer felt significant attachment to individual executives and instead transferred any feelings of loyalty to the company. After all, it was the organization on which they were dependent. The relationship between employee and manager became depersonalized and the relationship between employee and organization became animated instead. The work organization has taken on psychological significance in the way that an old school might: because people relate to it in the manner of children to an adult, it assumes a significance that would be obscure to an outsider.

Assumptions that the good employee is the willing-to-be-controlled-and-rewarded employee are implemented by elaborate job descriptions, position clarifications, and salary schedules. These in turn are supplemented by policies and procedures that delimit the area of individual freedom, thus centralizing control and standardizing operations. By being unaware of the psychological meaning of work organizations and by relying on a system of reward and punishment, executives fall into the trap that I have called the Great Jackass Fallacy.[4] While conducting executive seminars I frequently ask participants what the dominant philosophy of motivation in American management is. They almost invariably say that it is the carrot-and-stick philosophy: reward and punishment. Asked to close their eyes and form a picture that has a carrot at one end and a stick at the other, and asked what they see in between, the most frequent image they report is that of a jackass. Obviously, the unconscious assumption behind reward and punishment is that one is dealing with jackasses—that people are jackasses to be manipulated and controlled.

For over a hundred years there have been essentially no changes in the employer's assumption—namely, that the superior is giving rewards for services rendered. Today, of course, executives argue that they are much kinder, that rewards are more comprehensive, and that jobs demand less in return. Still, the organization is seen as having meaning to the employees only because it provides these rewards. No other psychological significance is recognized.

Behind the widespread belief that employees should be malleable lies a distorted image of them in the minds of those who have power. Although all executives know that a good manager must keep subordinates informed, make the most of their talents, and bring them into decision making, executives have doubts about their subordinates' capacity for initiative and leadership. New ideas regarding management practice may have been persuasive, but the basic conviction about the nature of people has remained unchanged.

Any way of thinking about people in any but simplistic terms is viewed as synonymous with providing "welfare" and being "impractical." All the average manager wants to do is to increase production or sales and this means two things: "sell them" and "sweeten the kitty." The selling emphasis is heavy, but people know when they are being "sold" and their massive resistance is a major managerial problem. The usual persuasions to sell fall on deaf ears. How many employees are motivated to work harder by the argument that the stockholder needs a greater return on investment? Employees also know when they are being conned. When managers are asked, "What about looking deeper into human motivation?" the usual response is, "I haven't time to do that."

Sometimes they do not even want to. An important executive in a large company recently took part in a management development seminar. After the seminar group had spent most of the first day talking about the complexity of human motivation, he interrupted the discussion with a painful and plaintive protest: "But I don't want to have anything to do with people." When he entered industry he had not anticipated having to supervise others. That was not part of his psychological contract. He knew engineering and he wanted to use this knowledge.

"The term 'organization,'" Philip Selznick points out, "suggests a certain bareness, a lean, no-nonsense system of consciously coordinated activities. It refers to an *expendable tool*, a rational instrument engineered to do a job."[5] The resistance of scientists to scientific discoveries is well known. Resistance of management and leadership to contemporary knowledge of human motivation is no less striking. This is partly because so many managers are trained in fields that are essentially objective—such as engineering, finance, or distribution—where the focus has been on the specific and concrete. The concern of such managers is with things that can be controlled. The need to deal with more complex problems frightens many people.

If executives cannot see—or do not want to see—the psychological implications of work, they also fail to notice the implications of some of the things that go on in work settings. In particular, three of the dynamics of organizational life create barriers to psychological gratification, either because they have always constituted barriers or because recent developments have changed employees' expectations so that rules that worked once no longer work effectively. These three are the practices of keeping adults in unadultlike roles, communicating in inappropriate ways, and motivating employees from authoritarian positions.

Adults in Unadultlike Roles

In organizations the focus of management tends to be on those below, who are supposed to be responsible to those above and who therefore must adapt their behavior. The executive's initial impulse is to try to force subordinates into a mold. This attitude, when it becomes ingrained, is much like that of the parent who tries to spank a child into being good. A philosophy that assumes that management alone is responsible for making decisions and resolving problems places adult employees in an unadultlike situation. They are merely told what to do and are paid for doing it. They are exhorted to be responsible and to invest themselves in their work, but they are often not allowed to assume any real or important responsibility for what they do.

Imagine two employees in a large American company. One, from his point of view, is a free man who is legally responsible for his actions, and as a citizen plays a part in the democratic process. Yet he is free only from 5 P.M. to 8 A.M. During that time he can voice his opinions and do as he pleases. He may be a leader in his union or the local commander of the Shriners. The other, from her point of view, is a free woman, largely responsible for bringing up the children in her family; for creating the moral, intellectual, and creative atmosphere of the household, and for ensuring that the household functions in practical terms. She may influence the school board by a protest or contribute to the community by leading a Girl Scout troop on Saturdays. Yet at 8 A.M., Monday through Friday, both of those employees lose much of their freedom. Major decisions about their work are likely to be made by someone else. If they are blue-collar workers, the way in which the work is laid out, the way in which they perform it, and the amount of time allotted to it may be determined by an industrial engineer. The lower they are in terms of skill and socioeconomic level, the more likely they are to be controlled by mechanical or automated pace and processes, and the less consideration they expect from higher management.[6]

The assumption underlying this rationalization of the work process is that both of these employees are machines. They contribute little to solving the organization's problems or even those of the work unit, whether it be focused on production, marketing, or finance. There seems to be a tacit assumption that they have little to offer the organization beyond their own limited task and that their ideas, judgments, and observations are of little value to the organization. This is true despite the fact that when employees are given responsibility for meeting task obligations, the results attained are better than when quotas are set by engineers.[7] Furthermore, when workers set their own goals, there is no attempt to resist quotas as there is when management relies on industrial engineering alone.

When all the responsibility is held by those above, much time is spent exhorting employees to do more. Never are workers confronted with the realities of the organization's survival, progress, and adaptability in ways that permit them to help directly: success or failure is always management's success or failure. Sometimes, after going along for the ride for twenty years or so, employees may find that they are no longer necessary to the organization: *a machine can do better what they have been doing for a working lifetime!* They are abandoned like obsolete pieces of equipment.

In spite of the current dramatizations of people-as-machines, there is a more basic underlying problem: management's failure to recognize the change in status of the noblesse oblige concept, as well as the change in the intellectual and educational levels of many of the workers. The gulf between manager and subordinates used to be vast; now it is often much narrower. Managers deal with other managers. The salesperson who sells electronic calculators, for instance, needs to have far more technological knowledge than she did when she was selling adding machines. Yet is this increased capacity acknowledged by higher management in its policies and practices? Often it is not, even though this same management will speak of having upgraded the sales force. The isolation of people who operate data processors and other information services is a growing problem. Data processing people and growing numbers in other technical roles tend to be more heavily identified with their function than with the organization. Organizations have not spent enough time orienting them to the work of the organization itself, giving them information, or integrating them into the business as a whole. The result is a high turnover among such personnel. Since the intellectual gulf separating them from management is narrower, the lack of interaction is even more offensive. Frequently, then, the lack of communication is not the true barrier—it is the way in which people look at their subordinates. Human nature and the nature of power in our society being what they are, people want to interact with those at a higher level, to ally themselves with power. So, in an organization, people pay more courting attention to those "above" them, sensing nuances and playing to the boss's interests. On the other side of the coin, the same dynamics cause them, often quite unconsciously, to look "down" on those below them in the hierarchy—"down" in a disparaging way, finding negative qualities and using them to make scapegoats of subordinates. There is a parallel to the pattern apparent in some families where fathers or mothers, intent on fulfilling their own ambitions, abandon their children by failing to acknowledge their needs. The real barrier to communication, then, is the condescension and contempt through which messages are filtered.

Communicating in Inappropriate Ways

Often when people are spoken to directly, they seem not to hear. Recently a manager was told directly by his boss, and in the presence of others, that certain kinds of financial controls were going to be instituted. The boss was surprised when, weeks later, his subordinate acted as if he had never heard what the boss had originally said. A similar situation occurred in another company where a large number of people had been told about a forthcoming reorganization, only to act subsequently as if they had never heard of it.

Communications is a glib phrase that covers almost every kind of interaction. Most people who talk about communication and those who try to communicate well do not take into account unconscious motivation. In both of the above examples, the mechanism of denial served to shut out the words. Most organizational development activity, without a comprehensive personality theory, has no concept of aggression or, therefore, of depression, with the result that it fails to help managers understand why events such as these occur.

When communications are perceived as shocking, traumatized people go through the shock, recoil-turmoil curve that Ralph Hirschowitz has described.[8] They cannot hear, much less hear correctly, and repetitions will not necessarily reach them. Furthermore, people do not want to hear from those whose behavior demeans them. Organizations often go through the motions of letting workers in on what is happening, and fill newsletters with everything except what the employees really want to know. Recently, for example, a paper company published a newsletter full of organizational small talk and family social events, but included not a word about ongoing labor negotiations that could be expected to have significant impact on the company. Employees had to read about the progress of the negotiations in the town newspaper. The message is: "You don't really want to know or need to know. Let's make believe these things are not happening."

Managerial publications are disproportionately preoccupied with communication and communications problems. Most writers assume that failures in communication take place because superiors have not made their words clear enough for subordinates to understand. And what is the assumption on which *that* belief is based? "If the subordinates really knew the meaning behind the superiors' words and the logic behind the superiors' thinking, they would accept both and act accordingly." Large expenditures of money to improve communications, with few demonstrable results in productivity, are testimony to the widespread acceptance of this belief.

There is considerable scientific evidence to indicate that the way in which messages are received depends on the values and attitudes of the receiver.[9] A man who had disliked a book in manuscript form saw it a year later in print. He asked if this were the same book or whether it had been rewritten. The two versions were in fact the same. Seeing much of it for the first time, he approved of what he saw because the differences that had existed between him and the author a year before had been resolved. Now he could look at the book more objectively. The words were the same, but the relationship between sender and receiver was different.

The emphasis on the relief of symptoms by better communications is part of the generalized focus on "those below." The focus is apparent in both executive development and supervisory training in industry. One of the most frequent requests that comes to psychologists from top management is that psychologists train first-level supervisors in human relations. Rarely does top management understand that the way in which these supervisors handle people is a reflection of the way in which they and their subordinates behave.[10] Although management often seeks to solve its problems of relationships among people by training, the manner in which it sets up its training programs frequently is self-defeating, and, more important, produces even greater difficulty.[11] No amount of training will undo the influences and examples set by higher management. Efforts to ameliorate the symptoms by various forms of human engineering are themselves inhuman because they fail to deal with the core of human problems, people's problems.

Motivating Employees from Authoritarian Positions

The authoritarian traditions of business leadership that originated in the nineteenth century have been only slightly modified to a more benevolent but little less authoritarian style of management in the late twentieth century.

At least the style appears to be authoritarian. In some cases, it is not really so. Although a lot of what we hear about authoritarian modes would seem to be covered by the theoretical work on "Theory X," the sources of the behavior may be more varied than was originally supposed.[12] True, personality may account for authoritarian behavior, but as Otto Kernberg says, speaking about the reinforcement of authoritarian pressures derived from the institution, "A leader's authoritarian behavior may stem from features of the organizational structure and not necessarily from his personality."[13] It seems important to look beyond the individual and try to discover what aspects of the organization—most particularly the hierarchical model that characterizes most organizations—contribute to behavior that appears authoritarian.

Because of the way that the hierarchical model distributes authority, people may find themselves in positions of power without having had any training in the use of authority. Well-trained in other areas, for other tasks, they are nevertheless ill-prepared for managing the people whom they supervise. It is as if an engineer unusually skilled in designing engines for power boats were suddenly to find himself the captain of a large freighter: commanding the freighter calls for coordination management and for decision-making skills that are quite different from the skills needed to design an engine.

Furthermore, executives find themselves in multiple roles and feel multiple external pressures. Attempting to juggle the requirements of several—sometimes conflicting—roles, they may resort to commanding rather than leading in order to be able to make some progress in any direction. Actions that look authoritarian may really stem from an executive's urge to act and to avoid risking the accusation that he is someone who does not know how to take charge. In trying to fulfill some personal image of what a good manager is, executives sometimes muster a take-charge manner and come across as impulsive and insensitive, whereas a more reflective and less hurried manner might send quite different messages to their subordinates.

At this point, people's personalities may push them into action that appears authoritarian, but that results from a dimension of character that is not essentially authoritarian: the degree to which they can tolerate ambiguity. Highly impulsive people may need closure on a question sooner than will those who are more deliberate and reflective. As a result, they may push for a decision and urge action, but do it because they are impatient and not because they are exercising power for its own sake.

Authoritarian practices, then, may be what an executive resorts to under pressure. They may also be reinforced by the expectation of employees who, out of their own dependency needs, want executives to be heroic. "A hero," writes Henry Fairlie, dispirited by the lack of heroes in our times, "is not just someone whom we admire. He is someone whom we idealize. The hero has some very definite attributes of his own, but it is we who give a special significance to them."[14]

When workers look to an executive to be larger than life, to carry the responsibility of their sense of purpose as well as her own, this can place yet another demand for action on the executive. If she cannot resist this call, unreal expectations are set up: employees expect the executive to have the answers and sound the call to action. When the executive does, they may be disappointed in the note she strikes. When she does not, they are disappointed at the silence.

The underlying assumption of the organizational leader might be stated as: "We hire you, we pay you, do your job. We will control and direct you. If you obey these controls and directions, our operations will survive and you will have income. Furthermore, we will provide you with fringe benefits so that you may have your pleasure off the job." Such an assumption requires a continuous spiral of buying the employee off. Part of the repetitive round of the increasing monetary demands that are the product of labor negotiation stems directly from the "buying off" psychology of leadership and is inherently self-defeating. Management complains that increases in wages do not result in corresponding increases in motivation to work. The management that operates on this psychology, and almost all American managements do, not only fosters dependency by arrogating to itself the responsibility for the success of the organization (see whose pictures are in the front of most corporate annual reports) but also is much like

the parent who buys off a child with presents because there is
no time for significant relationships.

In recent years this problem has been accentuated by what
has been called the "paper curtain."[15] More companies are
seeking young management trainees directly from college.
There are fewer opportunities for people to rise from the
workbench through the ranks to the presidency of a company.
A class of working people has been created who themselves
will have little opportunity for advancement. The paper curtain accentuates the alienation of lower-class employees from
higher-class executives and from the organization as a whole,
leaving them with the feeling that no one really cares about
them. Not surprisingly, there is a higher incidence of psy-
chosis and serious mental illness, among people at the lower
socioeconomic levels than among those in middle and upper
classes.[16] Mental health is poorer among those alienated from
the processes of work, the work organization, and its leadership.

As pressures, social forces, and cultural cross-currents
have begun to ferment in the last two generations, it has become increasingly difficult to motivate and to manage people
from a position of power. Authoritarian methods no longer
work consistently. Even if they did, they have become unfash-
ionable. They do not work because they are based on premises
that no longer hold true: that an organization can control people, that it can promise protection and security in return for fe-
alty. Executives cannot be certain of delivering on this promise
because they do not hold the cards. They may deliver on
today's assurance for today, but they cannot deliver on the future. Authoritarian methods fail, furthermore, because smaller
units of the organization, closer to the marketplace, have to
change rapidly in response to marketing changes: a superior
often cannot tell executives what to do because he does not
know the situation—they do. On the other hand, some of the
human relations methods that have been advocated have
turned out to be extremely superficial ("increase communications," "take an interest in the men,") because they failed to
take unconscious motivations—drives, defenses, problems of
identity, mastery, dependency, attitudes toward power—into
account.

Consequences of Selective Blindness

The consequences of management's failure to acknowledge psychological and sociohistorical considerations are readily evident. In the past, one of the major consequences has been the withdrawal of power from business leadership and its transfer to labor leadership. Management, failing to confront its own mistakes, long attributed the rise of labor to the manipulation of the masses by unscrupulous agitators. Psychologically, the behavior of labor leaders in any industry has been a mirror image of the style of management in that same industry. Rough, tough management groups spawned rough, tough union leadership. Labor power has been one of the managerial consequences of ignoring psychological data.

Now management is learning to hear what its employees have to say, but, as reflected in attitude surveys, it still tends to listen largely in one way: "Just tell me what you feel. Tell me what's wrong, and I'll remedy it." Until management moves toward a two-way, working relationship with employees, it cannot expect to help in any but short-term ways.

A second consequence is the resentment, fear, anger, and disillusionment that so often characterize the relationship between executive management and both middle management and line-level employees. As long as top management assumes that its power is its own, it tends to operate unilaterally. No matter how well-intentioned, unilateral action is seen as threatening by those who are affected by it. To whatever extent people are subject to the action of someone else, they are less able to predict their own future and to exercise control over it. Furthermore, if unilateral action of a benevolent kind can be taken, then there is always the possibility that destructive unilateral action can occur. There is a large body of evidence concerning employee sabotage of unilateral management action and the subsequent guilt of the saboteurs.

More serious are the impaired relationships with the work organization. A reciprocal relationship is an important asset to the mental health of a person.[17] If this relationship is impaired, it becomes a source of stress and tension rather than a source of support and personal enhancement. From the company's point of view, the employee's identification with the company and its goals is undermined.

A third consequence is the recent pressure in organizations to promote young people rapidly in order to be more competitive. Management has filled high-level spots with young people. Now younger people, having been in one position for some time, are pressing to move up. Companies that are not expanding as rapidly as they once did are having difficulty keeping their promises of rapid promotion to the bright young men and women they hired during the expansion years.[18] There are thus fewer slots for the even younger people behind them. The pyramidal structure carries within it the seeds of its own defeat. To compensate for the unavailability of promotion slots, companies have resorted to title inflation, participative management, and lateral transfers—none of which will work well. Sometimes they have added more slots in order to give the illusion of promotion. But in fact the slots have been too close together, with too little differentiation between them, making it difficult for superiors to exercise power and authority over those who report to them.

Many organizations are concerned about how to keep such people motivated. The hierarchical model, with its penchant for creating more defeated people than victorious ones, makes for a self-fulfilling prophecy. There is a pile-up of "career" people who are destined to stay in their grade and are often depressed. Organizations run the risk of becoming stagnant as restless people merely mark time or seek positions elsewhere. Young executives today show signs of being committed to working in accord with their ego ideals. They want to act and interact—they do not want to be put on hold or to fade unobtrusively into the background of organizational life. And they will not stick around for nothing. Businesses with attitudes and policies that go against the grain of the young will not be able to attract or keep managerial talent in the coming years, notes John B. Miner.[19] There must be changes in organizational structure, in processes like compensation and in assumptions about motivation.

Finally, leaders as well as subordinates suffer as a result of executive selective blindness. Too often, executives try to solve this problem alone, when it is also the problem of those below—those who are trapped in slots, unable to move up because there are no openings, often unable to move even laterally because the same situation pertains in other organizations. And because executives accept the assumption of authority and hierarchy, avoiding interaction with those less powerful than they, it is very difficult for them to develop an interactive model with their subordinates and join together to find solutions.

Managers, sensing the difficulty in traditional modes of management, have tried to eliminate the problems in different ways. Some have taken the easiest defensive road by denying the reality of underlying psychological needs and by saying in effect, "My job is to make a profit and to make this organization survive. I'm not going to be concerned about how the people feel. They will do what I tell them or they won't be around here very long." Others have struggled in more painful ways. One company president has unwittingly abandoned the leadership of his organization. He has become so concerned with some aspects of the psychology of his situation that he has forgotten he is supposed to be a manager. He appointed a vice-president to fulfill one of the major organizational functions, and then he was surprised when people in the organization began to look to the new vice-president not as a vice-president but as the executive vice-president. As a matter of fact, the man was not the executive vice-president, and the president could not understand why so many people turned to him in this way. What the president did not see was that, in his preoccupation, he was not leading. Furthermore, he was so taken with what he considered to be democratic leadership—but what was really nonleadership—that he thought an organization could run itself if only it were sufficiently democratic. Nonleadership is one thing; leadership that makes believe it does not lead while retaining the effective power to manage is another. So long as the power is centralized, there will be expectations about how leadership should use it. When the power is not being used by the nominal leader, people will turn to someone else. By the very structure of the organization, they have no right to use the power themselves. Functionally, they cannot anyway. Someone must. No organization can function without a leader.

Another president, when he started his company, had determined to give special attention to the motivation of his people: he would give them something to work for. He intended to accomplish this by working with his men on the line, by showing them that he was democratic and that he was not going to dictate to them simply because he owned the company. He still does not know why he is having so many difficulties in the organization and why there is so much bickering among the top-management group. A general cannot lead by being an infantryman.

Another company president took a different approach. He would have no trappings of business in his office—no desk or any other office equipment. Instead, he would have a living-room suite so that anybody who wanted to would feel free to come in and talk with him. This, however, was strictly a gimmick because he quickly made it plain that he did not want to talk with anybody. He would call meetings and then not appear; he would keep people waiting indefinitely. He would assign a group of men to a task; after months of work they would return with a set of plans to which he would say, "But anybody would know this plan isn't good for anything." In his eyes, he was challenging and stimulating his men. He did challenge them—never again to open their mouths.

Yet another chief executive resolved the problem very effectively. He has only one chair in his office—his. This means that nobody can talk to him for more than a few minutes and all who come in must stand up. He effectively cuts himself off from his people and manages to deny the reality of his power position.

The failure of executives to take charge and give active leadership can be as devastating to an organization as frankly autocratic leadership. Nowadays this kind of failure is masked by a soft understanding—or misunderstanding—of democratic management. Too many executives have become afraid of disciplining their subordinates and children. To exert control, they think, is to become "Theory X," or authoritarian. Some are afraid they will not be liked. Yet those with less power require control and guidance from those with more. In addition, they need a model of effective parental behavior. As Roy Schafer points out in his paper on "The Loving and Beloved Superego," all relationships contain ambivalence.[20] Over time, a person builds up a residue of guilt about his negative feelings. When he receives just but not overly harsh discipline, he has a way to relieve himself of guilt and repair his relationships through an appropriate degree of suffering and sacrifice. Thus, he can free himself for adaptive functioning instead of provoking authority or seeking self-punishment.

Executives who abdicate leave their people nothing solid to work with and soon find themselves lacking necessary information for making decisions. Their subordinates become accustomed to acting on their own. Essentially they run the company themselves and merely report their decisions to their boss. With no one to integrate or coordinate the various decisions and policies, in time they will be at odds with each other. Trouble erupts in spite of participative management.

Constraints on the Executive's Task

What the executive does not see has a parallel in the organizational structure: what cannot be seen cannot be addressed. For instance, the trend toward thinking of people and problems in terms of numbers, percentages, norms, and mass makes it increasingly difficult to conceive of social problems in human terms. Thinking solely in computer terms tends to eliminate or ignore those problems that cannot be computerized—in particular, people's feelings. Management cannot deal with problems it cannot "see." If it can conceptualize only computerized problems, others are likely to ferment until they explode. Among these may be the psychological problems of the middle class and middle management that result from technological change.

The issue is the same in science, industry, and government. With the pressure for publication, and especially for statistical documentation, scientists turn frequently to studies that lend themselves readily to "yes-no" answers and tests of statistical significance. There is, therefore, a tendency to lose sight of the richness and complexity of issues, to think not about the dimensions of a problem but the dimensions of experimental design.[21] Simple scanning of scientific journals demonstrates this trend. Reflective, integrative articles, not to mention comprehensive theoretical books, are comparatively rare in scientific circles. Even in the humanities, which are supposed to be concerned with human feelings and values, there are frequent complaints about computerized doctoral dissertations which yield little that is new and less that is insightful.

One dimension of the cost of focusing on problems that can be computerized is the failure to anticipate problems that may arise out of people's feelings. In my own experience, I have seen virtually dozens of consultants' reports gather dust on executive office shelves because, despite the weight of their evidence, they have stopped short of the human problems of introducing change.

It was the fear of narrow thinking and lack of consideration of nonmeasurable matters that led Norbert Weiner to point out that the computer, if used by the military, might produce a victory but at the cost of "every interest we have at heart, even that of national survival."[22] This is not to say that we should abandon or ignore the contributions of computer technology. Some problems need only the weighing of objective facts for their solution. Traffic control is a simple example. Others require the consideration of aesthetics, moral values, stereotypes, prejudices, and opinions, in conjunction with facts. It may be more economical to run electric transmission lines through an expensive residential area, but what will the residents think about it? Should a highway be put through a redwood forest if it is cheaper to do so than to skirt the forest?

Questions of judgment about human social problems must take into account something more than easily obtained facts. A critical question has to do with who is responsible for social decisions.[23] Given masses of facts, and cost-efficiency decisions based on those facts, it is relatively easy for a deliberative body to avoid responsibility by saying in effect, "The computer said so." A number of noted physicists who were involved in the development of the atomic bomb have continued to raise the question of responsibility for the consequences of their work. Are they responsible for the results of their technology? Does a chemical company have any responsibility for how people use pesticides? For the ill-effects of chemical waste buried near residential communities?

Issues of judgment and responsibility are becoming harder to cope with as the average citizen feels less and less knowledgeable. Even members of Congress complain that they cannot critically examine what the executive branch proposes. This means people are compelled to trust someone who presumably knows the answers. They themselves are likely to feel helpless about solving problems.

The problem of mechanistic-statistical thinking is not just

a problem of the data-processing machinery available to us. It has a more complex background, related to the American drive for power—economic rewards, materialistic achievements, political position. Psychological evidence indicates that high power motives and high achievement motives taken together not only produce wealth and power, but also a high incidence of isolation, insecurity, and stress.[24] High achievement motivation in a culture is correlated with such psychosomatic symptoms as ulcers and high blood pressure; high power motivation is correlated with increasing rates of murder, suicide, and alcoholism. More important is the fact that material achievement—wealth and productivity—is purchased at the expense of original thought. People who "strive" hard all day want only light entertainment afterward and seem to have neither the energy nor the interest to think deeply when they feel they must *act* rather than think. In this kind of a culture there is strong pressure toward simplistic, statistical thinking, computers aside.

The development of science in the United States has followed a parallel trend. American scientists have been heavily oriented toward experiment rather than theory. Although they have produced a dazzling array of technical achievements ranging from a cure for infantile paralysis to flights to the moon, a disproportionate share of the fundamental theory from which these achievements have been derived has come from European scholars.[25]

These two trends—the shallowness of thinking that is correlated with the drive for power and achievement, and the technically oriented style of American science—only make more vivid the varied forces pressing toward mechanistic thinking in the business world. This pressure is further increased when both forces are joined, as in the fact that in 1965 "38 percent of approximately 1,000 top officers of the nation's 600 largest nonfinancial corporations had degrees in engineering or natural science, or equivalent on-the-job experience."[26] Furthermore, the strength of this combination of forces is increasing. The proportion of top executives with engineering or science degrees jumped from 7 percent in 1900 to 20 percent in 1950 to 38 percent in 1964. Business schools that emphasize scientific management orientation—a combination of computer-based technical thinking, engineering orientation, and high achievement motivation—may be preparing executives for the business world to come, but it will be a world in which human feelings are systematically denied.

The narrator here describes the kind of double bind that can occur when an organization's policies are in conflict with accepted standards of behavior and when top management is closing its eyes, preferring to ignore an admittedly sticky situation rather than come to grips with it.

"I am a writer/editor for an advertising research firm known for its accuracy and honesty. The company was just getting started when I first began to work here four years ago. Jackson, the vice-president to whom I report, used to come in at night to help when we had more work than the staff could handle. He would run the stapling machine, the mailer, pitching in wherever help was needed. In those days we had a powerful feeling of what Jackson called 'esprit de corps.' Bonuses were handed out frequently. Good work was well rewarded, with my salary rising 100 percent the first year I worked here. People were happy and felt vital to the operation.

"Success has diminished that feeling. I realize that growth makes it almost impossible to maintain that special sense of closeness. We are certainly far more efficient now, no longer having to work all night to get a job out, and, as one wagster put it, you can now tell the secretaries from the bosses.

"If it weren't for the 'good ole days' I would leave. A problem of ethics in the field has arisen. It grew from an error when one of our sample cities was improperly set up for a major client product survey. Data from that area represent an important segment of our sample. Since the data were wrong, I suggested we return the client's money, redo the survey, and make sure an error like this never occurred again. The client company, however, is not known for its tolerance and had been less than satisfied with our more recent work. Jackson decided that since we had data from our other test centers, we would go with that and write the report from those figures. This was done, but a comparison showed such a large statistical deviation from the norm that our statisticians (and I) were concerned. Jackson then made the decision to have five people sit in a room and 'write-up' data. These papers were shoved in with the legitimate batch to make up the final sample. The client report, which I had to write, was based on these pseudo-statistics.

"I talked to Jackson about it, telling him I felt a little soiled. He assured me that the situation was 'a freak thing—it won't happen again.' I accepted this, but it has happened again. An entire sample was made up this way for an old client whose product's advertising has changed little over the years. Although I realize that the figures from the made-up survey closely approximate the data we acquire in our usual manner, the whole thing stinks as far as I'm concerned.

"What should I do? I have talked to Jackson. He obviously isn't interested in listening to me. I'm fairly sure the partners know what's been going on. They were around the day we did the first faked data. If I go somewhere with my story the firm might be discredited, lots of good people would lose jobs, and I would be known throughout the industry as a 'fink.' "

Analysis

Where Is the Pain?   The narrator has pain because of the conflict between his own standards and the manipulation that is taking place in his organization.

When Did It Begin?   With a recent error in the statistical sampling.

Ego Ideal   The narrator expects himself and his superiors to act with integrity. He feels that he cannot in conscience continue with the organization and the dishonesty of the organization, but at the same time he feels he has an obligation to his organization and his superiors. He recognizes that to admit the mistake would threaten the relationship with an already disgruntled client. At the same time he finds it hard to live with himself when false data are being reported. Furthermore, he doesn't want to be known as a fink and to have a reputation as a squealer.

Affection   Apparently the narrator likes the people that he is working with, the organization he is working in, and the work he is doing. He apparently has related well to those people and they to him and speaks of esprit de corps and closeness.

Aggression   The narrator characteristically funnels his aggression into work and into doing a reliable and trustworthy job. He is able to speak about his disquiet and discomfort in the face of the manipulation of the data, and apparently, if he must, he will be able to take a stand with respect to his own standards.

Dependency   Apparently the narrator is highly dependent on his superior, the organization, and his relationship to them or he would have left the organization earlier. He might have to go to another organization, perhaps even another industry, in order to get another job, but apparently, for whatever reasons, he needs to hang on and to sustain that relationship.

Is It Solvable?   Probably.

How?   The narrator must recognize that he cannot continue to badger his bosses to correct their behavior without incurring their wrath as he exacerbates their guilt. He also needs to recognize that as long as he remains in the organization, there will be a conflict of conscience. His best option is to leave the organization for another role where he will not be made uncomfortable by dishonest dealings.

Problems of conscience are troublesome problems because they usually require definitive action with limited options. In this case the narrator is faced with a clearly dishonest and unethical situation. His superiors are unwilling to act responsibly and he has little choice but to live with them or to leave the organization.

If he chooses to leave, he doesn't necessarily have to tell his story elsewhere.

PART 2

Redefining Leadership

Once the psychosocial terrain has been at least partially mapped, the executive task becomes less illusory. What is the executive expected to do in contemporary society? What is the organization to do? And with whom are they to do it? In this section some of the major dimensions of executive and organizational tasks will be sketched.

The question is often asked, "What business are we in? What is the broadest possible conception that will enable us to retain maximum flexibility yet not dilute our efforts?" This section addresses itself to similar but more comprehensive questions: "What is the broadest social function of the business institution? How can it be conceived of so that it retains its basic economic purposes yet adapts itself flexibly to social evolution?"

Answering these questions does not mean abandoning the historic role of the business organization or trying to substitute other purposes. Rather, it calls for shifting the emphasis to those aspects of the managerial role and organizational effort that, in the past, have been largely regarded as secondary. This discussion reconfirms the fundamental importance of human relationships for economic as well as social purposes by showing that what is often considered superficial has become the heart of the contemporary business matter.

SIX The Tasks
of Top Management

hat is it that we want business leaders to do? The discussion so far suggests three major tasks: they must manage their business, be effective social engineers, and maintain democratic values.

Top management must manage the business so that it will survive. This requires bringing out "the great energies and talents of its people," as Thomas J. Watson, Jr., has noted, and is probably the most significant element in the difference between success and failure.[1] Watson argues cogently that neither size nor present demand for the company's goods and services is a real indication of its capacity to survive. The capacity for perpetuation lies in continuous regeneration. Contemporary behavioral science research, as we saw in Chapter 2, shows that there is indeed the possibility of a "fountain of youth" in organizations. Organizations can create social and psychological climates that are conducive to the creativity and flexibility of organization because they permit the people in them to grow. More than the company's success is at stake: in addition to the returns paid to investors and the monetary and psychological rewards to employees, business provides the underlying financial stability for social institutions such as colleges, hospitals, research institutes, and even federal, state, and local governments.

As social engineers, business leaders direct numbers of people and organize systems of service or production, managing them in communities and wielding considerable civic power. They exert personal and organizational influence to improve schools and social services and to produce the goods and services that contribute to our standard of living. They influence vast segments of society, for good or evil—for instance, by conserving or depleting natural resources. Business leaders are being called upon to help explicitly in managing these parts of society, to assume responsibility in circumstances where they have long exercised power. One of these leaders, Irving Shapiro, chairman of the board and chief executive officer of DuPont, estimates that he spends from 30 to 40 percent of his week on activities outside DuPont: "We've got to help make the whole system work, and that involves more than just having a safe workplace and providing jobs for the number of people we can hire."[2]

This is not to say that a sense of social obligation is generated only at the top levels of management. Pressures from workers, too, can affect company policies. Polaroid's ultimate withdrawal from South Africa, for example, began with pressure from black employees in the United States who objected to Polaroid film being used to make the passes that South African blacks must carry. In fact, it is the worker, as an employee and consumer, who holds the power to make corporations accountable for the public welfare, according to Karl-Valentin Ullrich, a German economist who has taught at Harvard and the University of Freiburg. Ullrich says that "the free market system needs social responsibility from corporations if it is to be preserved," and advocates a corporate director who is entrusted with the company's social responsibility program, a kind of corporate ombudsman who could mediate among the public, the employees, and the corporation when company policies are called into question. Ullrich contends that corporate social responsibility makes "good business sense" from both the employees' and company's standpoint because employees who have pride in their company find meaning in their work and do their work more efficiently. He adds that European employees whose companies have excellent reputations for their social policies often wear buttons with their corporation's name printed on them.[3]

Other social critics caution about organizational involvement. Peter Drucker insists that the sphere of influence of large-scale organizations must be limited to what is necessary for the fulfillment of their social functions. "All around us," he says, " 'responsibilities' are being asserted by large-scale organizations—businesses, unions, universities, military services, and what have you—which are simply not grounded in the necessary function of the institutions. Let us not forget that 'responsibility' always carries with it 'authority'; whenever any institution asserts its 'responsibility' it must have authority in the area . . . The job our large-scale organizations have to do is so big that they need a great deal of authority; and the impacts they make, of necessity, are so great that they carry heavy responsibilities. But let us make sure that they do not go beyond this, no matter how well-meant, how attractive, or even how badly needed such action may be."[4]

Yet business executives have no choice but to see themselves increasingly as social engineers. Business leadership, already required for many governmental tasks, will be called upon to manage other social institutions. This new demand can, potentially, put executives in an awkward spot if they see a conflict between their obligations to the corporation and their obligations to the community. Frederick Pollock observes that planning ahead for social responsibilities is difficult because anyone who assumes executive functions in a large business organization today must be prepared to identify "body and soul" with the organization.[5] Nevertheless, the business executive has a dual responsibility because a business is a "profit center" for a community as well as for its immediate employees. Unless it produces economic, political, psychological, and other "profits" for a community, it should not be there.

Since executives serve, they are in many ways elected leaders, and, as time goes by, judgments of *all* those who are affected by their power will be heard more frequently. This means that people will expect them to extend leadership and not merely increase controls. They will look to the power of leadership to help them expand the psychological rewards they can obtain from their work, and the material rewards, in terms of living standards, that are to be had in the broader society.

In some ways, people undoubtedly expect too much. There has been a lot said about the sense of deprivation that people experience because they can no longer make a complete product (the Volvo plant experiment, along with others that have explored group work procedures, interchangeable jobs, and group compensation, attempted to make up for this sense of deprivation).[6] Some observers say that since workers are divorced from their products, they see no particular significance in their contribution to productivity and, as a result, their sense of purpose in life is diminished; these observers then argue that to recover a sense of worthwhile achievement, the employee must look beyond work for his greatest satisfactions. To a large extent this argument is based on a misconception about the past. Historically, few people were ever creative—most simply struggled for a livelihood in a primitive fashion until the industrial revolution made it possible for large numbers to have a higher standard of living. The employee's sense of deprivation probably lies less in the loss of the experience of shaping some *thing* than in the experience of shaping his or her own world.[7] It is the loss of responsibility and the failure to use adult capacities that make us feel childlike, useless, inadequate, and incompetent. These experiences of loss have been particularly salient in the large group of socially immobile people from whom the chronically unemployed are drawn. Now, because of technological change, the same kinds of loss experiences threaten middle-class, middle-management people. In acting as a social engineer, one goal of the executive is to mitigate this loss experience in the interest of the survival of a democratic society as well as of the particular organization.

The executive's third task is to take the lead in developing and strengthening the social forces that uphold the American democratic heritage and to combat those that threaten it. The business leader has too often allied himself with the past instead of the future. He has talked too much about returning to bygone eras, opposed every major protective innovation from child labor laws to social security, and has attacked governments while simultaneously seeking government money and protection.

As a leader, the executive cannot lag behind; he must lead. Society expects this because of the cultural conception we have of authority figures, the tremendous power that executives have (and will have more of), and the changing expectations of the people who are moving into the middle class. Executives are expected to manage the business, and any aspects of society that relate to the business, in ways that will sustain the beliefs Americans hold dear.

Values of freedom, opportunity, and democratic decision making are the core of American initiative and vitality and way of living. As a nation, Americans will not let these values be threatened from the inside. They will neither relinquish democratic values nor tolerate increasing authoritarianism. If executives appear to threaten rather than sustain these values, then ultimately, as Watson noted, society will constrain the corporation to the point of taking it over.

One Model of Leadership

The executive's perspective on the business must be visionary, including not only where it stands today but where it should be twenty years from now. This calls for a process of continuous reappraisal about risk and social responsibility. Bernard Muller-Thym points out that modern business came into being only after World War II, when it became the primary organ in our society for the creation and management of wealth: "Since wealth is generated not by production or any other functionally defined operation, but as the net effect of the total system, the task of the design and management of the total business now appeared with a specificity and separate identity which had not been recognized before."[8] Thus, top-management work became useful, separate from what a subordinate could do. According to Muller-Thym, the unique top-management tasks include:

1. Design of the business and all the separate businesses that may be included in its structure.

2. Optimization of corporate resources.

3. Management of perpetuity. Management education is part of this task since it looks to the creation of a managerial group, advanced in prudence as in managerial competencies, flexible and ready for the needs of the enterprise at any point in the future.

4. Management of innovation.

5. Keeping the business relevant to the culture, society, and polity in which it functions.

6. Keeping the aims of the business and its conduct well related to those larger aims that lie outside itself (this task springs from the design and goal-setting activity).

How does this theory translate into practice? Some would say that these observations are little more than wishful thinking, and even less true for small organizations than for large ones. From a survey of 903 top executives, Ithiel de Sola Pool concluded that the job of heading a small company is different from that of heading a large one; he designates four hundred employees as the dividing line.[9] The head of a small firm is a production manager and a salesman. Much of the work is inside management: considering the efficiency of subordinates and how they spend their time, and evaluating the methods they use to process the firm's work. On the outside he addresses his main efforts to selling. The head of a large company, in contrast, devotes himself to two quite different concerns: the firm's public and its investment and expansion policy. Heads of large companies look more broadly at the national scene and the market, considering how their organizations can be better placed within both.

Pool adds that presidents of modern companies seldom envision themselves as people of great power. Often they feel more vulnerable than many of their subordinates. Perhaps they have brought nothing with them into the firm but their own brains and experience, and can act with a free hand only as long as the results are good. They may be fired at will by the directors, and often are. Although they are proud that they have done something notable in rising to the top, the reward at the top is income, recognition, and status—but not unlimited power. The president, too, is just an employee.

With more data at hand, more pressure for performance, and more effective ways of measuring performance and competition, Leavitt and Whisler have argued that top management positions are becoming increasingly tenuous and that company presidents are more likely than before to move from one organization to another.[10] This may raise questions about whether a business organization will have enough continuity of management to foster and develop the kinds of psychological ties that meet people's needs and expectations. They predict that there will not only be top-executive team operations, which already exist in such large organizations as General

Motors, but that top-level performance will be more accurately evaluated by colleagues, a practice likely to produce greater emphasis on performance and less on conformity. In their view, the higher turnover likely to occur at top-management levels will actually be conducive to greater flexibility.

Responding to Change

Responsiveness to the environment and to the changes taking place around an organization is probably the most fundamental requirement of leadership. Consider the changes that have taken place in the past ten years: organizations and their leaders must contend with inflationary pressures, the decline of the dollar, and an ominous shortage of oil. The capital shortage means there is not enough money to invest in all the possibilities. And although oil may be the most dramatic example of depletion just now, it is not the only one: we are running low on timberlands, unpolluted waterways, fish in the ocean, and soil on the land. There is increased competition from overseas; Japanese, German, British, and Dutch companies are buying American companies, reversing a trend that we had become used to. The development of good overseas management schools, too, has changed the way business is done in other countries. There is an increase in mergers and acquisitions, and simultaneously the threat of legislative and judicial actions to curtail them. In some areas markets are saturated. Coupled with the slowdown in the economy are the rising expectations of women, minorities, and the nation's less privileged sons and daughters.

How are organizations, then, to "hang loose," as Fletcher Byrom says, "and listen for the winds of change?"[11] Decentralization of power is one avenue for putting more power in the hands of the executives who are closest to the market and its changing tides.

Centralization of power is a major obstacle that leaders face in meeting the expectations of society. To what degree is power surreptitiously centralized and access to it narrowly circumscribed? There are a number of ways in which it is centralized: we can look at who has access to leadership roles and how power is used in the network of relationships among those who hold it.

Ten years ago, despite the unprecedented upward mobility of people from lower socioeconomic levels, an increasing proportion of those who had moved into the business elite during the past two generations came from well-to-do families of high economic but low social status.[12] The chances of a man becoming president of a major business organization in this country were considerably higher if he had graduated from one of the Ivy League schools or came from a wealthy family.[13] The reasons were obvious: they had contacts, social advantages, and an educational edge. Today this pattern has changed. Twenty years ago, in a study of one hundred corporations with the highest sales, Andrew Hacker found that presidents of these corporations tended to be grandsons of "old American families," with 60 percent belonging to Protestant churches.[14] Ten years later, Hacker found that the top men in the top companies were symbolic of a new breed of American. "The future corporation president can emerge from anywhere in the generous bosom of the American middle class ... It doesn't matter where he went to school and, in most cases, no one cares who his father was or what he did for a living. Among the top executives today there are more products of the Big Ten than of the Ivy League."[15]

This does not mean that educational milieu has no bearing on a young person's chances, because it obviously does. A *Harvard Business Review* article reported in a 1975 survey that nearly half of the executives interviewed had done some graduate work and over 43 percent had graduate degrees.[16] A recent study by Korn/Ferry International, a large executive recruitment organization, surveyed over three thousand senior level executives and presented this composite of the executive: a fifty-three-year-old white male, born in a medium-sized Midwestern city, educated at a large public university (where he worked to pay part of his college expenses), and possessing an M.B.A. from a private university such as Harvard.[17] To date, there are not enough women in similar positions for us to know if the same patterns will hold. But the dynamic that appears to hamper women on the way up seems to be the same as that which hampered men from less privileged families some years ago. Margaret Hennig and Anne Jardim point out that as women are drawn to management, one of the ways they find themselves at a disadvantage is that they are not automatically knit into the "old boy" networks that underlie high-level corporate power.[18] Women do not meet other women on the squash court, on the golf course, or at the club, and are therefore outside the loop of influence, excluded from sites where contacts are made and reinforced, business conducted, and decisions made. Conscious efforts to become members of these networks and to establish linkages of their own among women in positions of authority need to be part of the strategy of women in management.

An alternative to moving through the managerial ranks, for some people, is to achieve independent success either financially or in some specialized function, and then be brought laterally into the top-management hierarchy. This is what is happening in some government circles: although there is a well-established civil service equivalent to middle management, top management people are politically appointed, with rare exception, at top levels for their specialized knowledge and contributions. In this case, business organizations may come to look something like the family-dominated organizations of Italy.[19] In such oligarchic systems, the road to position for the outsider is marriage into the family. In American organizations even now, when it is no longer possible to count on the people inside in order to meet new corporate needs, outsiders with special knowledge and skills must be brought in. When American Telephone and Telegraph had to shift from a production to a marketing mode, for example, it was forced to change drastically its management-development policy. Like that of IBM, the policy had been to cultivate leaders from the ranks. But faced with the imperative to shift to a marketing orientation, its ranks could not provide all of the needed skills, and so people from the outside were "married to" the existing management structure.

Centralization of power is an issue that bears not only on *who* holds the power but on *how* it is wielded. In business circles, there are some chief executive officers who see themselves as peers, members of the Business Roundtable, while others, who are not viewed as part of the hierarchy in the same way, are excluded from the inner circle. The same thing happens within organizations, noncommercial as well as commercial. During the faculty strike of a major eastern university, it was discovered that the night before the board of trustees refused to ratify a contract already negotiated by the faculty union and the administration, the university president had met with seventeen specially selected trustees—out of a board totaling forty-eight trustees—to discuss how to sidestep ratification. Centralization of power does not necessarily proceed unchallenged. In this case, objecting to the strategy, one board member wrote a memo that said, "To allow attendance at such a rump session to become a legal substitute for attendance and voting on controversial issues at a duly called official meeting of the board is setting a very dangerous precedent, to say the least."[20]

Cultural factors influence the ways in which power is used. Frederick Pollock contends that in an age of automation a new kind of society based upon authoritarian or military principles may well evolve.[21] Something like a general staff of people could have power and information (information itself becoming a means to power), and could conceivably command all the other employees. Although day-to-day operations might be carried out by specialists—such as engineers, administrators, and public-relations men—the general staff would be the equivalent of military officers. In Pollock's view, we can now see evolving a homogeneous class of executives who hold great intellectual and material power and are superior to the vast mass of the population—a social class that will control the mass media. With larger businesses and larger power at hand, there will be an increasing tendency toward authoritarianism. Although his view may be somewhat apocryphal, what we do see now in organizations is greater control.

Social psychologist Donald Michael, recognizing that information can become transmitted into power, has observed that the existence of privileged information, resulting from automatic data processing and specialized knowledge, will lead to an authoritative unelected ruling class.[22] If the public does not have access to data on which to develop informed opinion, its capacity for political judgment will be limited. And if information of this kind becomes the major factor when decisions are made, there is likely to be a shift in emphasis from concern with people, and problems related to people (and from leaders who understand these matters), to leaders who can do computer thinking. The more we concentrate on efforts based on data that come from automatic data processing, the more difficulty we will have in coping with the ambiguous and illogical aspects of society. People who place their dependence on information that can be quickly gathered and statistically interpreted will be less patient with the slow, illogical, and emotional processes of democracy. There will be a tendency to deal only in the mass, with little consideration for the individual. Problems that lend themselves to statistical treatment will get first attention. Already this is happening: we see it in the emphasis on performance appraisal, forced choice ratings, and MBO's.

Michael's thinking coincides with Pollock's thesis: the general public will be alienated from its own productive and governmental processes and will become less sensitive to human dangers. As the population becomes more remote from a sense of influence on national and international events, it becomes more the victim of insecurity and ennui. Signs of apathy are already clear. In New England fewer people attend town meetings in the spring, and throughout the country fewer voters go to the polls in the fall. An apathetic population will zealously focus only on the occupational needs of the day and will be less able to contribute to the mastery of intergroup and social problems. This may lead people to withdraw from public participation and to reorient their lives to private recreation. Indeed, the "me" generation is accused of doing just that. Further evidence of Michael's point of view may be apparent in the proliferation of engineering and technical advances, compared to the relative paucity of advances in the social sciences.

Within a given organization, then, top management may find that cultural factors team up with personal factors to centralize power and reduce flexibility. Any move to decentralize obviously requires more than mere changes on a chart. To be successful, there must be deliberate efforts to change the thinking—the assumptions and unconscious motivation—of the people involved. Fletcher Byrom talks about it this way: "What we've done is replace one chief operating officer with five chief operating officers—five presidents. This is not an additional line in the hierarchy. We're eliminating one level. We used to have five division general managers, and, for all intents and purposes, these five presidents cover the same areas those managers did. We've moved them up and said,

'Look, you're not to think like a division general manager; you're expected to think like a president.' " Asked to explain the difference, he says: "By the end of this year, we'll probably have thirty division general managers instead of five. We want those division general managers to have the same authority the presidents had when they were general managers. So what we're saying is, the chief operating officers should start to manage after the fact. They're not supposed to make decisions on matters that are the responsibility of division general managers.

"Their responsibility is to make sure they've got a sensing system so that after the fact they can understand what is going on. And it ought to be, essentially, on a real-time basis, so that they have the opportunity to question the person who has carried out a particular action when they feel it's wrong, and see to it that we don't repeat any errors."[23]

Decentralizing an organization means that much authority is taken away from staff units and given to operating units. This places staff units in a consulting role, and along with their loss of authority they experience a sense of severe psychological loss. It is important to provide solid training and consultation immediately after such changes take place so the staff units can begin to practice their new role, to identify with it, and to recognize that they are acquiring new skills to enable them to operate in new ways, rather than being left with the feeling that they have been shunted aside by the changes.

If executives are held responsible for the work of subordinates, they must possess the power to see that it gets done. Sir Wilfred Brown defines managers as those who are responsible for more work than they personally can perform.[24] They must therefore arrange for others to do some of it, although remaining accountable for the manner in which it is done. But if held accountable, the manager needs certain authority over those who will do the work, such as being able to veto the appointment of subordinates, assess their competence for the task, and decide whether to retain them. It also helps to have some authority for determining their relative salaries. Without these authorities, an executive simply does not have command. Brown's definition provides an excellent guide for measuring whether authority and responsibility are being allocated in concert in any organization.

As an organization moves toward decentralization, another change in the hierarchy may be a diffusion in the system of reporting. For many years an axiom in management has been that an employee should have to report to only one superior. However, with greater and more widespread use of task forces and matrix organizations, more and more people have to report to more and more bosses. This means that each person has the job of integrating and coordinating the responses of multiple superiors. This kind of situation provides an opportunity for playing one off against the other, but in the long run this will be costly for the subordinate. Having multiple bosses is a difficult problem for the subordinate because often they will be vying for power and the subordinate will be caught in the middle. Instead of being able to depend on coordination from above, people will have to do their own coordinating. This means that, in these flexible organizations, much coordination will have to come from below.

Balancing Obligations

If the executive is to manage the business for survival, be a social engineer, and maintain democratic values, he must act positively and avoid known pitfalls. One pitfall is the danger of equating gimmicks with control.[25] For example, the problem of the trend toward a power elite, with subsequent alienation of middle management from top management, will not be solved by building small scattered plants to maintain a personal touch between levels. With more centralized control, such a solution is only a gesture. Unless real power lies at the plant level, relationships will be tenuous so long as the people in the plant know that the power lies elsewhere. People have little reason to identify with a manager who is powerless to work on their behalf or to seek their help in the solution of mutual problems.

Another pitfall is to fail to understand the deep relationship between an organization and the community. The community can be seen as the surrounding town, whose inhabitants are affected by the company's expansions, contractions, and closings, or by the strikes, pay increases, or benefit reductions the company implements. But it can also be the wider community—all of the people who buy its products or receive its services. Much of the discussion about profit motives and social responsibility—as if these were two conflicting interests, competing for priority—does not take into account the perceptions people have simply because an organization exists. The corporation is a social invention and has been given legal rights (and obligations) similar to those of an individual. Like a person, a corporation can be taxed. Like a person, it can be sued. Companies, like people, can merge, and can dissolve earlier mergers that become unsatisfactory. The parallels are numerous and obvious. Organizations often fail to understand that the agreement they have drawn up with the community involves more than property rights: they have entered into a psychological contract with the community. And the bigger the organization and its assets, the greater its influence and the more its decisions are felt.

The lines of obligation are not always clear. An example is the issue of recalls. At what point does the hazard of a car or a toy become conspicuously the responsibility of the organization that (perhaps carelessly) made it, rather than the responsibility of the consumer who (perhaps foolishly) used it? Parker Brothers, the toy company, introduced a toy called Riviton in 1977. That Christmas one of the 450,000 sets was involved in the death of a child, who put a quarter-inch long rubber rivet into his mouth and choked to death. "It was a freak accident," said Randolph Barton, president of the company. "After all, peanuts are the greatest cause of strangulation among children, and nobody advocates banning the peanut." Ten months later, with Riviton sales on the way to an expected $8.5 million for the year, a second child strangled on a rivet, and Barton decided to halt the sales and recall the toy. Although manufacturers can be taken to court for product liability, Barton says the recall was prompted mostly by "our sense of moral obligation . . . The decision was very simple. Were we supposed to sit back and wait for death No. 3?"[26]

Industry is frequently accused of ripping off the government and the public, but private organizations are by no means alone in violating the psychological contract with the community. People are also angry about the inefficiencies of government. The situation offers business a golden opportunity to show what it can do about meeting social and public needs, and to enhance its public image in the process.

Government agencies have not had conspicuous success running hospitals, prisons, military services, or other public services. Conscientious private businessmen, on the other hand, could successfully manage such institutions if they set high standards. Public-service ventures have already been adopted by some corporations. Closing mental hospitals, for instance, has resulted in many patients going to private nursing homes. Businessmen who operate good facilities are thereby serving a social need. Other needs are not being dealt with adequately, however: facilities for criminal rehabilitation and juvenile offenders and housing for the elderly are just a few of the areas in which business could intercede, and budget cutbacks have released many professional people who could operate such programs.

In Sweden the law prohibits an industry from having more than 20 percent of its business in national defense work, thus assuring that the responsibility for defense will be widespread. In this country it might not be a bad idea if a certain percentage of the business of large companies was devoted to public service. Multidivision businesses could make important social contributions by having one division that operates human services. Responsibility for such services would then be more widely spread, and they would have the advantages of good business management and the flexibility of private enterprise. Chief executive officers could become business statesmen, conceptualizing the kinds of services their organizations can render and the conditions under which they can be done honorably and profitably. This seems more constructive than trying to improve the negative public image of business through economic education.

A different kind of long-run accounting, in which the costs of the various styles of management can be computed, is needed to clarify the relationship between an organization and the community. Which one should bear the costs of pollution? Of unemployment? If Ford, pioneering the five-dollar-a-day wage, hires workers and then lays them off after three months (as the original Henry Ford did), should the company or the city of Detroit be held responsible for their welfare?

The concept of "social accounting" or "social auditing" has been widely discussed since the early 1970s, when a number of large corporations devoted a few pages of their annual reports to "corporate social responsibility." Today the trend in this country is fading, but a large number of organizations have expanded efforts to provide a social balance sheet that documents both the positive and the negative effects that companies have on society. Norton publishes a special report that cites efforts in minority unemployment, ethics, and energy conservation. General Motors' *Public Interest Report* discusses safety, consumer satisfaction, environment, and South African investments. Bank of America has two committees— one of bank directors and another of bank executives—that have developed public- and social-policy goals. And Abt Associates, a social-science research firm, has published a social audit of its operations.

In Europe, the trend is toward an increase in social accounting. Beginning as a result of pressure from protest groups during the early 1970s, large corporations such as Migros in Switzerland and BASF, the German chemical giant, have seen this as a way to diffuse potentially damaging criticism and legislation. Social accounting practices play to mixed reviews. The Migros report—which in 1979 acknowledged that it paid women less than men, that many of its jobs were boring, and that the emissions of nitrous dioxide had risen 2 percent over a four-year period—was hailed by some as a milestone in social accounting. Critics of these confessions attack the "do-gooder" tone of many of the reports, and point out that total objectivity is often lacking (a report by Deutsche Shell, for instance, failed to include a section on pollution).[27] Nevertheless, the concept of social accounting suggests possibilities for improvements in assessing an organization's impact on society and in refining the ways information on these issues is presented to the public. In creating social devices to encourage and support more expansive and long-range thinking, businesses can continue to become institutions of problem solving and learning. In doing so, they will continue to remain the social ladder on which new generations have the opportunity to rise.

Responding to change—one of the major tasks of top management—can engender all kinds of difficulties, as is apparent in the dilemma of this narrator whose company, through merger, finds itself involved not only with a new product but with new people.

"Our company, a major international electronics concern, recently bought a small but rapidly expanding firm in the Northeast. This firm, a family business, has developed two particular lines of equipment. The first is similar to the general type of work done by our corporation. The second is a new product, and is the main reason we were interested in acquiring the firm. We agreed that the merger would take place over six years, during which the two lines were to be split off from each other. Near the end of this period, a decision was to be reached as to whether the firm would have two heads (one for each product line) reporting to the corporate president, or whether it was to be amalgamated under a single individual. For the past three years the company has been reporting to me through its president, who is also the principal owner. I would then report to the corporate president. Now I am going to move to the Northeast to help develop and expand the first product line. I will still be reporting to the corporate president.

"The problem is that the nephew of the firm's president, Charles, who is a vice-president of the company and in charge of the second product line, has been very resistant to some of the changes that have been necessary to bring his firm into our corporate structure. None of these changes has been undertaken without the full consent of his uncle or without general approval of the major subordinates concerned with the changes.

"Charles's uncle, president of the firm, will be retiring at the end of the merger period. The decision about splitting the company will have to be made before his retirement. Charles wants to have control over the entire operation. He indicates that if he is not given control, he may leave, taking with him the people who are loyal to him and who have the expertise in the second product. It is vital to the corporation that this product be developed into a national line. We need all of these people to do this.

"The firm is still operating as a unit under the control of the president, with whom I have had a very good relationship. He remains nominally in charge, but I am responsible to the corporation for the first line and Charles is in charge of the second. The personnel of the company, which is the key issue here, work in both lines. Charles and I will need to share them.

"My problem is how to smooth over potential conflicts and develop a good relationship with Charles and the employees who are loyal to him. He sees me as his strongest rival for the top spot. What can I do to help smooth the way for whatever the corporate president decides to do?"

Analysis

Where Is the Pain?   Both the narrator and Charles are feeling the pressures that always accompany this type of merger. The narrator has a very difficult responsibility placed upon him by his corporate president. He is, essentially, to smooth out any problems that are developing because of the merger and to prepare the important personnel for more direct contact with the corporation. The narrator is supposed to create loyalty to the product, to himself, and to the corporation. Charles is, on the other hand, fighting to retain as much control as possible over what he perceives as "his" company.

When Did It Begin?   When the merger period began, approximately three years ago.

Ego Ideal   The egos of both Charles and the narrator are heavily invested in this situation. Each wants the new arrangement to work. Each wants to maintain his own measure of self-esteem in doing the job well. Charles knows that the narrator was the company overseer for the past three years. He feels this has lowered his status and power. If Charles is not given the "top spot," he will have suffered further ego damage. He is probably also aware of the corporation's concern about his ability to handle a national organization.

Affection   In the past, Charles has been obtaining his affection from his uncle, from those subordinates who are personally loyal to him, and from his ties to the family organization. This safe source of affection is seriously threatened as he perceives the narrator's position beginning to encroach on his home turf.

Aggression   Charles is showing his aggression by being openly critical and hostile to the changes the merger has brought. He is trying to use his power and position to pressure the corporation into giving him the "top spot."

Dependency   Charles has in the past been able to depend upon his uncle for support. He obviously feels he has the support and loyalty of all the important employees. His uncle, however, could be seen as having deserted him, leaving Charles at the mercy of the corporation. The narrator is secure in his relationship with the corporation and its president.

Is It Solvable?   Perhaps, but it will take patience, time, and care—particularly on the part of the narrator.

How?   The narrator will have to become a source of support for Charles and attempt to let him see that he is not competing for the "grand prize." If he can help Charles perceive the ways in which it is necessary to deal with the corporation, he can become Charles's mentor and, if the narrator becomes the overall controller of the firm, he can help cushion the blow to Charles's self-esteem. If Charles can be made aware of the narrator's and the corporation's intentions, he will be able to understand his own position better.

SEVEN The Business as an Educational Institution

I f executives are to meet the three major responsibilities of top management—manage the business, be effective social engineers, and maintain democratic values—they must, at the same time, view the business as an institution for problem-solving and learning. This can seem like just one more responsibility. In fact, though, treating the organization as an educational institution increases the chance for perpetuation. The educational aspects of business-as-usual need to be spelled out so that we can recognize and evaluate them as formal processes.

In identifying existing learning activities or in planning new ones, one requirement holds: the activities must meet the needs and expectations of people while simultaneously contributing to the vitality of the business, the economy, and society at large. People must be able to use the organization in which they work to channel their drives and meet the obligations of their consciences; any activities proposed must provide experiences of mastery and must enhance people's self-image and their aspirations for partnership with power. They must help people act directly, both individually and in concert, to tackle the personal and social problems that confront them. Three kinds of educational processes serve these purposes: training programs, in-service education, and intellectual acculturation.

Training

As an instrument for solving problems, the business organization could be used to deal with pressing social issues much more effectively than it has been to date. So far, two major social devices have evolved to deal with the problems of displaced and chronically unemployed workers. One of these is broad-scale retraining and rehabilitation, an ongoing effort financed by the federal government and carried out at the local level. The other is the negotiated pay arrangement, which results in financial advantages as a result of labor-saving efforts being shared with workers who are displaced by these efforts.[1]

Both devices have serious shortcomings. The first program assumes that people can and will be retrained, and that after they are, jobs will be waiting for them. Efforts have been made. The Zenith Radio Corporation became involved with a pilot program that used CETA (Comprehensive Employment and Training Act) funds and that trained laid-off employees in a comprehensive course in basic electronics and repair.[2] Lockheed developed remedial skill training in specific jobs for disadvantaged or unemployed workers in its Georgia and California plants, and found that the turnover, quality, and quantity of the work in these sites was equal to that at other plants.[3] The results of community training efforts have, however, been mixed and often disappointing: critics say that candidates were not sufficiently motivated for retraining, had insufficient education for higher-level jobs, or did not want to move. Modest success was reported when the retrainees could go directly to new jobs from their training, and better success was achieved with on-the-job training. The best results occurred when companies retrained their own employees and constructed new plants near the sites of the closed obsolete plants, as DuPont did when it was closing its outmoded chlorine-making facility at Chambers Works in New Jersey.[4]

These results were hardly surprising. Community retraining programs generally fail to take into account the relationship between people and the organizations in which they work, as well as the demoralizing experience that occurs when they are separated from their work organization. Disillusionment sets in, which dampens the motivation to be retrained and to risk establishing new ties to another organization where the same process may occur again. "I like my job," says an executive in Allen Dodd's novel *The Job Hunter*, after having found a new position, "but I have no faith in its permanence or the permanence of any relationship between a man and an organization."[5] Echoing this, a retired person said, "You don't prepare for the fact that you are standing alone and unprotected against the world. This realization hits you about three weeks after you retire. The company is no longer standing there beside you, or behind you, to tell you what to do, when to come or when to go, to speak a word for you in court, to defend you against outsiders, to tell all and sundry that, since you are one of its very own, you are a good and honorable guy—and does anybody want to fight about it?"[6] Speaking about this sudden alienation in medical terms, the late Dr. Harold G. Wolff summarized: "In short, prolonged circumstances which are perceived as dangerous, as lonely, as hopeless, may drain a man of hope and of his health; but he is capable of enduring incredible burdens and taking cruel punishment when he has self-esteem, hope, purpose, and belief in his fellows."[7]

Little wonder that comparatively few displaced people take advantage of rehabilitation opportunities, particularly when trainers often have difficulty in finding new job openings for their protégés. Well-intentioned programs frequently become only temporary devices to occupy people's minds before they are once again left to their fate, particularly if these people are not given support and incentive that will stimulate them to want to learn and to find new opportunities where they can use their new skills.

The negotiated pay arrangement, too, has the appearance of a solution without providing any real answers. True, it softens the shock of displacement and change by providing a financial cushion and even job security. But in many instances negotiated pay is no more than a temporary expedient because the displaced people will still have to find other jobs (and in this way they become part of the problem their company retraining programs are supposed to solve) or they work part time and have financial security but lose some of the psychological value of working consistently. Short of a miracle, these methods are not likely to make impressive dents in the ranks of the residual unemployed. Nor will they alleviate the problems of those who are being displaced or capitalize on the psychological values of work. But if we take seriously the psychological meaning of the work organization to the individuals who work in it, their expectations of leadership stemming from their psychological needs, and their egalitarian traditions, we may be able to come up with other options.

Suppose a number of people are to be displaced from a plant because of technical innovations that increase plant efficiency. When a plant must displace people from their jobs, both the company and the community incur major financial costs. The community must pay for individual rehabilitation and for unemployment or welfare benefits. It must also offer economic incentives to entice companies to set up a new plant. The company usually must pay separation bonuses and the costs of moving people to other locations, if it has them. One choice is to turn them loose individually and attempt to retrain them for jobs that still need to be found. Another choice might be to use the money that would be spent by community and company to establish a new kind of business in place of the one that is being automated or closed. The corporation could use some of its staff, plus the resources of local and state industrial development commissions, to create an initially subsidized new business under its own corporate name. Displaced workers could be retrained as a unit and as staff functioning as a group in the new business, while retaining some of the ties with the original organization. If the new business were too far afield from the direction of the corporation, or if the corporation did not want to maintain it as part of the larger corporate structure, it could be sold or reconstituted as a complete, functioning unit. In addition, if employees and management could make such a shift together, the integrity of the work group within the organizational structure could be maintained.

Some results of company retraining efforts, compared with community retraining efforts, suggest that it is more than just a nice idea. At least one small company put the theory into practice by taking over not only the physical plant but all of the employees of another company that was vacating the site. The new management felt that it would be considerably cheaper and more efficient to employ an already organized and cohesive work group than to hire new people individually.[8] Owens-Illinois entered the sugar business in the Bahamas when its timber operations there had to be suspended for twenty years.[9] And the United States Army reduced its psychological casualty rate and raised efficiency and morale when it began to send unit replacements overseas instead of individual infantry replacements.

Some will argue that such a plan puts an undue burden on the host corporation, which already bears a tax burden, a bonus burden, and an increasingly heavy social burden, all of which pose problems for the economy and the society as well as the business. The concept is not new, however. Many companies did something similar during World War II, developing and operating facilities for the federal government with activities that were far from the basic business of the contracting corporation. After the war, Pan American Airways operated the Cape Kennedy facilities. Many other companies operate large enterprises on a contractual basis for the government. Some have even gone into the formal business of training school dropouts and unemployed workers in community programs.

There is another option that would build on the psychological meaning of the organization: the in-company training program for the displaced or unemployed. There has been some success in this sphere already, particularly with dropouts and young men and women who might become unemployed after high-school graduation.[10] Detroit's Federal Department Stores took a group of dropouts who lacked the minimal education and could not pass the elementary psychological tests to qualify for rehabilitation; the company trained them to be successful department store salesmen.[11] Control Data opened a plant in a ghetto neighborhood—and backed its presence with a promise to keep it open. The plant is still going, providing a source of employment and training for people in the surrounding area. Efforts such as these could include more young women who receive aid for themselves and their dependent children, if communities would establish complementary day-care centers. These nurseries, besides caring for children during the day, could provide social and psychological stimulation for them and ensure that they are given adequate food and medical care. A dual focus plan such as this would serve both to habilitate the adult and intervene to prevent the same social tragedy from handicapping the child. It could interrupt the vicious cycle of generations on welfare rolls.

In Sweden, anyone who loses a job or is threatened by unemployment in a declining industry is eligible for a free training course; Stockholm pays subsidies to private firms for training expenses. In West Germany there is a program for continuous training and retraining.[12] Americans now are urging a closer tie between education and work. "I'd like to see employers given some kind of credit for making more work-study opportunities available," says Seymour Wolfbein, Dean of Temple University's School of Business Administration.[13] And Wharton professor Bernard Anderson says, "We have to be prepared, I think, to make a much larger investment than we have made to date in employment and training programs ... We should have a national program that combines counseling, work experience, skills and training, and the creation of specific jobs in order to ease the transition from school to work ... I think most employers would be willing to take on workers who have fewer skills or are less well trained than those normally hired, if some incentive were offered to underwrite the cost of on-the-job training."[14]

Whatever the options for dealing with the impact of technological change, most people want to see increased technical efficiency in manufacturing and data processing. Management can help maintain a favorable public climate by demonstrating that it has carefully considered the impact of technological change on employees and that it wants to help solve related problems. The more management demonstrates its willingness to lend a hand with the social problems of unemployment, the more it will be respected for using its power constructively.

Apart from the special problems presented by poverty and the need for rehabilitation, there is the general task of training young people in marketable skills and increasing the proficiency of craftsmen who already have basic skills. At the present time this is largely handled by vocational and technical schools. The idea of a vocational school to train young men and women so that they can be employed is good; in practice, however, vocational schools operate under severe handicaps. Their equipment tends to be outdated because their budgets are too small; their teaching, divorced from the realities of the working world, tends to become obsolete, too. Students rarely work on products that will actually be sold or take on responsibility for rejects and errors. Without the concrete prospect of a job plus the psychological bond to an organization, it is difficult for many students to invest themselves in training.

Vocational training would be more effective conducted in the context of businesses. The same formal curricula could be followed and apprentice criteria could be maintained, but the training would be enhanced by the serious overtones of real business. This was illustrated after World War II with the establishment of on-the-job training, which offered appropriate compensation for employers if established standards of training, supervision, and performance were maintained. Today it would be in the employer's own interest, as well as that of young men and women, to have continuous skill-training programs in businesses where specialized competence is important. In addition, many millions of dollars allocated for school construction could be saved.

In-Service Education

The problems of displacement and unemployment are not limited to blue-collar or hourly-rate employees. Technicians and managers can become obsolete, too, and this presents a pressing issue for all businesses. The engineering student of a decade ago, for example, would barely understand today's courses. Schools of engineering are urging the conservation and development of engineering manpower, and the dean of one school has called for a national attack on the problem of obsolescence by means of broad and versatile programs for continuing education as a long-term investment and responsibility.

To counteract obsolescence among executives, many American companies have established their own education centers or joint programs with universities. Xerox has a campus-like education center at Leesburg, Virginia, from which it directs the activities of ninety-seven training branches around the country.[15] Digital has a center in Maynard, Massachusetts; American Telephone and Telegraph has one in New Jersey, and General Electric's center is outside New York City. Goodrich uses facilities at Kent State University. The City University of New York has a two-year business degree program for Citibank in the company's offices; in the New York–New Jersey area, Pace University conducts some courses at AT&T offices.[16] The Small Business Association of New England arranges educational courses for companies that do not have their own, and Wharton and other business schools provide traveling experts who lecture on finance, marketing, and other special areas. At the Harvard Graduate School of Education, people come from industry to talk about educational jobs in management. In short, education is big business, outside university schools of management as well as within.

Training people for basic wage-earning tasks is one thing; preventing obsolescence is another. But neither of these methods by itself strengthens the leadership function. This is the goal of management development and a major part of perpetuating the organization.

In addition to training the unemployed and training the already employed for more skilled tasks, every business organization must continuously provide advanced education. Knowledge is the linchpin of contemporary culture. Everyone is now required to learn at an accelerated pace, and a competent understanding is needed to deal with a widening range of decisions about social problems. Intellectual obsolescence is so much a threat to both man and organization that learning must become a formal part of work. Some companies already require managers to be involved in at least one period of instruction each year; many more will soon be doing so. It has even been suggested that businessmen take sabbaticals.

Although rapidity of change is a severe problem, it is not the only one: the composition of the work force is becoming sharply different. The ever greater numbers of people entering technical and professional fields are not as startling as the fact that there are more professional physical scientists than general clerks, and more engineers than typists in the federal civil service. Like business, the federal government has had to provide for specialized training at full pay, plus tuition and subsistence costs. Although the numbers entering graduate school remain high, students frequently do not enter directly after their senior year, but work for a few years first. They are also more likely to go into areas of specialization than into academic disciplines.

It is not enough to put the burden on the individual, as-

suming that those who want to advance will be sufficiently interested to take the initiative in seeking out more advanced
training. A business has too much at stake to leave the initiative for combatting obsolescence to its employees. The person
who is not able to keep up with a job is not the only one who
suffers; the organization suffers too. For its own survival and
perpetuation the company must use education as a strategy of
preventive maintenance against the social corrosion of occupational obsolescence.

Intellectual Acculturation

Manpower planning is a major executive task—so much so
that 85 percent of the chief executives in a recent survey listed
it as the most critical management undertaking for the next ten
years.[17] If the name of the game is perpetuation, then the issue
of succession is perhaps *the* fundamental executive task. But
manpower planning cannot go on independently of strategic
planning; the company needs a comprehensive overview of its
current position, its desired position, and the best course of
action for attaining its goals. Strategic planning is impossible
without people, and organizational development is impossible
without strategic planning. They go hand in glove.

The difficulties in finding well-qualified men and women
to fill top posts are well documented. Although people get
training early on—and may continue it in training programs
in-house—there is a growing need for intellectal acculturation,
for three reasons. First, the larger and more complex the organization becomes, the broader the kind of understanding that
is required and the greater the need for a capacity to abstract.
Second, as the behavior needed by management becomes
more specialized, the more people are pulled in and out of
roles. Third, business organizations have tended to attract
technical people who have more training than they do education, and the organization, by its need to focus on the tasks at
hand, tends to stamp out emerging capacity for abstract
thought.

Succession is always a problem. Choosing one's successor
breeds its own difficulties, so that while it is impossible to
know how many chief executive officers unconsciously select
successors who are bound to fail, there are signs on all sides

that the hand-picked successor meets more problems than had been anticipated. If the task is to identify professional managers who will take over the reins in a family business, there are as many difficulties in handling the CEO who has become a company legend (and may still lurk in the wings, breathing fire) as in dealing with the demands of the environment outside the organization.[18] In short, two things can be said about the task of developing top-executive timber. If an organization is interested in survival and perpetuation, no task is more important. And in far too many companies, no task is more pervasively ignored or postponed.

If senior executives think about the football analogy described in Chapter 1, in which the organization uses modular teams that can be put into play for their particular talents and then withdrawn from the fray for a while, what happens to the players when they are temporarily benched? The concept of using entire teams of people, then benching them, is radical enough to intimidate many. Yet at any one time in a large organization, there may already be a number of key people who are pulled out and sent to various educational courses. The team approach simply extends this practice and does the same thing on a refined basis. It systematically uses the time of a group of people, in between plays, to educate them and make them better candidates for top-management positions.

One way to manage the time of benched players is to keep them so busy with tasks at hand and so immersed in the details of daily organizational life that they lose sight of what goes on in the rest of the world. Although this is a common organizational practice, it compounds a problem that is serious enough without further complications—the problem of developing organizational talent to move into positions of leadership in the future.

There is another way to occupy players temporarily benched: their time can be used deliberately and constructively to improve the players' skills and groom them for higher-level executive positions. Skilled in particular tasks, many men and women come from backgrounds with a narrow cultural outlook. As thoroughly at home in one kind of community or region as they are in one kind of job, they lack not only the cosmopolitan outlook that will help them assume broader responsibilities, but also the knack of learning new skills and perspectives. They frequently have technical backgrounds in accounting, information systems management, and finance; even their undergraduate courses in college may have been primarily in the sciences. On top of this, organizations tend to pressure people so that they do not have much time to look around.

However, top-level positions require that the people who fill them have the skills of generalists—that they be able to survey the entire field and understand the dynamics behind its problems, and also be socially at home in a wider group of people. Clearly, there are individual exceptions—people who read, subscribe to publications, enroll in courses, travel, discuss, and change. But there are not enough. The firm of Yankelovich, Skelly, and White, which polls public attitudes toward contemporary issues for reports to executives, also polls the managers of client companies on the same topics. Managements are often unhappily surprised to find out that their own people are less thoughtful and less well informed than comparable management groups in other organizations, and that they are considerably behind the population at large.

This does not mean that one political point of view, for example, is more acceptable than another. Nor do these polls indicate any lack of "right thinking." Rather, it is the level of overall thinking that seems deficient. It makes no sense to blame the victims. Generally these are men and women who have made the most of their opportunities and who, in the process of several job changes and geographic moves, have clung to values and lifestyles that were familiar and reassuring, even as they moved into new businesses and social areas and were exposed to new ways. For all people, change is a matter of taking what is new and integrating it with what is old, tried, and compatible.

But just as new is not always better, old is not always best. Ideally, organizations would like to provide growth opportunities for people in middle management, so that over a number of years these people can become more thoughtful, more sophisticated (in genuine, not artificial ways), and more capable. Unfortunately, a different pattern often prevails. Left alone and unnourished, at least in direct and formal ways, people fend for themselves. Suddenly, at forty-seven, a manager is in line for a job as vice-president with almost no time to prepare for the role and the demands that go with it. What the players need, as they move off and on the bench, is some form of direct training. It may be in the form of in-house educational programs, or a course that stretches thoughts to consider the connection between major literary themes and present social problems. It can be an executive training course at one of the country's major schools of management. Or, in particular cases where people are likely to spend significant amounts of time overseas or dealing with international companies, it could be direct training through a course that presents the history and culture of a country in Europe, South America, Asia, or Africa.

What is needed, then, are formal ways to instill wider perspectives in people who will eventually be eligible for greater responsibilities. It is an acculturation process as well as an intellectual one. What people think is important; how they behave in various situations—professional, social, or in the no-man's-land that is both—is just as important.

American business and industry have been heavily involved in management development since the end of World War II. As late as a generation ago, a reasonably intelligent and diligent man could succeed in becoming the head of a business. Now men and women can no longer depend on these virtues alone for achievement. Today's business complexities call for experience and breadth of education, both formal and informal, that will enable an executive to lead professionals. Executive manpower shortages were predicted fifteen years ago.[19] They still exist because there continue to be more executives whose strengths lie in concrete rather than broad-gauge thinking.

The evolution of the "paper curtain" and the often unrealistic academic requirements for many jobs have put a ceiling on upward mobility. If, in addition, middle-management positions will no longer provide the apprenticeship training necessary for advancing to higher levels, and if seniority is less and less useful as a basis for advancement, then there will have to be a range of avenues—not only engineering and scientific—through which people can become executives.

Management cannot rely on business schools or universities for more than background training for business leadership. Even if all of those who enter management ranks were to go to schools of business, such schools cannot mold a complete professional product any more than any other professional school can. We speak of the practice of law and the practice of medicine not only because professional people have a body of professional knowledge, but also because they must continually refine and update it in practice. So it is with management.

Furthermore, practitioners in management do not always concur with what is being taught, or fully analyze the ways in which the organization will profit from changes in executives' behavior. When university executive-development programs are good, they create problems: they change people's behavior. In fact, business leaders' favorable reactions to university programs appear related, in part, to the programs' minimal influence on participants. Authors of a study of this phenomenon even assert that "it could be the program's undoing if it were to significantly alter participant attitudes and behavior."[20] This reaction reflects the common failure of management to relate organizational objectives to the people who carry them out. Participants in training programs seldom know what their companies are trying to accomplish by sending them or whether anything new will be expected of them as a result. Few people select the programs they attend or have a clear basis for deciding what they need to learn. On the other hand, by formulating policies about what they expect from people who attend different programs and by designing channels for putting participants' new knowledge into operation, companies stimulate more effective use of training programs.

Despite the major contributions of business schools and their work toward establishing programs for generalists, there are limits to what they can do. They continue to be hampered by limitations inherent in academic institutions: they are often divorced from the real and daily problems of the subject matter they teach. It is difficult to get from a business school the kind of executives an organization needs, because the schools are too narrowly focused on analysis. There is no "practicum" for leadership. No business school operates a business as a medical school operates a hospital, so it is nearly impossible for them to teach those subtle elements that translate the subject matter into finished skill—the feel and artistry of the leadership role. To acquire this skill, apprentice executives need a chance to work on real problems; even more important, they need the opportunity to work side by side with master executives experienced in solving such problems.

There are two kinds of professional schools where students are not taught by those who are themselves expert practitioners in the field: teachers' colleges and schools of management. Apart from some who teach in departments of education (as contrasted with other departments like psychology), there are few professional teachers in schools of education. Similarly there are few expert managers in schools of business. Faculties are composed largely of a wide range of specialists—in accounting, law, marketing, personnel, and behavioral science. Students in a business school are likely to major in one of these areas and get a smattering of the rest. They become specialists, whereas an executive by definition must be a generalist. Only after they have risen in the hierarchy are they expected to be responsible for the functioning of other specialists. Even then they do not view themselves as generalists—executives per se—with a general knowledge of all the areas that they must organize.

Some critics complain that management often has been on a misguided self-development binge.[21] But formal management-development activities are imperative. All organizations must have systematic ways of replenishing, developing, and producing their own leadership if they are to be masters of their own fates. Many do. What, then, is the best course of action for those that do not?

Currently, management-development activities are left largely to training departments. Learning is relatively divorced from role and function. What is left out is the executive as paradigm, as role model. The implication is that business leaders will themselves have to provide continuous intensive leadership training within organizations. To teach decision making, for example, is not merely to instruct in rational analytic process, but to teach the extended process of building the organizational context for decisions.[22]

This line of reasoning does not imply that executives must abdicate a leadership role. Only if they continue to carry out this role will there be a psychological basis for teaching. If the business is a problem-solving institution and if executives are problem solvers within this framework, then the activity is their subject matter. Their role is their strength. Executives can teach in two ways. They can do what they ordinarily do and let others learn from observing—a hit-or-miss system that fails to take into account elementary psychological principles about how people learn best. Or else—and this is clearly preferred—they can do what they ordinarily do, but at the same time build into their daily activities formal teaching circumstances and conditions that facilitate practical learning.

Specifically, executives must be concerned with developing their subordinates' capacity for leadership. Not only do businesses need continuing sources of leadership for their own survival, but a democratic society needs leaders as well—and there are never enough of them. Gifted young people tend to enter graduate or professional schools, where they assimilate attitudes appropriate to scholars, scientists, and professionals rather than leaders of society.

In the process of teaching others, the business leader also must take steps to offset the creation of a power elite drawn from a limited number of universities and business schools. Drawing instead on a conglomeration of people from many sources with a vast variety of skills, the executive's teaching efforts can facilitate the development of extensive perspectives, capabilities, and sources of leadership contribution.

The collective impact of a series of actions is never more astounding than when it gives rise to a new social ideology. Daniel P. Moynihan points out that the social revolution that started when Britain granted independence to India in 1947, leading to the breakup of most of the great empires of the world into independent states, grew out of the general corpus of British socialist opinion between 1890 and 1950.[23] Disestablishment of ancient privilege, guaranteed liberties, and liberal social policies was a prominent issue then. The citizen suddenly became a very important person. When these ideas were transferred to colonial populations through the British educational system, they were taken on as principles for action. The United States was surprised by the spate of new nations that resulted only because we had not recognized the ideology as a distinctive one—one that people expected to live by.

In a similar way, new business school programs and internal education efforts are continuously feeding the kind of revolution we see in organizations. People have learned to expect to have an effect, and they will. Organizations are expected to be self-correcting, and they will have to become so. Any company that does not take the force of these ideas into account and that does not find ways to relate to them will in the long run ensure itself a position in left field.

CASE HISTORY 6

This case history presents an instance in which a very capable but increasingly difficult subordinate is creating problems that affect the working atmosphere of several departments. It is not Barney's technical abilities that give rise to the tensions, but his personal style. The annual employee evaluation offers an educational opportunity: it can be used to stretch Barney's thinking about what he does, and why, and how it might be changed, if only moderately.

"About three years ago I took over a staff department in which Barney heads one of the major functions.

"Barney, a hefty six-footer, is fifty years old and happily married with two grown children. He not only is one of the most knowledgeable people in his specialty in the entire country, he also has the ability to constantly ferret out engineering and operating problems and arrive at solutions that lead to huge savings for the company. He probably saves us nearly one hundred thousand dollars a month. Since we installed a new accounting system about a year ago, the savings he makes are readily visible to the whole top-management group.

"Barney and I have a very close relationship. He is constantly telling me that under his prior boss he was always frustrated and was seldom able to effectuate his ideas, which resulted in unnecessary losses to the company. Often he will leave a little gift of one of my favorite cigars on my desk, or do something for the secretary.

"In his day-to-day activities, Barney is required to interact with other departments, particularly the engineering department. He has always been proud of the fact that he is 'never wrong,' and he puts other people down when he gets defensive about it. This inevitably leads to conflicts, though in all fairness to Barney, I must say that others go a good halfway toward creating them.

"About a year ago, I told Barney at annual employee review time that he needed to improve in interpersonal relationships with other departments. All other ratings were very high. This criticism bugged him so badly that he mentioned it to me at least once a week during the past year, and he began to give me long, drawn-out explanations of each recent conflict situation.

"Five years ago Barney had a tumor removed from his brain. This caused some slight reduction in motor control, but not to any noticeable degree. However, since then he has worried about his health, and I suspect that he is fearful that he may be having progressive deterioration of his mental abilities. If there is any, no one has seen any sign of it. What we do see is increasing emotional vulnerability.

"Barney has another habit that is disturbing to the upper-management team. He frequently drops into the president's office and spends time preselling his ideas. He does the same thing with the executive vice-presidents. This is time-consuming for all of them and is really not necessary because there is no trouble getting his programs through anyway.

"I am now faced with another annual employee evaluation. I have not yet decided how I will handle it or what should be said to Barney. The trouble is that this problem employee has more value to the company than most non-problem employees."

Analysis

Where Is the Pain? The engineering department and to some extent the top management team are annoyed by Barney's behavior. The narrator is facing a more immediate problem—Barney's performance appraisal. Barney is hurt if he is criticized, but otherwise his behavior brings no ill effects to himself.

When Did It Begin? The problem appears to be chronic. Although an operation five years ago is mentioned, the narrator notes not a change, but an intensification of behavior.

Ego Ideal Barney wants recognition from every quarter. Being never wrong is his way of earning it. His security is thus dependent on being perfect. Such people are usually overly sensitive to criticism.

Affection   Barney's most important source of affection is top management, as is indicated by the fact that he goes to them to sell his ideas even though he does not need to. He wants to see their approval himself, hear how valuable he is. He is a kind of love addict. He wants everybody to appreciate him, and he leaves small gifts to ensure that he will be liked.

Aggression   Most of Barney's aggression goes into work—finding problems and solving them. However, it is clear also that he feels anger toward anyone who does not recognize him sufficiently, such as his former boss or those in the engineering department.

Dependency   Barney shows very little independence or interdependence. He trusts only his own brilliance to win him the approval he wants. Thus, a tumor, and even the process of aging, will be excessively threatening to him. Many people whose intelligence is a source of much ado early in life obtain so much pleasure from people's response that they continue in this pattern instead of growing up emotionally. Barney seems to be like this.

Is It Solvable?   Barney's behavior is deeply embedded in his personality and is not likely to change. However, the narrator could do several things to make the situation more livable.

How?   The narrator has a good relationship with Barney. He can use it to advantage if, instead of rating Barney down, which we know will only increase his defensive behavior, he enlists Barney's help in solving a problem in the engineering department. The narrator should explain that now that Barney's spectacular achievements are widely known, he has become a threat to more ordinary achievers, especially those in the engineering department. Then they can discuss ways in which they could work together to help the engineers. To top management, the narrator should simply explain why approval is so important to Barney. They will feel less annoyed if they understand the significance of their responses.

EIGHT

The Role
and the Learners

When the subject of teaching leadership is raised, several questions are inevitably asked. Leadership for what? What kinds of leadership will the organization need for perpetuation? When planning a formal or informal course of instruction, executives need to ask what immediate and specific practices will concern the leader of tomorrow, how these will differ from today's practices, and what knowledge is available to help prepare leaders for their tasks.

What Is Leadership?

Contemporary leaders have much to say about leadership, and their views can provide a starting point for constructing a description of the role. Responding to a survey, a number of presidents of large American companies commented at length on the qualities they wanted to see in their successors.[1] A summary of their views would go something like this: A desirable successor is a person with a general knowledge and an understanding of the whole organization, capable of fitting specialized contributions into profitable patterns. To be able to understand as a generalist, the person needs a wide range of liberal arts knowledge together with a fundamental knowledge of business. With this as a base, a leader will be able to view the business in global historical and technical perspec-

136

tive. Such a perspective is itself the basis for the most important requisite, what one might call "feel"—a certain intuitive sensitivity for the right action and for handling relationships with people.

Most statements about the requirements for good executive performance are vague. John F. Kennedy is reported to have told Arthur Schlesinger that he did not know what the duties of the president would be: according to Schlesinger, Kennedy wanted to keep things flexible. "How presidential decisions are made," Schlesinger says, "in particular remains a mystery to me."[2]

The same mystery surfaces when experts speak about other kinds of leadership roles. From some thirty years of editorial experience John Fischer concludes that most editors are utterly incapable of explaining what they do, or why.[3] "This doesn't mean that they don't know; it is simply that they can't put it into words which will convey much to outsiders." The primary piece of equipment for a good editor, Fischer believes, is an instinct or hunch that signals what people will want to read a month, a year, or a decade from now. "Equally important, and often harder," says Fischer, "he has to keep out of print those things which in his judgment don't belong there." This knack for projecting into the future, for estimating what people will be eager to read at some remote date, seems to be associated with three characteristics: (1) a certain ordinariness (good editors react, in their bones, the same way most of the readers will); (2) in addition to curiosity and intellectual companionship with the readers, the enthusiasm of an adolescent in the throes of first love; (3) simple ruthlessness (happy are they who are born cruel, for if not they will have to school themselves in cruelty). Without ruthlessness, editors are unfit for their job, because kindly editors soon find that they are publishing worthless material. But ruthlessness must be combined with a genuine liking for writers and sympathy for their work. The same three characteristics could be said to make good executives. Business leaders need a sense of resonance with subordinates, rather than alienation as a result of perceived differences in status; they need, if not a passion, an enthusiasm for their tasks; and finally, they need the courage to take charge and the clarity of vision to reject ideas or plans which, after a considered review, look tangential, ineffectual, or futile. Like the editor, too, the executive needs to be able to distinguish between a useless idea and the person who generated it, taking care not to send messages that equate one with the other. Bruce Henderson of the Boston Consulting Group agrees that business decisions are not as rational as executives like to think: "Intuition disguised as status, seniority, and rank is the underlying normative mode of all business decision." He says that this cannot be helped. "Too many choices must be made too often. Data is expensive to collect, often of uncertain quality or relevance. Analysis is laborious and often far too expensive even though imprecise or superficial."[4]

The fact that final decisions are often intuitive is exactly what makes it so important to have a fundamental body of knowledge about psychological matters. Intuitive decisions are based on unconscious processes. But these processes cannot be turned to advantage without an established frame of reference. Douglas McGregor has pointed out that good leadership is essentially dependent on the manager's conception of what his job is—of what management is. It depends also on personal convictions and on beliefs about people.[5]

Although leadership may be a component of management, it is not necessarily synonymous with it. Distinguishing between the concepts, Abraham Zaleznik has said that managers tend to view work as a process that involves people and ideas interacting to establish strategies and to make decisions. They tend to have impersonal attitudes toward goals. They act to limit choices and work from a conservative base, and are able to tolerate mundane, practical work for their own survival. Leaders, however, work from high-risk positions. They are concerned with ideas and relate to people in a more intuitive and empathetic manner. A leader pays attention to what the events and decisions mean to people who must work with them. Leaders seem to feel separate from their environment and from other people. They may work in an organization, but they do not belong to the organization. They do not find their sense of self through a social identity, the way most managers do. They work to develop fresh approaches to large problems and to offer alternatives and options that people can work toward. Leaders, according to Zaleznik, have no tolerance for mundane work.[6]

The executive's perspective on his business must be visionary, including not only a clear view of where the business stands today, but, more important, where it should be in twenty years. The executive's task is one of continuous reappraisal, assessing risk and measuring social responsibility. He or she must be able to act fast on the basis of quickly assembled facts in order to resolve complex problems.[7]

Henry Kissinger, writing about Charles deGaulle, said that sound relationships depend less on a personal attitude than on a balance of pressures and an understanding of historical trends. "A great leader is not so much clever as lucid and clear-sighted. Grandeur is not simply physical power but strength reinforced by moral purpose. Nor does competition inevitably involve physical conflict. On the contrary a wise assessment of mutual interests should produce harmony."[8] What is leadership? To ask is to beg the question. Except for the most general and often the most peripheral tasks, the reality of the leadership role, that for which the executive is to prepare others, defies simple mechanical classifications. Nevertheless, leaders can prepare others to assume their mantle. Flexibility, imagination, psychological strength, and judgment are all qualities that executives can help cultivate in those they supervise. Such adaptive skills are subtle, and subtleties of this kind are most likely to develop in the process of identification—the unconscious assimilation of the behaviors, values, and perceptions of more capable people.[9]

Styles of Leadership

If the executive is seen as a teacher, and subordinates as learners—apprentices in the art of leadership—then the differences between master and apprentice provide a useful tension that helps learning to occur. But other differences are significant as well, differences that distinguish organizational styles and the work modes of people who are drawn to the organizations.

The "personalities" of organizations are partly a product of the ego ideal of the founder or head, who holds up a certain standard of behavior and sets up a particular kind of structure, thereby attracting certain kinds of people. They, in turn, attract more of their own kind. As the company builds policies and practices with which these people are comfortable, the corporate personality endures. By the time they are in place for a couple of generations, the system has eliminated people who do not fit, and a personality type has become well established.

For example, employees of AT&T have over the years looked upon "Ma Bell" as maternalistic. The company has always provided exceptionally good workers' benefits, and could be counted on to take care of its own. Its public image has reflected this dependability: AT&T was traditionally the soundest of the "widows-and-orphans" stocks. It has also tried to be a model of service, as shown in a well-known advertisement in which a telephone operator sits at her switchboard while flood waters rise around her. The psychological contract between the company and its employees is one of dependency (although it has been eroded in recent years by economic pressures; more employees have been forced out, jobs have been eliminated by attrition, and there is pressure on executives to be more competitive).

IBM has a very different personality. Once paternalistic like its founder, Thomas Watson, it now has the aggressive personality of a marketer, an attitude that more companies are beginning to emulate. People in marketing are less inhibited, in the positive sense; they grapple with a more hostile environment and are thus more competitive. The path to success at IBM is through sales, and there is intense competition among salesmen, reinforced by a system of quotas, "100-percent clubs," and the like. IBM represents marketing aggressiveness at its best, because of the high-quality products, guaranteed service, and powerful ideal of integrity that back up its marketing efforts.

At Sears, Roebuck and Company the style is more egalitarian. The organization was originally set up to give a great deal of independence and flexibility to store managers. Sears had an unusually "flat" organizational chart, with only three levels of management. As many as thirty store managers would report to a single person; because they were not closely supervised, managers had great freedom to use their own judgment. Recently, though, Sears has succumbed to the general pressures to economize by centralizing and computerizing nationwide sales and promotions. Even so, Sears is more flexible than many other national retailers, who tell their managers not only what products to sell but also where to put them on their shelves.

Just as most people find their own families more congenial than others, so they are more at home with a certain kind of corporate personality. Someone from a traditional Italian family may be able to get along as a second-in-command to an authoritarian boss, whereas a person with a different background might not. In a traditional Italian family, the sons respect the *padrone* and know they will eventually take over if they patiently bide their time. A rigid Germanic upbringing suits a person for the highly disciplined atmosphere typical of machine-tool factories, where precision and quality control are essential.

One of the more interesting examples of a "fit" between individual personalities and corporate personalities is the Federal Bureau of Investigation. The FBI traditionally attracted many Irish-Catholic lawyers, probably because they felt at home within the agency's rigid structure (which was a lot like that of the Irish-Catholic family and parochial schools) and comfortable with the sharp distinctions between right and wrong characteristic of the late J. Edgar Hoover.

A mismatch between the personalities of employee and corporation can sometimes risk disaster for both.

Who Are the Learners?

If what is to be taught cannot be explicitly defined, and if much of what is learned develops subtly out of a relationship with the leader, then the learning process can be encouraged if leaders have a concise picture of the kind of people with whom they will be involved. What kind of people are the followers?

Usually the executive will teach people who are younger. Even if they are not chronologically younger, one condition always holds: at that particular point in their relationship, the executive has more power. The executive's strength serves as an attractive force for most subordinates, who would like to become as strong as he. By being strong, the executive attracts and holds their attention, so that the power itself can be used as a device that facilitates education. Of course, if it merely stimulates fear or exacerbates the subordinates' dependency, it will be almost useless in teaching leadership skills.

Describing contemporary college graduates who are entering corporations, Eugene Jennings notes that they recognize that authority is important and therefore relate to it properly. By "properly" he means that they have limited trust of authority figures: they detach themselves when they can no longer learn. The "brighter" ones who move along steadily and get to the top have what Jennings calls "maze brightness."[10] Such people are sensitive to the values of the organization and to the differing values of various departments. They recognize which values have higher priority for the organization as a whole. They have, further, the capacity to understand the exercise of power, which means both the institutional right to take action and the capacity to apply power. They also know the boundaries and limitations of the possible, and the avenues by which they can make the most of their aggressive drives.

The young men and women whom the executive will teach are not only highly intelligent but also want to use themselves and their lives effectively. A person's work is a major way of justifying existence. Today, bright young people are not looking only for jobs. Wittingly or not, they take John Gardner's concept of self-renewal seriously: "For the self-renewing man the development of his own potentialities and the process of self-discovery never end."[11] Such a young person, according to Edgar H. Schein, comes to the organization asking, "Will the job provide an opportunity to test myself, to find out whether I can really do a job? . . . Will I be considered worthwhile?" In most cases, Schein adds, a college education gives graduates a sense of being special, of having attained something not available to all members of society, and of having special skills which, the assurance goes, will be considered valuable in any job situation. No wonder they are particularly vulnerable to failure or to rejection by the organization. As Schein observes, one inevitable outcome of prolonged education is the expectation of continuing to grow and develop. The expectation generates questions like these: "Will I be able to maintain my integrity and my individuality? Will I be able to lead a balanced life, to have a family and to pursue private interests? Will I learn and grow? Will the organization in which I work meet my ideals of the rational business organization described in economics and business courses?"[12]

Students today are more flexible and better prepared both academically and socially. Their attitudes toward industry have changed; they may want to be successful, but many are determined not to become "organization men" and will not trade their integrity and individuality for security. Able, sensitive, and intensely concerned, particularly where they have been influenced by academic values of questioning and learning, they rebel at the thought of the "stereotyped" life of the businessman. They trust fact not authority; they want to examine assumptions, and the many idealists among them still want to remake society. They ask a business how its goals fit their goals, especially their wish to make a social contribution. They do not believe that business has seriously come to terms with the major social problems of the world. If young people want to deal with these problems, then they will be attracted to those businesses that promise to help alleviate hunger, disease, and poverty.[13]

A decade or so ago, students were disillusioned with "the system." At the time, Daniel Yankelovich told the Institute of Life Insurance that a number of the nation's best-educated, most promising young adults had lost enthusiasm for their business careers.[14] He said that there was a "crisis of purpose" among the top 10 percent of those people between eighteen and twenty-five whose family affluence had already assured them of economic achievement. "For many, the problem of finding meaning and purpose through the pursuit of traditional goals remains achingly unsolved," he reported.

Today, there is a new synthesis. Most students want to "make it", and many still want to have a say in changing society. But increasing numbers see a degree in business administration as the "golden passport" that can help them do both.

"People realize that the M.B.A. offers more than a good salary," says Boris Yavitz, dean of Columbia's business faculty. "They see that in business, government, and society at large, you have to deal with complex issues—and business school is a way to teach people to cope with the unstructured messes of the world."[15] Students are being drawn to business programs, both undergraduate and graduate, in unprecedented numbers. A recent survey of college freshmen indicated that nearly one out of four planned a business major. In 1978 an estimated 47,600 students received M.B.A. degrees, as opposed to 18,101 ten years earlier. Another big change is the number of women enrolled: many schools report a 40 percent female enrollment.[16] Although a desire for money and power may be part of the motivation of these men and women, many feel the urge to influence society in constructive ways. High idealism is sometimes part of the package. A black student entering Harvard's graduate school of business said he believed that the power to effect social and political change has passed from lawyers and politicians to businessmen: "My ultimate goal is to get the company I work for to donate money and other resources to social causes I think need help."[17]

Not all students are this idealistic. Nor are all of them well prepared academically. While prestigious graduate schools look for students with well-rounded backgrounds, others are not as determined to choose applicants with a track record in the humanities and social sciences, as well as in the physical sciences, engineering, and business. As a result, executives may find that although they have a greater number of new M.B.A.'s to choose from, the numbers alone do not guarantee a rich crop of experienced young people, able to think through the psychological and technical problems that they will meet in their organizations.

Up-and-coming young men and women are not the only ones whom the executive is to teach. Many will have been in the company for years, and some will be older than their boss. Among them will be people who have long been shelved, some who have been passed by, and some who are highly successful in their own right. Failures or successes, they share two problems. First, they are bombarded by a literature that extols youth, creativity, and flexibility, and as a result will too easily believe that they are less useful than someone younger with more formal education. Second, the contemporary emphasis on change is bewildering to many people who have loyally served in an organizational structure that only yesterday appeared to be so important. Their personal goals may be less obviously altruistic and self-fulfilling than those of their younger colleagues, but they, too, live with many of the same enduring aspirations. Most are capable of increasing their competence, and a major aspect of the executive's work will consist in helping them do this.

In fantasy the leader is omnipotent—at once a generalist and a specialist, individually mobile yet cooperative as a member of a team, intellectual but with an acute sense for the commonplace. He is supposed to be a "man"—aggressive, charismatic, and stable—and at the same time exercise restraint and self-control. But sometimes he cannot embrace these seeming contradictions. Sometimes a woman, herself caught in role conflicts, cannot either. Sometimes each of them succeeds.

Younger people are likely to have technical brilliance but lack the wisdom needed for humanness. This they must learn by working with the artist. They, too, want to become diamonds in their own right—bigger, more brilliant than their predecessors—and they should. There is one qualification: they want not only to sparkle, but to be useful as well.

Leadership is an art to be cultivated and developed.[18] Like any other form of art, if it becomes stereotyped it is no longer art but merely replica. An artistic achievement is varied in texture, composition, symbolism, color. It is dynamic in the eyes of the viewer because it takes on new meaning with each perception. In short, it lives. So it is with the work of the good leader. In different circumstances, at different times, with different problems, leaders choose different modes of action. It is this flexibility, together with a conception of and appreciation for the role, that makes leaders like diamonds—solid, strong, yet many-faceted and therefore sparkling. This is why leadership cannot be learned by prescription or content; it must be learned in a relationship, through identification with a "teacher."

CASE HISTORY 7 | An organization invites trouble when its top people neglect the role of teacher implicit in the role of leader, as did this narrator's predecessor, who "made all decisions himself." Having inherited a valuable technical person, but one who has had no opportunity to make mistakes under stress—and thus no chance to overcome the tendency—the narrator recognizes the need for a different approach but has not found quite the right one.

"I am a vice-president in a large, national corporation where I head a technical department. My problem concerns Raymond, the man who's second in command to me.

In the year I have been with the company, I have continually run into difficulties over Raymond's hasty decisions.

"Raymond is liked by his peers and has excellent knowledge and experience. When in a relaxed frame of mind, he can make appropriate decisions. But when he's under stress, he becomes erratic and impulsive, often with disastrous results.

"My predecessor made all decisions himself, and thus Raymond had no opportunity to make such blunders. The company prefers a more democratic management style, which is one of the reasons I was recruited.

"Raymond seems to feel some loss of face because he had been placed briefly in my position before I came and then had to move back. Apparently he has to give an immediate answer in order to make a good showing as an executive and to counteract his hurt pride. Although disappointed at not being promoted, he also felt relieved. He told me that he did not feel ready for the job I've taken. When I'm present he consults me freely and works very cooperatively with me. Even if we don't agree on some things, he is loyal to me. The problem arises only when I am away.

"Much of the work of my department involves quick decisions and fast thinking. Often we are called upon to give a red or green light to a product, based on whether it meets certain standards. If the situation is unclear, it is essential to wait until we have enough evidence to go one way or the other. When people approach Raymond with such a decision, he usually gives a quick yes-or-no answer. In one of his recent erroneous decisions, he cost the company a considerable sum of money.

"Raymond has come to be known as a soft touch. I have begun to notice that some people now make a habit of consulting me when they know I'm out of town so that they can deal with Raymond. Recently a man from marketing approached Raymond for support on a new program line which I have opposed for some time. To my chagrin, he gave his approval, and the wheels were set in motion by the time I returned.

"I have discussed each of the major incidents with Raymond, and in every case he is genuinely apologetic. I have suggested that he try not to feel pressured when approached by people in my absence and he agrees with me that it is never wise to make a decision without careful thought. Nevertheless, the blunders persist. What can I do?"

Analysis

Where Is the Pain?   The vice-president feels the pain acutely, and undoubtedly others in the company suffer from Raymond's behavior. There is no indication that Raymond feels much pain.

When Did It Begin?   Raymond's impulsive decisions are a product of his personality and probably could be traced back to his childhood. The effect of his personality on the company became a serious problem when, for the first time, he was assigned high-level responsibility.

Affection   Raymond's needs for affection get in the way of his good judgment. For people like him, the pressure of having to make a decision means risking loss of affection. Saying "no" might alienate someone.

Aggression   Raymond is described as being well liked. We presume that he gets angry, as all human beings do, but he seems to bury these feelings. Anger is not pleasing to people, so he cannot express it.

Dependency   Raymond's needs for affection and his inability to assert himself combine to make him a highly dependent person. If he can lean on others, they will make the decisions and "face the music" of people's disapproval. When he worked under his previous superior, he was in an ideal position. He had the status of holding a responsible position without the burden of having to take a stand on anything. Most people would have found this situation intolerable.

Ego Ideal   Raymond's aspirations conflict. On the one hand, he wants to hold a responsible managerial position.

On the other, his overriding need is to please people. It is clear from the presentation that when the chips are down, being liked is more important than doing his best on the job.

Is It Solvable?   Raymond is capable of thinking rationally only when his needs for dependency and universal acceptance are not involved—that is, when he is not under pressure. He does not need training in decision making, for he is already competent in this area when he is relaxed. The problem lies at the heart of his personality, so talking to him about his mistakes doesn't help. His personality isn't going to change, but change is possible in his environment.

How?   The vice-president should tell him openly that he is the kind of person who cares a lot about having people like him and show him how this concern gets in the way of his decision making. The vice-president should give him examples of situations in which his need to be "nice" has led to blunders. He can explain that such needs are an asset in certain jobs, like selling, and can enlist his participation in selecting some other assignment in the company that fits his personality more comfortably.

NINE

The Executive as Teacher

The task of training leadership in an organizational context is not easy. Unless this role can be formulated to encompass all other executive tasks so that it meshes with other responsibilities, the executive will only be left frustrated.

Although the perspective here focuses on top management, the development of leadership capability is the responsibility of everyone who supervises another person, so the issues to be discussed here apply across organizational levels. There are no recipes for the leader's teaching role. There is, however, a wide range of data that can be marshaled as a guide.

The Teaching Role

Just as there is no single way to lead, there is no way to teach. Every executive brings his or her own unique talents, skills, and personality to the executive task. And there is as much diversity in the teaching role as in the other roles of the leader. Psychologist Joseph Adelson points out that there are many styles of influence, many modes of connection, that bind the student and teacher to each other. Building on the work of anthropologist Merrill Jackson, Adelson proposes five types of teacher-leaders.[1]

1) *Shamans.* These leaders heal through the use of personal power. They focus their audience on themselves. (Although tribally women sometimes hold these positions, the role of shaman, like the other teacher-leader roles described here, has traditionally been seen as reserved for men—an assumption that is being challenged in the culture of the organizational world, if not on a tribal level.) When their skills are combined with unusual gifts, shamans become charismatic. They have power, energy, and commitment, which they use to organize people around them.

2) *Priests.* Priest like leaders claim power through their office. They are agents of omnipotent authority, and the people who organize around them see themselves as set apart from others. A priestly structure is characterized by continuity; it has a past and a program for the immediate and distant future, a hierarchy with roles and places in a hierarchical ladder.

3) *Elected leaders.* These people endure trials and self-transformation, training, or some other form of rite to achieve their position. Elected leaders derive their power from their own experience and from the mandate of those who back them.

4) *Missionaries.* Usually mission involves a utopian view of the future and a program for achieving reforms. Much of contemporary business leadership incorporates the priestly, elected, and missionary types. Power is delegated by the most powerful. People in one company or unit are differentiated from others. There is continuity, hierarchy, and election. Most organizations have some kind of mission, however prosaic.

5) *Mystic healers.* These are altruists who seek the sources of illness in the patient's personality. Translated into teaching-leadership functions, these are the leaders who try to discover the statue in the marble, who discern, like Michelangelo, what could be created from the raw material. This style of leadership requires not only acumen but considerable sensitivity, as well as the flexibility to vary the teaching approach according to the student.

The shaman, referred to in management literature as an "authoritarian" leader, is most effective in crisis situations. At such a time the organization needs a strong figure to follow. The danger is that the subordinates will remain powerless and never learn how to use power except as charismatic leaders. Since they have been rendered powerless, they are rarely able to become charismatic. So the organization is threatened when the leader departs. It either declines in power and effectiveness, brings in outside management, or becomes vulnerable to "pirates." Authoritarian leadership is characteristic of many first-generation organizations, run by the leaders who built them, but it is conducive neither to the personal growth of subordinates nor, as a result, to the survival of the organization.

The priestly type of leadership, incorporating the sense of "election" and the conviction of the "missionary," has all the advantages and disadvantages of rigid structure. Subordinates can see themselves as part of a tradition and can readily measure their progress. The danger lies in the organization's pressure to conform and in its potential for molding people in the image of a system at the expense of their individuality and originality. Sometimes the phrase "military mind" is used. Subordinates become imitative and always carefully correct, establishing what Adelson calls an "ersatz identity." They play the part, but they may often lose their sense of self as the price of "belonging."

Mystic healers have the most demanding of all roles, but their style of leadership is potentially the most productive for the organization. It requires the leader to renounce personal pursuit of power in favor of building strength into the subordinates and into the organization. If survival is the main goal of the organization, and if a successful leader is one who can build survival potential into the organization by seeing the most in and getting the most out of people, this style of leadership will become more widespread.

Leaders who put their followers before themselves are easily misread as weak, vacillating, overkind, or irresponsible. As a matter of fact, theirs is the most difficult type of leadership to carry out because it is the most realistic. It comes to grips with the psychological and social data about human motivation that are usually ignored—at great cost to management, the organization, and the employees.

The management philosophy of the mystic healer calls for a sensitive and delicate molding—what the behaviorists call "shaping." Many people recoil at the use of the word "molding," thinking it implies that the executive will manipulate and control the life of the subordinate. This is not the case. Inevitably, a company's system of compensation and appraisal, modes of leadership, and varieties of opportunity all contribute to eliciting or suppressing the potential of the executive-to-be. People are never really free to grow, independent of the influence of those who exercise power over them. Unless leaders face this reality, they deceive themselves with clichés like "All development is self-development" and "The best will rise to the top." Leaders do have influence on their subordinates. If they can accept the fact, then the question is only how to use it most wisely.

Following the Grain

To begin with, executives must understand that they cannot shape other human beings into a preconceived form. Talk in the past about silk purses and sows' ears has had such a judgmental ring that it has clouded another basic issue: for many needs, silk is of no use either. Executives who try to change people will meet with resistance, or will cause them to fail as a result of conflict between the momentum of the subordinates' personalities and what their superiors want them to be.

What then does shaping mean? It means to follow the grain of the person and help it achieve refinement in a form that it could not achieve by itself. Just as the sculptor follows the natural grain of a piece of wood, so the leader must discern the real strengths of the subordinate and encourage them. Instead of providing a prescribed range of experiences for all promising young men and women, executives need to discriminate. What obscure talents does this employee seem to have and what experiences will foster them? Where does he sparkle most in his relationships? What challenges give a particular woman greatest satisfaction? With what kinds of bosses does she work best?

The executive must consider how to bring together a range of people whose talents complement one another, and must stimulate each to further growth. This approach is certainly different from the more usual managerial maneuver of pitting a group of young people against one another, dissipating talent in rivalry and defensiveness and discouraging cooperation.

There is always a danger in such efforts—the tendency to try to shape people in one's image, or drive them to become what one had wished to become but could not. The danger is best avoided if executives try to discern and understand what the subordinates themselves are and what they are striving to become. And the leader must not help too much—this will only encourage the subordinates' dependency at the cost of autonomy. A subordinate should have enough stress and frustration to understand the complexity of human relationships, to learn that there is pain in leadership, to discover how easy it is to hate when you are frustrated, and to realize that building relationships of trust with others is a slow and arduous business.

A second danger is that the executive will try to be a psychotherapist for the subordinate. In an effort to be understanding, bosses may either dig too deeply into someone's life or assume that they must solve all personality and family problems for their subordinates. There are capable professionals who can do this, and executives should not try. The executive's work is to teach the subordinate about the job the subordinate must do. Certainly executives should be helpful and compassionate. Still, personal pressures and problems, though they temporarily impair performance and learning, cannot be excuses. Respect for human personality means to hold adults responsible for their actions. It also means demanding what adults are capable of giving to the immediate task; otherwise subordinates feel guilty and superiors feel cheated. The consequence is mutual contempt.

Has the leader a right to mold and shape? Of what use is maturation, experience, and wisdom if not to be instructive for those who are younger? Leaders not only have the right—they have the obligation.

Settling down to assess each subordinate in this way may seem like a large order and a distraction from the job at hand. "Forget it—I have to get my own work done," is a common reaction among executives when the idea is proposed to them. Although the reaction is understandable, executives who give in to it do not acknowledge the real needs of the organization. Developing the skills and expanding the strengths of subordinates *are* major aspects of the executive's task. If other kinds of work take up all their time, executives may delude themselves into thinking that they are putting forward their best efforts for the organization, but in fact they are not. Executives who continually emphasize tasks at hand at the expense of organizational development are not responding to the primary needs of the organization. This emphasis is actually counterproductive: it exploits the organization in the short term without taking into account what is necessary to keep it alive and healthy in the long run.

There are no prescriptions that the executive can follow in acting as a teacher. In the organization, as in any classroom, teaching is a matter of doing what comes naturally, taking care to make opportunities for showing what it is one does, how, and why, and how the same strategies could be adapted and used by the students. This is what is known as the "shine—and show them" approach. Executives do the best they can and point out what has happened, how a problem has been identified and solved, and how the students (in this case, the subordinates) could apply similar techniques to solve the problems they encounter in their own work.

Executives can say, "Watch me," do what they normally do, and still incorporate some formal teaching arrangements. "Formal teaching arrangements" may have a formidable ring. Executives shrink from the thought of devoting half the business day to seminars for learning, while other work is left undone and while executives and subordinates turn self-consciously into teachers and students. But this is not the idea at all. The process of example-setting goes on all the time. Executives behave in certain ways, sizing up problems, considering the resources (manpower, supplies, and finances) that can be utilized to meet them, and making decisions about procedure. Subordinates, likewise, watch what they are doing and how they do it. Learning takes place all the time. What can be made more explicit is the act of teaching. And rather than usurping the business day, it can happen during, say, one meeting a week, when the executive, choosing a particular problem that is fresh in everyone's mind, discusses its various aspects with subordinates already at least partially familiar with it. The executive can use the problem as a case study, explain its history and present implications, and show how it has been solved.

Becoming more aware of possible teaching strategies can help both the leader and the learner. One important technique is the private discussion. In contrast to a group meeting, the private discussion gives the executive an opportunity to work with a subordinate in a more direct, one-to-one way, by talking over the current situation and suggesting possible improvements.

Executives are apt to run into several problems here. Style of discussion can be one. Listening closely to the way people talk offers clues to their relationships. Kenneth R. Mitchell found three distinct patterns in a friend's speech: (1) the public speaking pattern, which marked his friend as a learned man; (2) the ordinary speech pattern, which contained a mild regional accent and a casual, ordinary vocabulary; and (3) the pattern used with cronies or intimates which was occasionally spiced by colorful, vulgar language.[2] The patterns were rarely mixed, except under extreme emotional distress (when confronted with a crisis, Mitchell noted, his friend's intimate speech changed to his ordinary pattern). With their styles of speech, people draw boundaries around their different roles, unconsciously changing the way they talk to fit their immediate role. The executive might find it useful to tape conversations with subordinates and play them back, to see what boundaries have been established and whether these boundaries might become barriers to further communication.

Indirectness is another problem for many managers and executives. Rather than speaking straightforwardly, they allude to what they have in mind and expect their subordinates to read between the lines. Most people cannot. Many managers complain that they have difficulty when their superiors approach them indirectly. Some continually press their superiors for clarification. Most, however, remain uneasy and in doubt. Executives have a responsibility to tell subordinates *exactly* what they expect of them and to do so straightforwardly.

Directness, however, does not rule out being diplomatic, and directness should not be confused with aggression. A lot of executives like to think of themselves as tough and aggressive. Indeed, many (including recent American presidents) think that toughness is the essence of the ideal executive.[3] Many bosses think they can motivate their subordinates with actual or implicit threats and tough, macho poses. They do not want to appear in any way soft or flexible, in part because they think others will then take advantage of them and in part because they think such behavior is an admission of inadequacy or failure. But people who talk tough are often rigid and insensitive, unable to respond to reasoned arguments or to change with changing events.

Talking tough closes off communication. The very word implies insensitivity and harshness. Good leaders can take harsh action when necessary, but they do not rely on rough, bullying behavior to get things done. People who are preoccupied with toughness are actually hung up with feelings of helplessness. They swagger to ward off others because they fear anyone could deliver them a harmful blow.

Direct talk can include criticism of a subordinate, but an important facet of performance appraisal is the manner in which criticism is given.

> Criticism can be used and met constructively or destructively. It can be the means by which people receiving it climb, or it can be used to bolster the critic's vanity.
>
> Criticism in its highest sense means trying to learn the best that is known and thought in the world, and measuring things by that standard.
>
> But let us look at the other kinds. Captious criticism takes note of trivial faults; its author is usually unduly exacting or hard to please. Carping criticism is a perverse picking of flaws. Cavilling criticism stresses the habit of raising petty objections. Censorious criticism means a tendency to be severely condemnatory of that which one does not like.[4]

Executives are likely to become more careful about how they apply criticism as they acquire a deeper understanding about the effect they have (greater, probably, than what they believe it to be) on those who work with them. Ordinary actions by a supervisor can have profound effects not only on subordinates' feelings about themselves as professionals, but also on the way they conduct their work. Margery Jean Gross Doehrman points out that the supervisor/supervisee relationship is important in ways not ordinarily recognized in the standard conception of the relationship.[5] She notes that in supervising somebody, it is difficult to change one's professional self because there is an inevitable fear of change, even when one is learning new skills. When growing to a new level of responsibility, there is always concern about whether one will measure up, and that is quite normal.

Executives should realize that while their knowledge, status, and training inspire feelings of admiration among subordinates, they may also inspire fear, envy, and hostility. This is the common ambivalence in all power relationships that is magnified by the subordinate's dependency on the superior. Managers are always startled to discover that people who report to them are afraid of them. There are several reasons for this fear: (1) a manager exerts power over people, (2) people are dependent on the manager, and (3) they are vulnerable to his criticism because of his quasi-parental role.

Managers find it difficult to understand fear. They do not see themselves as intimidating figures. They would do well to ask their subordinates if they inspire fear, and if so, when and how. Merely raising the issue will reduce fear. The answers might make it possible to do more to help people feel less afraid. Sometimes a subordinate thinks that his superior expects more from him than he feels capable of producing. The superior, in turn, may patronize her subordinate or feel hostile when challenged by him, thus magnifying the difficulties on both sides. In the back of her mind, a superior may also be concerned that the subordinate will become a competitor.

All executives should be sensitive to the unknown and intense effect they have upon their supervisees as well as the effects supervisees may have upon them. Superiors, since they are in a more powerful position, need to give more thought to what is going on among their people and how they affect them. Anything and everything that happens in the supervisor/subordinate relationship affects, in turn, the work of superiors with subordinates. These issues should be central in supervisory and managerial training.

In arranging private discussions to talk things over, executives often find that many people do not want to talk—especially about their feelings. There are several ways in which executives can support people who find it difficult to open up, all of which revolve around demonstrating that the executives care about how the people feel. First, executives should be specific about their interest. They should ask directly about a situation that they think the subordinate might be reluctant to bring up. Second, they should be personal. It will help if they talk about some of their own experiences that they think might have relevance. Third, they should generalize. If they know of certain experiences that the subordinate is bound to encounter, they can say, for instance, "Most people around here sooner or later run into so-and-so, who seems to act as if the department were his private possession." If the first encounter has already occurred, the subordinate should be encouraged to describe what happened and tell how the situation was handled. Here, however, executives must be careful not to prejudice people or lead them to support internal factions. Fourth, executives should direct the conversation away from the subordinate. Those who find it very difficult to talk about themselves usually deal with emotional issues better by looking at what someone else is up against or how someone else might feel in a certain situation. Such people could be asked to discuss the problems of their own subordinates.

Everyone finds certain kinds of talks anxiety-provoking. The uneasiness is generally rooted in the unconscious feeling, left over from childhood, that words can kill. Executives cannot make unconscious anxiety disappear, but they can make themselves more comfortable if they take it into account. In such situations, executives can rehearse with a trusted peer beforehand and thus anticipate the subordinate's probable reactions. They should try to put themselves in the other person's shoes. Sometimes what may seem uncomfortably like an attack on another person is only a reflection of the executive's differing values. What is important to the superior might not be equally so to the subordinate.

There is more to talking things over than talking, however. There is also listening. This is especially important in a talk that is at the same time a serious negotiation. Negotiating is one of the most difficult and least understood of the arts. Both sides have to be winners. Putting somebody on the defensive is always disastrous. The answer is to learn to listen.

Listen for what? For a person's values. Executives must consider what type of work environment will make subordinates look good to themselves, considering the pressures, and then help them create such an environment. For instance, a union leader must prove to his people that he has fought hard for them, and so he has a need to draw out negotiations. No quick, easy solution can satisfy him. Likewise, an independent person must have a situation in which she herself can pick out the solution from among many options, so that she feels she has control. People may not reveal their values, but if executives stop to imagine themselves in the subordinate's shoes, the person's basic priorities will most often be readily apparent.

Talking to a subordinate—whether the conversation is a brief talk or a critical incident performance appraisal—can help only so much. There is a limit to the growth that can be achieved within a classroom, and students are therefore often placed in some kind of internship or practicum where they can try out their new knowledge and build competence. Similarly, there is a limit to what an executive can teach a subordinate within the confines of a conversation. To build on new information or improved insights, subordinates need new chances to try out what they have learned.

Executives can give them these chances by putting them in situations where they can try to do what they have been thinking and talking about. The challenge is to work out assignments to see how people respond. Organizational life, like life outside the company, presents spiral opportunities, fresh chances for people to manage a particular kind of situation more successfully than the last time they encountered it. For instance, people who tend to overcontrol can be encouraged, in private discussions, to see that their energy is needed for certain kinds of work, and to relinquish some of the tight control kept on other tasks. Obviously it will be important to reassure these subordinates that their skills are respected and needed, since a usual motive for maintaining such close hold on the work is the fear that other people will take over, do it better, and displace them from their territory. Then, in a position that poses less threat than before, subordinates can be given the chance to delegate more responsibility.

Executives can send subordinates to represent them in certain ways, such as visiting plant sites or acting as delegates at an association conference. Listening for feedback, executives may learn something from the way in which the subordinates conducted themselves. At the plant, did one of them use the visit as an opportunity for self-aggrandizement, to boast of achievements or give his own orders in the boss's name? Or did he act in a collaborative and constructive way with the supervisors at the plant?

Sometimes executives have a problem with a subordinate because there seems to be no problem yet. This happens especially with "jets" who may not have been in one place long enough to fail, or to see and account for the consequences of their actions. An unbroken chain of overnight successes does not reveal much about such a person's ability during a crisis or over the long haul. If the person is just a star passing through, this is not extremely important. But if it is someone who may have a longer tenure in the organization, executives must learn more about the real person behind the bright lights. One way is to place the jet in a difficult situation and see whether the person succeeds or fails. In this case, it is important to help forge a mentor alliance that can provide a flow of information, guidance, feedback, and support for the subordinate in this new role.

The Mentor Alliance

Mentors are not new. What has changed is our understanding about the relationship between an older, more experienced professional and the unseasoned apprentice. In terms of management "professional" is the right term, since the leadership qualities needed today at the top levels of organizations are those of professionals expert in directing a team of people rather than the qualities of specialists skilled in marketing, engineering, or finance but inept when it comes to working with a group.

A professional note has always been implicit in the meaning of the word "mentor," defined by the dictionary as "a wise, loyal advisor." (The original Mentor was the trusted counselor of Odysseus, and later of his son, Telemachus.) A mentor, a particular kind of role model, offers specific examples of what to do in order to qualify for a particular job or kind of work. The emphasis is on skills and behaviors. The role need not be professional in today's usage. Just as a student can form an alliance with a senior doctor, lawyer, or teacher, so can an apprentice learn from an experienced cabinetmaker, weaver, or house painter. Frequently the mentor demonstrates not only behavioral skills, but the underlying attitudes as well. Philip Abelson, editor of *Science*, has said that the professor's most important role is to motivate the student to pursue continuing scholarship throughout his life, and to acquire a sound value system and the capacity for independent thought.[6] For young cabinetmakers, it is not enough to learn which tools are used or which woods serve best for a desk or a sideboard; they must also acquire the carefulness and attention to detail that characterize the master.

The mentor alliance, so far, sounds like a one-way street, with the mentor sending messages and the apprentice absorbing them. It seems to be based on a premise similar to a classic view of teaching, which holds children to be tabulae rasae—empty slates on which experienced elders write the messages they think children need to know. Like this view of education, however, the one-way mentor alliance is out of date. Mentors today offer more than a distant example of behaviors and attitudes: they also offer the junior partner the chance for close engagement as an adversary. Abraham Zaleznik, writing about the training of leaders, says the mentor method can help potential leaders develop their full capacities by giving them the chance to work in a one-to-one relationship with other leaders.[7] Potential leaders must have the opportunity to challenge their mentor, to allow their competitive impulses and behavior (within bounds) to surface, and to have healthy interchange with superiors. Junior partners flex their muscles and develop their skills by engaging with their mentors, sometimes in friendly disagreement, and sometimes (as they gain confidence and begin to know their full strength—and in order to prove their strength to themselves) in open confrontation, break, and separation.

Mentors may be good teachers, but may be unwilling to share power. An interview with three past presidents of the Jewel Companies highlights this important aspect of the mentoring relationship.[8] For Franklin Lunding, mentoring—the "first-assistant philosophy"—was the company's basic philosophy. Mentors and learners help each other and the business, Lunding says. "I needed him [learner George Clements] more than he needed me. What I loved was that all you had to do was give him a go." Clements in turn groomed Donald Perkins for the presidency by sharing his power with his successor. "What's more important," he asks, "me being right or Don learning?"

Mentors who guide and teach may run the risk of overcontrolling. They can be like perfectionist parents who have a lot of knowledge and experience to share, but who want their children to be mirror images of themselves and to do things the way they themselves have always done them. Often these people can give up power only when they have a cloned replacement. Younger people need not only politically seasoned and technically experienced mentors, but freedom and responsibility as well.

Since the vast majority of people in management have until recently been men, the history of the mentor alliance has been a masculine one. As those who write about management have observed, one of the obstacles women have faced in efforts to prepare themselves for leadership roles has been the lack of women as role models. This does not mean that managerial women have had no mentors, only that their mentors were usually men, and one study conducted in 1964 suggests that they are likely to have been their fathers. Of twenty-five women enrolled in the M.B.A. program at the Harvard Business School, all had had extremely close relationships with their fathers and had been involved in an unusually wide range of traditionally masculine activities in their fathers' businesses, starting when they were very young. Their families had encouraged them to pursue interests that caught their attention, regardless of whether they were considered girls' interests or boys' interests, and at an early age they developed a preference for the company of men.[9] Women in management can use female role models, but a study of cross-sex mentoring suggests that they also need male mentors who can help them understand men's thoughts and behavior. When female therapists acted as mentors to young male therapists, they shared their feelings and sensibilities with the men and helped them cross sex barriers that impeded their work with female patients. The young men became more sensitive to the nuances of female psychology. They were not so quick to assume that women's anger was irrational, and they examined in greater depth women's psychological histories. By responding positively to a trusted female mentor, these young therapists learned to respond more seriously to their female patients.[10]

As more women enter management careers, cross-sex mentoring will become more important in business. Women managers are working in what is still mainly a man's world. They need male mentors who can help them appreciate and master the fine points of male psychology. Women are often baffled, for instance, by the dynamics of team play that most men take for granted. Good male mentors can explain the subtle blend of competitiveness and cooperation that characterizes so many male relationships. When women are more attuned to male psychology, they will be able to participate in the real sources of power and influence—the informal relationships and social contacts through which men have traditionally established their careers and won their promotions. Similarly, women mentors can help men understand the fine points of women's traditionally nurturing roles. With sensitive cross-sex mentoring, managers can break down some of the sex barriers that inhibit understanding and cooperation. It is a way to map out territory so that men and women will not be so alien in one other's worlds.

Future studies should yield interesting information on the nature of the mentor alliance, between men and men, men and women, and women and women. Sex is one factor that can play a part in forging a mentor bond. Others include ethnicity, professional interests, family background. A number of factors, often unconscious, go into the choice of a mentor. In order to understand the mentor alliance more fully, it is helpful to know more about the process of identification.

The Process of Identification

Identification is one of the most important aspects of the teaching situation; successful teachers must be good identification figures and learners must be able to learn from them by identification. This process begins in childhood.[11]

Identification, Freud observed, is the earliest expression of an emotional tie with another person. "A little boy will exhibit a special interest in his father; he would like to grow like him and be like him, to take his place everywhere. We may say simply that he takes his father as his ideal." Children also identify with their mothers and imitate their behavior. By identifying with the mother first and imitating what she does, they acquire skills and develop their earliest competences. As they grow older, though, they come to resent their mother's efforts to take care of them, interpreting her aid as interference. With each successful act of identification with the mother, children make the mother less necessary.

A boy's identification with his father is an essential step toward becoming a man. It involves not only love for the father but also rivalry with him. A girl's identification with her mother works the same way. Identification is not simple imitation. For identification to succeed, children must first love, then imitate, then assert their relative independence to practice the behavior they have learned. Furthermore, every step of development is hard won and is bound to be fiercely defended. Such aggressive defense occurs frequently when parents forbid or compel certain acts.

As they grow, children differentiate themselves from other people. Rivalry develops, for instance, when a girl observes that another person has greater strength or skill in some area than she, and wants that particular personal asset for her own. This rivalry, in turn, begets competitive struggles with those whom she admires. Instead of simply imitating all of the behavior of the loved rival, the child becomes more selective, adopting only those traits of the other person that fit her social context, her stage of development, and the skills she already has. As she experiences successes and failures, pleasures and disappointments, she learns about her own capabilities and weaknesses. These experiences contribute to children's selectivity of identifications. For example, a child who finds that he does not have language skills comparable to those of other children his age may be reluctant to learn them if they are not evident at home and he has no place he can use what he is being taught in school. This is one of the problems of teaching disadvantaged children.

The identification process gradually centers on rival figures, because the child wants to become as powerful as they. This is critical for the child's identification with the parent and particularly for the development of the superego. Aggressive feelings, hostility, rivalry, competition, and a sense of separation are as important to the identification process as affection for the admired person. Any kind of identification implies, "I don't need you; if you don't want to do it for me I can do it myself; and if you don't want to give it to me I can give it to myself." When the child makes selective identification, he or she is saying, "In this respect I like you and want to be like you, but in other respects I don't like you and don't want to be like you; I want to be different—in fact, myself."[12]

Identity—an enduring and consistent image of oneself—arises out of all of these choices for identification which fit together with innate and acquired capacities. Identity is a continuous sense of internal harmony which makes the future a flowering of the past.

Identification serves many purposes for the child. It promotes learning and forms the basis for the ego ideal. In normal development, the ego grows through the process of identification, a process of voluntary psychological acquisition which continues through a lifetime. However, if development is hampered, children may fall back or regress to an earlier stage where they could exercise their capacities without interference.[13] In this sense, the forward motion of development is like that of an army: when attacked it falls back to a previously prepared solid position. When natural development requires further activity and progress is blocked, children may fall back to an earlier, more passive level.

Through identification, children learn their native language and subsequently acquire other intellectual knowledge. The process also teaches them how to deal with the demands of their environment and of their innermost feelings. Psychiatrist Joost Meerloo, taking a global view, points out that all civilized action is learned from parents and former generations.[14] In the course of growing up, people absorb and internalize from their environment and its history and culture the many meanings condensed in unity. A young man or woman may learn about and identify with an important personality, such as Joan of Arc or Abraham Lincoln, without ever having met the person.

Identification is a generalized process of learning how to behave and what to become, an evolution that continues into adulthood. Identification occurs among adults when one person has a strength that others want to acquire. In organizations the leader, the power figure, has certain strengths; subordinates want the ones that fit their needs. Sometimes leaders have more strength than they realize; we speak of such "added strength" as charisma.

The leader seems so strong partly because of transference. People who are neither peers nor challengers have affection and respect for those who hold high formal positions. As long as leaders enjoy this affection and respect, they are more likely to keep their positions in the structure of authority. This is one reason for the advantage that political incumbents often have over their challengers.

Transference is a result of the nature of people's early relationship with their parents.[15] People look to the leader, as they looked to their parents, and see someone who can satisfy or frustrate their needs. If they cannot identify with the ego ideals or goals of the leader, or if the leader cannot help them reach those goals, they will no longer follow.[16] This dynamic is played out in organizations especially. People become affiliated with an executive in order to achieve certain goals. Nothing else, except external compulsion, can hold them together. They have been brought together to achieve the purposes of the organization, but they also have their own purposes. In identifying with the leader, in looking to him as they did to their parents, they expect him to be instrumental in obtaining the goals that will serve both the organization's purposes and their own.

It is not merely that the leader controls compensation and appraisal, or offers routes to certain concrete satisfactions. Identifying with the leader enlarges people's capacities by helping them meet the demands of their superegos and to develop their sense of identity. They want to see themselves in certain ways, and here is a chance: the leader needs them. Mahatma Gandhi, for example, served just such a purpose for his followers.[17] Because they identified with him and responded to his moral challenges, his followers were able to mobilize unsuspected inner resources.

A leader meets the ego ideal of a group as well as of the individuals in it. By acting as the focal point of unity, the leader knits people together into a social system.[18] With such a leader, said Freud, a group is capable of high achievement, abnegation, unselfishness, and devotion to an ideal. Without such a leader, the group falls apart because people lose their medium for establishing ties with one another—identification with the leader. A group without a leader is a mob. Every group needs a leader and moves toward a leader, someone with a strong and imposing will which the group, having no collective will of its own, can incorporate. When leaders stand for an idea and are accepted by their followers, they acquire what Freud calls "fascination" or prestige. To maintain this prestige, leaders must go on being successful. Prestige, as Robert Waelder puts it, is the reputation for victory. "Loss of prestige may therefore embolden all enemies and dishearten and demoralize all friends and so bring about a radical change in power relations."[19] In times of transition and conflict the ego ideal of the leader becomes an especially important social anchor for the followers.[20] The pattern is familiar. As adults, the members of a group identify with a leader as they would with a parent because the parent represents what the child would like to be. This is not childish behavior, however—it is the appropriate way for adults to move on, reaching ahead to meet new challenges. Adults, no matter how well educated, sophisticated, or competent, still need the purpose that comes from pursuing ideals. Inspiration is largely the transmission of ideals as a basis for action, and ideals are considered through a role performance—the way people act as part of the positions they hold in a social structure, whether this structure be a family, a community, or an organization. In identifying with the leader, subordinates establish or expand a professional model for themselves.

Although group leaders are transference figures at first, ideally as time goes on they become examples of how to look at the world in a more rational way.[21] Rather than weakening their followers, they build up their strengths. As the followers become more mature, the gap narrows between the followers' level of competence and that of their leader.

Identification is not simple imitation but the process of adopting aspects of the model that "fit" the person who is identifying. So it is not the same as making the subordinate just like the superior. In fact, the executive might say to his subordinates, as Emerson did in his essay "Self Reliance": "Insist on yourself; never imitate. Your own gift can present every moment with the cumulative force of a whole life's cultivation, but of the adopted talent of another you have only an extemporaneous half possession."[22]

Emerson's advice is not always followed, and in some organizations identification can become little more than imitation. This is what happens with priest-like leaders who rely heavily on molding men to fit the system. The result is called, in clinical jargon, "identification with the aggressor."[23] When superiors are threateningly aggressive toward their subordinates, the subordinates become anxious. They tend to cope by impersonating the aggressor, assuming or imitating his manner; thus, the subordinate makes himself not the frightened person but the one who frightens. In an organization, there may be people at each level displaying hostility downward, and subordinates whose subsequent growth is warped. Identification with the aggressor stimulates competition among the followers for the special attention and affection of the leader. There may seem to be democracy in the group, but underneath it is clear that the group goals come from the boss alone. The leader is seen as a depriver, and the goals, being the leader's alone, are to be defeated.

This is quite the opposite of creative and constructive identification. Positive identification lets the followers absorb those aspects of the leader that suggest a strong, helpful, understanding figure who respects the efforts of the followers and who, in addition, has shown them how to do the work they want to do.[24]

Positive identification has another outcome. Selwyn Becker points out that when people anticipate a mutually beneficial outcome, they would rather share it with someone like themselves.[25] When they expect to cause discomfort to someone or to suffer discomfort as a result of another's actions, they would rather that the other person were dissimilar. When the group's mode of identification is imitation, there is a tendency for senior executives to avoid situations where they must be realistic with their subordinates—to try to persuade subordinates to a different way of doing things rather than to point out their failures. This in turn means that feedback is disguised and the underlying message unclear. If subordinates fail to succeed in imitative roles, Becker notes, superiors take this as their own failure, a personal insult and a reflection on their capacity as managers. Obviously, imitative identification limits the range of solutions a group will examine.

Under ideal circumstances, the leadership climate does not promote simple imitation of one hierarchical level by the level below it.[26] Rather, identification is a process of interaction in which the values and role models offered by higher levels are transformed in keeping with the needs of the followers and the requirements of the organization.

Encouraging Positive Identification

If people learn most of what they know from others, and if being able to learn from others depends on being able to identify with them, then one of the leader's basic tasks is to create the conditions for identification. At the same time he or she also creates conditions for identification with others in positions of authority. What are the conditions of a relationship in which this can happen?

Most adults seek closeness to other people, not only for exchange of affection and support, but also to attain a sense of completeness. Something of this is seen in the wish to give and receive affection. It is also seen in the desire to be near the source of power, to have close social relationships within organizations, and to identify with the leader. The need for "oneness" with the environment leads people to use the work organization as a psychological anchor point and their relationships with the work organization as a way to maintain the feeling of psychological continuity.

Not every person seeks closeness with every other person, nor do all need closeness to others and to organizations in the same degree. Karl Menninger indicates that people need a range of contacts of different degrees of intensity and intermittency: very intimate (as in the family), moderately intimate (as with friends), less intimate (as with acquaintances).[27] And they also need some privacy, a chance to retreat from contact altogether.

Relationships can be sustained only if they are gratifying or pleasurable. Adults expect the leader to recognize worth, work, and achievement, and to be responsive to their needs. They also want rewarding social ties in their work. Above all, they want to respect themselves as competent adults.

A gratifying relationship for the child is one that provides support, protection, and guidance. Even in adult situations, persons with less power require support and guidance from those who wield more. In varying degrees, they require the boss to help them grow on the job, represent their feelings to higher management, show them how to do better, and not exploit their dependency. From the organization they seek support, security, and the gratification of legitimate dependency needs.

In their work, adults seek greater mastery of themselves and use work as one way of controlling fantasies. The work organization provides avenues for mastery through the use of skills and competences. It reinforces psychological defenses and self-control. In social relationships the egalitarian tradition discourages submissiveness and encourages individual self-determination and democratic responsibility.

In a democratic society adults are urged to aspire to leadership, to envision themselves as free, and to take initiative and be responsible. They demand that their leaders maintain democratic values. In their work, adults find the opportunity to gain money, status, and power. They also seek to reinforce their position in society, their role as providers for their family, and their sense of worthiness. This comes in part from the work itself, in part from their role in the organization. In their ambitious strivings they expand their egos and fuse and channel their drives in keeping with the demands of the superego and reality. All of this is true for both men and women. Although a woman may have some ambiguous feelings about pursuing these goals, work will mean as much to her as it does to any man, especially if she is the head of a household and responsible for her family.

A continuing part of the whole identification process is the need to express aggression through rivalry with or rebellion against favored models, from whom people can "take" aspects of behavior that contribute to growth. The child must consolidate views of the "good" parent and the frustrating or "bad" parent into a single view of the adult as both good and bad. By learning to accept others as imperfect, children learn to accept themselves as imperfect, to establish multiple identifications and to consolidate them into an identity. Adults do much the same: they turn to different people, in both social and organizational relationships, to learn different skills and to obtain help in fostering their diverse talents. They take traditions from society, aspirations from leaders, values from religion, purpose from institutions, and ideals from parents, welding them into a more or less harmonious composite and thus maintaining psychological equilibrium.

Mutual Means

When people seek to fulfill these needs in an organizational setting, through their relationships to each other and to their leaders, they do so by efforts that Irving Knickerbocker has called "mutual means."[28]

Executives who see themselves as leaders and teachers recognize that the essence of their task is to enhance the capacities of their subordinates, and to enable both themselves and their subordinates to accomplish their mutual goals and fulfill their joint needs. Leaders must create these common means by their own efforts and the activities of their followers. If they are successful in creating such means, they will not need to persuade subordinates to follow: subordinates and leaders will discover by their own experience their common objectives and their needs for one another and the organization. Leaders will then have identification by consent.

The concept of mutual means becomes more important as traditional organizational structure yields to new forms of organization. These are likely to have one generic feature: temporary, expedient work groups.[29] Whether these be called task forces, project groups, or something else, they will be concerned with accomplishing a given task. They are also likely to have one central dynamic: instability. Groups will be formed, finish their work, and dissolve, and new units will be formed from previous groups for new tasks. But the varied groups will share one property —whatever their task or composition, they will all be part of the same organization.

There is a military metaphor for what is happening in organizations. In World War I infantry divisions were organized along traditional chain-of-command lines. Some men gave the orders and others followed them. Masses of men and armament were mobilized to bring overwhelming force to bear on a given point or line. They were in relatively stationary positions for long periods of time. But today a contemporary bomber crew or mobile combat unit is a highly trained group of specialists who work in intimate proximity with each other and who must function as a team. Often such a unit is far from its base of command. Frequently decisions must be made at the combat site. Such groups cannot be commanded like infantry divisions of a bygone era. Commanders have many such teams at their disposal, each physically distant from the others, each with its own mission, and each always on the alert. Commanders are first, trainers of their units, then strategists; the units become their own tacticians.

Business executives today are likely to find themselves with organizational units that have the same qualities as mobile combat units. They work with teams of skilled personnel who are charged with functional responsibility, oriented toward results, and subject to rapid mobility requiring flexible adaptation, while they simultaneously seek to meet their own needs. Mutual means does not entail "being nice to people" because "in the long-run it is good for business." Rather, the strategy works with psychological realities that result from the nature of the task, the organization required to accomplish it, and the people who are performing it. The word "mutual" assumes greater meaning as the traditional hierarchical concept of authority diminishes in importance. People must do for one another what in a more paternalistic and authoritarian structure superiors did for them.

CASE HISTORY 8

The mentor alliance, involving as it does both admiration and competition, can be expected to change as the relationship between mentor and protégé changes. Sometimes it is the protégé who chafes against real or imagined restraints imposed by the superior. Sometimes, as this case demonstrates, it is the mentor who suffers as the younger person gains strength, becomes an equal, or even—at least in the organizational hierarchy—a superior.

"My association with our company goes back to the time when I was hired as a salesman eleven years ago. In college, I had been interested in going into psychology, as I had always liked working with people, but upon graduation I was inducted into the armed services where I spent three years. When I came out, I was in no mood for school but felt a real urge to get out into the marketplace, so when one of my father's golfing pals said he would help me get a job with the company where he worked, I was eager to try it. It turned out to be the best move I ever made.

"Brian, my father's friend, had just become district manager, having been the company's top salesman two years in a row. We developed a very warm relationship and became good friends, although he was a little older than I. I really appreciated the time he spent teaching me the ropes, so that I learned my new responsibilities and became confident in my new role sooner than I would have otherwise. Working out in the field gave me a good grounding in the company's operations, and after seven years I was made a district manager, on a level with Brian. We remained cordial. I still consulted with Brian on occasion, but I did not see so much of him since we were now concerned with different districts.

"A year ago the company was bought out by a national merchandising corporation, at which time I was fortunate enough to be made regional manager, thus becoming Brian's superior. This promotion came after a restructuring of the regions, in which Brian remained in charge of virtually the same district, and marked the watershed of our relationship. I still feel as warmly toward Brian as before. He had been like a father to me. My being his superior, in itself, is not the problem.

"Whenever I see Brian, I feel a distinct coolness on his part, a withdrawal—for instance, as happened recently when we met accidentally at the airport. I was very glad to see him, especially away from the office, and invited him for a drink. He declined and turned away, mumbling something about his luggage. A short time later, I saw him in the waiting area reading a newspaper. I felt really rebuffed. This incident points up his general change in attitude. In our regional meetings, his behavior is very proper, very correct, but he is silent and uncooperative; he doesn't contribute freely the way he used to. I always valued his advice and was grateful for his help. It pains me to realize that Brian feels so uncomfortable with me now that he cannot think of me as a friend and goes out of his way to avoid me. Our working together has been radically im-

paired and, in addition, I can no longer benefit from
Brian's wisdom. It bothers me especially because the company is losing the best efforts of a valued employee. And
yet, I hesitate to talk to him frankly because I feel I am in a
very difficult position. What can I do to improve things?"

Analysis

Where Is the Pain?   Both the narrator and Brian are in pain.
The narrator speaks openly of his distress, while Brian's
behavior clearly signals his pain.

When Did It Begin?   The difficulties in their relationship
began as soon as the narrator became Brian's superior.

Ego Ideal   Brian's self-esteem has suffered a severe blow—
a natural reaction on being outdistanced by a subordinate,
and especially by a protégé.
   The narrator values being considerate to other people,
He feels secure when his wish to please is fulfilled, and
takes Brian's coolness and "proper" attitude as rejection.
Normally both his working relationships with people and
success in his job performance are sources of gratification
for him.

Affection   Warm feelings on the part of both Brian and the
narrator were an integral part of their relationship in the
past, but Brian's behavior indicates that he no longer feels
friendly. The narrator states that he is pained by Brian's
avoidance—that is, his lack of affection.

Aggression   Privately Brian rebuffs the narrator. In front of
others, he behaves correctly, but does not volunteer any
help, even though his reluctance may interfere with the
operation of business. He is showing his anger and aggressive feelings, unconsciously lashing out against the narrator. He wants to hurt him.
   On the surface the narrator sounds as if he still wants to
be as friendly as ever with Brian, but he has been rejected
by him, which raises his anger. He uses the expression
"watershed of our relationship" and in fact the nature of

their dealings *has* changed. He has been denying his aggressive feelings.

Dependency   In the early days, the narrator relied on Brian for advice and guidance, respecting him greatly. The narrator was at first like a son to him, then an equal, and now like a father. This is similar to what happens in a family, when a son outstrips or overthrows his father, and has serious psychological implications. Unconscious feelings about such a possibility go back to early childhood, to a time when thought was equated with deed. To the small child, thinking hostile thoughts about a father is the same as attacking him, perhaps even killing him. The narrator does not want to have hostile thoughts about his former "father," and tries to deny them.

Is It Solvable?   Possibly. The narrator can at least take steps to try to ease Brian's pain, but whether the problem is ultimately solvable depends on Brian.

How?   The narrator's inability to confront Brian may mean that he feels guilty or that he is really angry and cannot show it. He must try to clarify the situation openly and frankly. He should call Brian in and give him a chance to express his true feelings, questioning him as neutrally as possible about what has gone wrong in their relationship. In this way the narrator may help Brian get his bearings.

PART 3

Moving toward Action

To be a professional is to apply knowledge and skill. To be an executive is to act and to implement. The professional executive does it all. This section elaborates the steps of executive professional action by delineating the psychological role of the executive, specifying and elaborating the human needs that he or she must meet, and integrating much of the literature on the psychology of management. By doing so, it counteracts some of the psychological clichés of the current management literature and tries to resolve executive confusion about what appear to be disparate points of view on motivation.

TEN Ministration Needs

People frequently have needs that they cannot gratify by themselves. Like an itch in a hard-to-reach place, they must be endured. Sometimes, if endurance lasts, the needs disappear. Those that are not met are usually psychologically veiled, leaving a point of vulnerability in the person.

Ministration needs call for someone else to do something. Often they are encompassed, though inadequately, under the heading of "dependency" needs, or the need for "inclusion."[1] While it is true that they can include the need to lean passively on another person, they extend beyond dependency. Frequently they are at the core of the relationship between people and the organization that meets their needs.[2] "Guest needs" might be a better name for them, since people with these needs will approach an organization seeking work, in part to gratify them. In this sense, the person is a "guest" and the organization a "host." Ministration needs include the needs for gratification, closeness, support, protection, and guidance.

Gratification

People's need for gratification in their work is self-evident. Part of the gratification, John Gardner comments, comes from doing something about which a person cares deeply. "And if he is to escape the prison of the self," Gardner adds, "it must be something not essentially egocentric in nature."[3] This means that some aspect of the work should be in the service of an ideal or to help other people. Such work is a way of giving.

Much of the gratification from work results from the fulfillment of other needs. When people feel a sense of gratification, they feel good about and within themselves. It is not necessarily equated with pleasure; to reach the summit of Mount Everest is gratifying but the experience is hardly physically pleasurable. Gratification may result from enjoyment, relief, discharge of tension, relaxation, rescue, reduction of fear, and many other experiences.

One form of gratification, described in the contemporary research of Frederick Herzberg and his colleagues, offers exceptional executives a guide to meeting the ministration needs of their subordinates.[4] Herzberg differentiates between those aspects of work that he calls "satisfiers" and those that he describes as "dissatisfiers." Job factors that provide the most permanent gratification, the satisfiers, are achievement, recognition, pleasure in the work itself, responsibility (stature more than status), and advancement. Traditionally, management has tried to make work more gratifying by offering good working conditions, job security, salary, and similar attractions. These fringe or "hygienic" factors are important because they are dissatisfiers if they are inadequate, but they do not produce the same long lasting motivation and dedication as the satisfiers.

What makes Herzberg's satisfiers gratifying is that they serve a variety of the facets of personality. Gratification derives from many dimensions of experience and personality. The problem in trying to understand and meet the need for gratification is that executives equate gratification with pleasure and look upon it as being a single, pleasant experience. They fall too easily into the trap of trying to please people by being nice to them; they become disillusioned when this effort fails, as it must. Motivation is more complicated than this.

Closeness

People can live or work next to one another for years, yet not feel close (we are concerned here primarily with psychological closeness). Organizations are essentially communities, groups of people gathered together for a common purpose. The more people are closely interrelated and develop a sense of community about what they do, the more likely they are to achieve their goals and purposes. A major function of the leader in any part of the organization, as well as of the organization as a whole, is to instill and sustain a sense of community, so that participants feel a sense of mutual support toward their common purposes and goals. As in families, all members of a community do not have to like each other. People may quarrel, fight, and have significant differences. Having differences is less relevant than the fact that being a community provides mutual support. In a community, people should know that no matter what their differences, they are better regarded and find more protection and support inside than they do outside. This is why leaders at every level in the organization should create a sense of community and maintain a network of relationships that transcends individual differences, points of view, quarrels, even dislikes. They should give people a sense of where they belong, who cares, and why they are there.

The need for closeness is most crucial when people begin a relationship with an organization. It is at this point that people become "attached," when they are most confused about the new job and the strange organization. They are more heavily dependent than at any other time in their organizational careers, and unless someone takes them in hand, they cannot begin their work.

Adequate orientation can help reduce anxiety. Much of the turnover among newly employed people is due to their concern that they may fail. They feel deserted, left to "muddle through," and are convinced that no one really cares about them. When careful support is given to new people, turnover is reduced and productivity is increased.[5] Effective support includes the very factors that are usually left out of an introduction to an organization: orientation to the idiosyncrasies of coworkers, encouragement to seek out answers to questions, and recognition of the initial anxiety.

One useful way of doing this is to have someone in authority talk informally with the new person or incoming group. The "orienter" should not only tell them how to get around the organization physically, but psychologically as well. He or she should point out the various barriers to action and how these are dealt with in the organization, how to address various superior figures, and the kinds of questions or behavior that may threaten another person or department. The orienter should meet regularly with the new person or group during the first several weeks of employment to give them a chance to express concerns about relationships with others, particularly supervisors, and to reinforce the guidance given earlier.

The same process can be followed with people who are new to a department even though they may be veterans in the organization. Management rarely recognizes the high cost in anxiety and dollars of the initial, confusing adaptive experience. One vice-president of a major corporation reported that it took him a year to learn his way around the executive suite after his appointment. All the time he was afraid he would take a false step that would indicate to his superiors that he was incompetent.

For the young man or woman just coming into the business world, the process of introduction into the organization is a particularly critical one. It must undo some of the distorted expectations and stereotypes that will interfere with personal attachment and subsequent success. Simultaneously, it must take into account the fact that the new employee comes with needs and expectations more refined and intense than those of a skilled blue-collar worker. As Edgar H. Schein has pointed out, if new people are to become effective, they must have or acquire the following characteristics: competence to get a job done, ability to accept organizational "realities," ability to generate and sell new ideas, loyalty and commitment, high personal integrity and strength, capacity to grow.[6]

When young people enter an organization, they customarily encounter two barriers: the organization's perceptions of them and its conceptions of how they are to be prepared for competence. Schein describes some specific biases about new recruits to managerial ranks. They are frequently perceived as overambitious and unrealistic in their expectations of advancement and increased responsibility; too theoretical, idealistic, and naïve to be given an important initial assignment; lacking the maturity and experience necessary for executive responsibility; unduly security-conscious and disinclined to take risks; reluctant to recognize the difference between having a good idea and getting it implemented. Although potentially a highly useful resource for innovative ideas, new approaches, and better management, recruits must be broken in before their resources will be any use to the organization.

Traditionally, the process of introduction and orientation is based on a tacit assumption that incoming people must learn to delay ambitions, suppress fantasies of achievement, and be "tamed." Most orientation programs assume that these controls are to be established by confrontation with harsh reality or by some degree of "caging." A wide variety of orientation strategies follow from this assumption, and most of them work against the newcomers' need for closeness.

In some organizations people are left to their own devices, to sink or swim. In others, they are confronted with an initial task that is intended to set them straight, the "upending" experience. Some managers rotate newcomers through jobs, presumably so they can learn while they are working. Others concentrate heavily on training, using work stints to reinforce training.

Schein advocates an integrative approach. After an initial period of work at a task for which they have immediate responsibility, newcomers undertake full-time training. Immediate responsibility appropriate to individual capacities makes people an integral part of an organization and therefore close to it and to others in it. Subsequent training communicates that they are held close—that is, held in esteem, and that they are being strengthened for further maturation and more effective mastery. This opportunity to confront problems responsibly and to look at experiences conceptually also provides a sense of increasing mastery and stimulates the drive to become even more capable. It is basic to the identification process.

The right kind of supervisor, able to give new people important responsibilities to ensure that they have a reasonable opportunity to fulfill them, can also provide closeness. Schein advocates an apprenticeship under a particularly supportive kind of coach, or a part-time work, part-time training setting that gently nudges new people into progressively more difficult tasks. To avoid or moderate unrealistic expectations, Schein urges that the work of recruiters be coordinated with that of the first supervisors.

The issue of closeness does not diminish in importance after the orientation program is over. Psychological needs always exist, felt more or less strongly in different situations.

Closeness can continue to be an issue in a number of ways. People in certain kinds of jobs, like service occupations, are more likely than business people to have close friends doing the same or related work.[7] Insurance companies, as another example, always want to know what to do about their divisional and regional sales managers. Most of these people are promoted from agency positions and initially have misgivings about taking on a managerial position. They tend not to do well, and the reason is that people become insurance agents partly to fulfill a great need to relate to other people. They can do so either by vanquishing them or pleasing them—usually the latter, which serves to sell policies. They get further pleasure by providing continuing service to their customers.

When they move from agents to regional managers, they lose this direct and gratifying contact. They may become jealous of the agents who work under them. In addition, prolonged close contact with subordinates requires that they learn to tolerate on a regular basis more aggression than they encountered in the more distant relationships with customers.

Such people nearly always need considerable training, coaching, and support if they are to adapt well to the managerial role. Supervisors should be neither surprised nor dismayed to find that many newcomers, once they see what the position entails, will recognize that they are not suited to it. Finding these people more appropriate positions is far better than leaving them to flounder and fail and suffer the consequences of defeat.

Closeness arises out of the division of labor.[8] People tend to identify with those with whom their own acts are coordinated—the "we" of a team or a company. People of similar personality types, closer to each other because they think in the same way, are superior in decision making when the issue calls for a choice among similar obvious alternatives.[9] People who are not so close, who come from different departments and levels, do better in exploring extreme solutions. The greater the number of followers whose values are similar to the leader's, the greater the leader's authority will be.

The universal desire to control personal psychological dis-

tance from others is an important component of the psychological contract that people have with their organization.[10]
One major, often unconscious basis for choosing a job or profession is how close a person has to be to others in the course
of carrying it out. Another version of the same issue is
whether a superior should visit subordinates in their homes or
be called by his or her first name.

Closeness is affected, too, by the nature of the organization's work. People are further from each other in an assembly
line operation than in a group task, in scattered selling assignments than in a chorus. Closeness is also governed by the size
and degree of formality of an organization. Ideally, no organization that exists as a separate identifiable entity should be
larger than four hundred people or have more than five hierarchical levels. No person should have more than six immediate
subordinates, in order to support them adequately and be
their contact for interrelationships with other work groups.
The larger the organization and the greater the distance separating people from one another and from the leader, the more
tension and alienation there is between superiors and subordinates.[11]

The closeness issue has several implications for leader-
teachers. They must recognize the basic importance of the at-
taching process. They would do well to define some of their
conceptions about incoming young men and women and how
they learn best, examining their validity and consciously correcting misconceptions. Once they have clarified their perceptions, they can design a strategy to foster closeness, and tailor
it to the organization. The orientation program that evolves
will be supportive and will also encourage responsible action.
It will automatically take account of the dependency needs of
new employees if such needs have been openly discussed
throughout the managerial hierarchy. Once having examined
the organization's work processes to see which aspects dis-
courage closeness, the leader-teacher can develop methods to
cut down on the distance.

This process will help reduce early turnover, but not for all
people. Nor should it. Many young people need to experiment
with several different kinds of jobs in several organizations to
find out which meet their needs best. In fact, it probably
would be a good idea to have young people leave the organiza-

tion after a few years: if they return after trying others, both they and the executive can be more certain that the person-organization fit is right. The more effective the orientation program, the more clearly the younger man or woman can visualize the organization and make a judgment about a future with it. Their choices, instead of being made negatively, can then be made positively, on the basis of satisfaction and need-fulfillment.

Managing Dependency

When newcomers enter the organization, the executive has to consider not only how best to integrate them into the work "fraternity," but also how to help them deal with feelings of dependency. "Psychologically," Douglas McGregor has said, "the dependence of the subordinate on his superiors is a fact of extraordinary significance."[12] This dynamic is paternal rather than fraternal. The subordinate's dependence on superiors reawakens emotions and attitudes that were part of childhood relationships with parents and that supposedly have long since been outgrown. However, young men and women coming into an organization are still struggling with their conflicts about becoming independent, even though they may be unaware of that struggle. The struggle is often reflected in problems with and about authority.[13] Ideally, supervisors themselves should have long since resolved their dependency conflicts. Inasmuch as most adults continue to have such conflicts to varying degrees, however, supervisors will have to be prepared to contend with both their own and the younger people's efforts to manage these feelings.

Promotions, too, involve questions of dependency. When promoting people, particularly to higher executive levels, it is essential to assess their capacities for using initiative and taking independent action. A good way to do this is to look at the way in which they handle dependency. Four aspects of this issue are especially relevant to good organizational fit.

First, some people are simply more interested in relationships with people than in asserting leadership and exercising power. Some cultures emphasize kinship ties and cooperative skills more than independence or competitive skills. People with such interests will probably not want to become leaders, but they will work well in teams.

Second, a high degree of dependency can be situational. When people operate for a long time under authoritarian leadership in a rigid structure, they grow used to it. Many people think they are failures because their bosses or organizations do not use them fully. These people frequently experience their work lives as a series of frustrated opportunities, largely because they expect so much of others. They want to move up, but they have such strong dependency needs that they wait for others to create opportunities for them. They need permission as well as encouragement to assert themselves. With gradual increases in responsibility and support from their new superior, some will be able to develop considerable independence, particularly if they have not been penalized too heavily for their initial mistakes.

The third kind of dependency relates to individual character. Because of difficult experiences in early childhood, some people are unable to take independent action. They will never make leaders, but they often do well working closely with someone more powerful than they who can always be ready to assume responsibility.

Finally, some people try to deny their need to depend on others by over-asserting an independent stance. Such people may make vigorous leaders, but they are likely to develop ulcers in response to their underlying, unresolved conflict. Also, they will leave behind a trail of unhappy and underdeveloped subordinates. Just as they cannot depend on others and share the decision-making process, they cannot let their subordinates depend on them for guidance and support. This creates a weakness in future leaders, because organizations that cannot offer adequate support for their people pose just as much of a problem as subordinates who are excessively dependent.

Support

The ability to provide psychological and moral support is one of the basic dimensions of good leadership. It is also a *sine qua non* of organizational life. Despite its importance, the most glaring deficiency in contemporary organizational functioning is the almost universal inadequacy of support. Executives habitually neglect the importance of being available to their people. They think it is silly to have to "hold people's hands." Wanting their subordinates to take initiative and to act independently, they try to model a self-reliant stance. All this is very rational, but it is not valid psychologically. People need to have access to their superiors, to be able to read their faces, to see recognition of their own existence reflected in their superiors' eyes. Managing by objectives does not alter this fundamental human condition. People need contact and support, and executives at all levels should recognize this as one of their primary tasks.

Even CEOs need a great deal of care. Unlike their subordinates, CEOs rarely have somebody to confide in, someone who can confirm their achievement, pinpoint their anxieties, and help them talk out their fears. Words from somebody whose judgment is valued are always necessary to alleviate anxieties. Members of the board should take on this responsibility. Either individually or collectively, they should have regular visits with CEOs, to hear them out, provide feedback, and enable them to relax in the company of their peers. In fact, board members should be picked for their capacity to do this. Most CEOs encourage the selection of board members who are capable and competent people, but the CEOs are reluctant to make demands upon their time. It is therefore up to the board members to offer support voluntarily to the CEOs.

Support for lower-level executives is frequently discussed, but not necessarily delivered. The suggestion that managers and supervisors meet with subordinates for a few minutes before starting the day's work is often greeted with the response that there is not enough time. But such meetings provide valuable opportunities to touch bases, lay out the day's work, anticipate problems, and gather momentum. They also serve to start the day with a sense of cooperative helpfulness, mutual support, and optimism.

The reasons? If people hear bad news on broadcasts on their way to work in the morning, they are likely to think that others are not very decent, honest, or altruistic. Stephen M. Holloway and Harvey A. Hornstein of Columbia University found that favorable news broadcasts produce happier people.[14] Holloway and Hornstein originally were testing people's integrity by dropping wallets on the street. They found that about 45 percent of the finders returned the wallets in a few days. But on June 4, 1968, the day Robert Kennedy was assassinated, not a single dropped wallet was returned. They concluded that people had been demoralized and that this made them socially irresponsible. They decided to conduct further studies of the impact of broadcast news on people's behavior. Support within the organization can help counteract feelings of pessimism and discouragement produced by social trauma.

Support is also needed when something immoral or inappropriate occurs. It is important for the head of the unit or the head of the company to talk to all the people in the organization, explaining the situation honestly and straightforwardly, answering questions, and allowing people to satisfy their curiosity and discuss their anxiety. Corporate leaders are sometimes reluctant to explain, feeling that it is better to dampen the issue and let it die out, but this does not resolve the psychological disturbances within people.

Matters of conscience are troubling to people. They need to have some way of justifying themselves and the organization—they need to explain difficult situations to their friends and colleagues, and they need some way to restore good feelings about themselves and the organization. If they do not have enough information to do so, they are left with secret uneasy feelings and a distaste for what has happened. They will feel that the leadership has said one thing and done another. These issues should never be washed away. Ignoring them will only create employee anxiety and hostility, which will take a greater toll upon productivity than the original controversy itself.

Even in day-to-day operations, when there is no moral or strategic crisis, people benefit from support in the form of feedback. As a rule, they do not get enough of it. One can ask people in almost any organization, "How do you know how well you are doing?" Ninety percent of them are likely to respond, "If I do something wrong, I'll hear about it." Too often this topic is discussed as if praise were the answer; it is not. What people are saying is that they do not have sufficient support from their superiors. Praise without support is an empty gesture.

As in the family, the most critical support comes from superiors who have greater power. Support includes more than approval and praise. Rensis Likert and his colleagues use the following questions in their survey research: "To what extent does your supervisor try to understand your problems and do something about them?" "How much help do you get from your superior in doing your work?" "To what extent is he interested in helping you get the training which will assist you in being promoted?" "How fully does he share with you information about the company, its financial conditions, earnings?" "How much confidence and trust does he have in you and you in him?"[15] Positive answers to these questions reflect a high degree of organizational support.

Support tends to produce effective solutions. A foreman who uses a problem-solving approach with his people, backing them up in their work, is more likely to obtain solutions of high quality and acceptance than one who applies extrinsic incentives.[16] Support is essential to learning.

Support is more than just something a person needs for self-serving reasons. It is related directly to both productivity and morale. Several studies indicate that the employee-centered, supportive, participative managerial environment encourages productivity, whereas executives who run their departments autocratically create high turnover and low productivity.[17]

According to a study by David G. Bowers, the self-esteem of foremen is related to their supervisors' supportiveness. There is also a relationship between a foreman's self-esteem and his estimate of what his subordinates think of him, but the research suggests that his estimate bears little relationship to the actual attitude of his subordinates. As his self-esteem diminishes and as his estimate of their attitude becomes poorer, he alienates himself from his subordinates; he assembles them as a group more often, but to exercise his authority rather than to seek their advice. His behavior toward his subordinates becomes less supportive.[18]

The destructive effects of pressure without support have long been known. A series of studies by members of the Institute for Social Research of the University of Michigan and by researchers in other universities show repeatedly that low-production groups are led by supervisors who are work-centered; they exert pressure for production but do not support their people. High-production units, on the other hand, are characterized by supervision that is employee-centered—less threatening and more supportive. High-production heads are more democratic, invite suggestions and participation of their subordinates; they delegate responsibility and spend less time in actual production work. Low-production supervisors tend to be authoritarian, dictatorial, and dogmatic.

To be effective, support must be integrated into managerial style and not put on as window dressing. There is a story about a foreman who used to yell, "If you don't do this job, I'll punch you in the nose!" After attending a sensitivity training group, he returned to the job and yelled at a worker, "If you don't do this job, I'll punch you in the nose! By the way, how's your mother?"[19]

At the other extreme, support does not mean being preoccupied with human-relations considerations at the expense of the task. Supervisors who are most competent have three kinds of skills.[20] To coordinate the activities of one organizational family with another, supervisors must have administrative competence; to integrate organizational objectives with individual member needs, they must have human-relations competence; to accomplish other assigned tasks, including the performance of technical operations, they need technical competence.

Support also implies realistic presentations of situations. People operate better when they know precisely what they are up against. Many wonder if this can be so when the realities are anxiety-provoking. Why feed people's worries? Because normal worrying is useful preparation for meeting difficult situations.

This principle is beautifully illustrated in a recent study by David T. A. Vernon, psychologist at the University of Missouri.[21] He observed three groups of children entering a hospital for minor operations. One group was given no advance preparation. The second group saw a film of a child wincing and saying "Ouch" as he received a shot. The third group saw a film of a child reacting calmly and without pain to a shot. When the children entered the hospital and received injections themselves, those who had seen the realistic movie showed the least distress, followed by those who had seen no movie. The children who saw the "painless" film experienced considerable distress. As Vernon points out, they not only had to endure unexpected pain, "but also feelings of betrayal and distrust in authority figures who let them down."

Companies, too, should help their people anticipate the future, and should not make facile promises meant to comfort people momentarily. How often, when a merger has taken place, are employees of the newly acquired company reassured that nothing will change? And then things do change. This is betrayal.

The healthy relationship between superiors and their subordinates could be described as a managerial alliance. They should be able to stand together to attack the organizational task at hand. This does not mean they are coequal—the leader has to be in charge. It simply means that they trust one another. A managerial alliance cannot exist when leaders manipulate their followers to make themselves look good, or when the followers try to undermine their leaders' authority. They give mutual sanction to their separate roles by focusing on the task.

The leader functions primarily as a model. He helps people define the realities they face and supports them in the process of addressing these problems. He must constantly redefine priorities and help people balance alternative costs of choices they have to make. He must exercise sufficient control to keep the group working toward a common purpose—at standards he himself maintains—so that people are not played off against one another.

The leader acts also as an umbrella. She shields her people from unnecessary psychological static arising from conflicts at higher levels, yet she transmits to them all the information they need in order to make appropriate decisions in their own self-interest. She protects them for the failures that are bound to come as they take risks on behalf of the organization, but she also represents them adequately to those above her. A good leader will support her subordinates by taking time to listen and talk with those several levels below her, so that they will know she stands behind their own supervisor.

The way in which the organizational structure is shaped plays as important a part in productivity as the attitude of the leader. According to Likert, an organization uses its human potential effectively only when each person belongs to a work group that has deep group loyalty, frequent and meaningful interaction, and high performance goals which it has helped establish. Likert proposes a principle of "supportive relationships."[22] To foster such relationships, the form of the organization should be one of multiple, overlapping groups in which each supervisor is a "linking pin"—the leader of the group below and a member of the group above. In addition, persons at all levels should be members of other groups (committees, representational groups, and the like) that help link the organization laterally. In such a structure, traditional methods of job organization and work facilitation ("scientific management") should be used as means to an end rather than an end in themselves. Traditional measurements of performance should be supplemented with periodic appraisals of human organization variables. All of these data should be used to appraise the health of the organization, and to find out where weaknesses exist and improvements are needed.

There will be a certain level of conflict, pressure, and tension in an organization when such a principle is used. Likert argues, however, that if this principle is implemented, all levels of the organization have more influence and the social system is tighter than it would be otherwise. Executives do not lose influence because others become influential; instead, they gain influence, since there is greater identification with them and less defensiveness.

The research of Eric Trist and his colleagues, performed at London's Tavistock Institute, further illustrates the point.[23] Trist contends that there is an optimum level of grouping, which can be determined only by an analysis of the requirements of the particular technical system employed by the organization. The most effective group does not evolve on the basis of people's friendship on the job, but rather on the basis of task orientation. Trist reports that grouping produces its main psychological effects when it leads to a system of work roles in which the workers are primarily related to each other by task performance and interdependence. When this task orientation is established, the worker has a range of mutually supportive roles, with respect to both improving performance and dealing with stress. As the role system, or "composite system," becomes more mature and integrated, it becomes easier for workers to understand and appreciate their relation to the group.

The effects of a composite system are demonstrated in the Tavistock research on mining groups. Trist and his colleagues report that work groups of as many as fifty members are capable, under certain conditions, of self-sustained regulation. When a composite group was formed of men with many skills and the group was made jointly responsible for all its tasks, the men rotated tasks, shifts, and activity subgroups among themselves. Comparing the composite group with miners working under traditional organization, the Tavistock researchers found that nonproduction work took up 32 percent of the time in conventional groups but only one-half of 1 percent in the composite group. The absence rate was 20 percent among the conventional groups and 8.2 percent among the composite groups. The conventional groups were never ahead of their cycle timetable; in fact, they were behind in 69 percent of their cycles. The composite group was ahead in 95 percent of its cycles. Productivity was 3.5 tons per man-shift in the conventional group versus 5.3 tons in the composite group.

Some would argue that support from peers also means control by peers, and that group participation will constrict the individual. Nowhere is the evidence about group support more impressive than from the studies of group risk-taking.[24] The evidence indicates that groups of people are more willing to take risks and tend to make better decisions than the same people would as individuals. Apparently, group risk-taking allows a greater diffusion of responsibility and fewer guilt feelings if there is failure. Some individuals are always better than the group average, but, on the whole, group decision making has much to recommend it.

Despite its many advantages, group participation in decision making and productivity is not a panacea. Robert Dubin has noted some of the constraints on participation and has pointed out that worker autonomy is only one factor contributing to differences in productivity. "When worker autonomy . . . is combined with two other dimensions of supervisory behavior found significant in combination in English factories, the combination still accounts for less than one-fifth of the variance in productivity. Furthermore, there is reason to believe that worker autonomy may be relevant to batch- or

unit-production technologies, but probably not to mass production technologies, and almost certainly not to continuous
process technologies."[25]

In other words, where there is no possibility of forming a
group around the task, then there can be no group participation in decision making. Whether certain technologies actually
do make it impossible to form groups is another question.[26]
People who operate as isolated technicians can still be brought
together to talk about the problems of the plant as a whole,
but often management does not think such people are capable
of discussion and decision making at the plant level.

Support, then, is a psychological platform based on style
of leadership, method of operation or production, interlocking
of roles, participation in decision making, and, sometimes,
simple human contact which makes help possible. A group of
subordinates are more likely to be supportive of one another
and, hence, cohesive when their respective skills contribute
directly to their joint and collective mastery of the work. No
amount of congeniality will supplant this requirement. Given
joint and collective task mastery, closeness will arise from the
mutual support. The members of the group will be able to
meet many of their own ministration needs. They will care for
and about one another.

There are many lessons here for the executive-teacher.
Support can be attained by managerial invention. Specifically,
executives can assess the supervisors that newcomers are assigned to, making sure they will be effective as agents of
growth. They should learn—if necessary, through studies of
subordinates—which supervisors are too aggressive or too dependent to support their people. Job descriptions and definitions of responsibility can help define complementary task
roles; often the work group itself can report what types of additional skills are needed to accomplish its job.

If the task itself is defined clearly enough, executives
should create mutually supportive groups whenever possible,
even when people seem able to accomplish their tasks by
themselves. If they do not need one another for task accomplishment they will not find it necessary to seek help, but if
they do need one another the channels for cooperation and
communication will be open. Such group organization also diminishes rivalry for the attention and favor of the superior and

fosters interdependence. Whether the group can work together depends on how well the leader facilitates the ability of the individuals to speak candidly about problems, both with the leader and among themselves. It is the leader's focus on facilitating work performance that makes support an instrument for individual and group achievement.

Protection

The need to provide protection, a dimension of good leadership, is rarely discussed in the management literature, and then only in terms of "safety" needs.[27] Yet employees expect that those who have leadership power will be protective in varying ways. A man who loses his job because of changes in technology usually feels that his company has not adequately protected him. A woman who signs a petition directed at a public official assumes that she can improve some condition and that her career will not be jeopardized as a result of her action. Protection is a major ministration function of a union.

When supervisors encourage efficiency while at the same time "going to bat" for their subordinates, their work groups react with high standards of performance.[28] When supervisors are not protective, subordinates respond to efforts toward efficiency with low standards of performance. When reward for efficiency is accompanied by close supervision, work groups attain their highest degree of cohesion. In such instances the supervisor protects each individual member and the work group as a whole by "holding them together."

Another form of protection is protection against the jealousies and personal maneuvers of senior competitors.[29] Still another, particularly for younger and more creative people, is protection from their friends. "The first restraining force for one who steps off the path of custom . . . is the clutching hands of intimates and colleagues," observes John Gardner.[30] Often supervisors have the same effect: "You don't get paid to think."

With so much pressure for action in the business world, the irreplaceable asset of the executive is the one most flagrantly dissipated: time. Superiors rarely recognize their responsibility to protect the thinking of their subordinates, thereby exacerbating the impulse to act at the expense of thought. Young executives in particular are entangled in the conflict between reflection and production.[31] Superiors must protect subordinates by requiring thinking time and by refusing to let subordinates equate busy work with deliberation.

A more common form of protection is that provided by a systematic program for evaluating individual skill, experience, talent, and achievement. Ralph Cordiner recommends establishing company-wide opportunities and moving people frequently within the company. Managers will thus be less likely to choose their successors from among those few people who report to them. A paper program is never enough. "The chief executive," Cordiner asserts, "should make it a point to know, personally, the most promising men in the organization who might someday qualify for the highest positions of responsibility. He should see that these men receive challenging and educational assignments that will help them stretch their capacities."[32]

Job definition and description, continuing education, adequate communication, and participation in decision making are all forms of protection. An open, supportive relationship with superiors and with the organization at large, in which subordinates can actively look out for their own interests, offers the most effective possibilities for protection.

Guidance

In business and industry, guidance is usually included in the areas of executive development, coaching, and counseling.

There are two schools of thought about executive development.[33] The life-process theory says that executives are products of years of systematic guidance. Executive development is a form of character building, and brief courses and programs are therefore useless. The other school says that executive development is chiefly a result of being exposed to the use of the right skills at the right time. These skills can be reinforced by an understanding of their psychological, sociological, and economic underpinnings. There is no clear evidence for either position and no inherent conflict between the two. Personality is an unfolding process; however, single events or brief experiences do have important impacts. Those who have devoted considered effort to executive development generally agree that the organizational climate of the firm—rules, procedures, methods, and skills that the leading executives in the firm adopt—determine what the potential executive believes and does. Identification once again becomes a critical issue.

Management development programs have been subject to diverse and often severe criticism. Raymond Katzell, for instance, describes some possible weaknesses in educational programs for executives.[34] He says that they apparently are not sufficiently integrated into a total program. Katzell contends that there is too little attention to the emotional barriers to affective action, and that there may be danger in overemphasizing administrative techniques at the cost of knowledge. Thus, he argues against isolated, gimmicky technique programs and in favor of a continuous process of learning. As would most psychologists, Katzell indicates that understanding one's own feelings is basic to self-controlled action. He refers to the lack of correspondence between development programs and individual needs or organizational climate. Sometimes such programs are directed to problems over which the participants have no control, or they may be inadequate to the issues they are supposed to address.

Douglas McGregor points out that elaborate programs for management development provide few opportunities for the career development of professional specialists.[35] He states the difference this way: for the professional person, promotion or advancement means receiving rewards and recognition for becoming more proficient at her professional work. Whether in private practice or in academic institutions, she is accustomed to choosing among alternative opportunities in terms of whether they will facilitate her proficiency. Thus, the ideal of many lawyers is to be a lawyer's lawyer. Management, on the other hand, is accustomed to exercising a substantial amount of "career authority" over its managerial employees at all levels. The individual is evaluated, promoted, rotated, and transferred in terms of the needs of the organization, almost irrespective of his personal career motivations. These incompatible points of view, McGregor says, are certain to come into conflict as professional employees become more numerous and indispensable to industry. The conflict in fact already exists, not solely because professional employees are becoming more numerous, but because executives are becoming increasingly professional and will therefore have more of the values of professionals.

Criticisms of middle-management development are more specific: (1) lack of acceptance of development among middle-management personnel, (2) lack of time among such personnel to attend programs, (3) difficulties determining the training needs of middle managers, and (4) inadequate time to present such programs. Typically such criticisms arise when executive development is delegated to training personnel who have little power to influence the organizational climate, who are asked to create "package programs," and who have little thoughtful support from top management.

Furthermore, when a self-improvement program is simply imposed on those lower in the hierarchy, they will view it with fear and suspicion. Some, bitter about being "sent to school," have little wish to learn.[36] They perceive such programs as criticism of their work, often do not understand what is expected of them, and look upon the program as a waste of time. Their anger becomes especially acute if they are evaluated on the basis of their performance in training, when they believe they should be judged only on their managerial accomplishments.

These criticisms argue for the planned, continuous involvement of executives in the definition and refinement of the career goals of their subordinates. Teaching should be formally conceived and integrated with ongoing executive work. If the prime task of executives is to coordinate and lead the efforts of others toward organizational goals, they must give careful attention to helping their subordinates understand and take into consideration people's feelings. Teaching content and function in the context of feelings makes it more possible for subordinates to use their combined learning for solving organizational problems and accomplishing organizational goals. The contemporary practice of teaching management content and human relations as if they were independent of each other, and of assigning the teaching to training directors or extramural programs, vitiates much of the teaching effort.

Narrowing the executive's teaching activities to specifics, he can ask the following questions as a basis for his efforts: What does the subordinate want to learn in the next year? How will this propel her toward more distant goals? How much can be learned in her present position? What does she need to know, but is unaware of? What does the executive or the organization require her to know and how much of it is to be learned in the present experience? Combining the answers to these questions in a general statement, how can this generalization be subdivided into monthly, even weekly, units of experience and teaching?

Often the most important things an executive has to teach are precisely those that cannot be easily specified. The executive should try to determine which are the most important lessons he has learned, which were the most difficult obstacles to surmount, which events caused the most pain. Although subordinates can only experience vicariously what the executive did, they can learn from his experience if it is introduced as a consideration toward better problem solving.

Suggesting that the executive ask questions and make plans implies that teaching by experience alone is uneconomic. A planned effort gives the teaching its proper perspective. It takes into account the range of content, and ensures that both subordinate and organization will receive their just due. This is not an argument for rigidity. The executive's "plan" should be the road map, and not be mistaken for the road itself. Like all maps, it allows for choices among alternative routes.

Second to the executive's own practices, the most useful device for teaching human-relations skills is coaching. "To be a coach," says Mortimer Feinberg, an industrial psychologist, "is to be both informational and inspirational. The coach integrates the unique capacities of the members of his team. He also lifts people up and out of themselves."[37]

An executive may feel inadequate to such a task. However, there is no reason why she cannot improve her coaching skills, provided that a sound series of actions is carried out with persistence. Walter Mahler suggests a plan for acquiring coaching skills that would include periodic instruction on coaching techniques built around both day-to-day coaching and more formal coaching as in performance reviews, with "bench marks" for improvement.[38] Inasmuch as the executive will be coaching in one form or another, it should not seem frightening to suggest skill practice and training in this technique while she is doing it.

The term "coaching" has been used to refer to the teaching of skills in the context of a personal relationship with the learner. "Counseling" refers to help with personal problems that interfere with the learning experience. Although the roles of teacher and therapist differ, there is common ground between them. Executives inevitably will find themselves treading on this common ground when they try to help alter some aspect of a subordinate's behavior that inhibits growth.[39] For example, the subordinate may resist needed and appropriate changes in his behavior, be preoccupied with trivia at the expense of the larger task, be unable to organize tasks to accomplish work, resent supervision, be unduly critical of others, or otherwise be unnecessarily irritating to others. Or he may be too sensitive to the aggression of others.

These are "pathologies" that interfere with growth, the negative side of the personality about which superiors may have to counsel subordinates. The specifics are to be found in many books on employee counseling.[40] Counseling may also facilitate "blossoming." The counseling process, ideally, is a mode by which the subordinate continually evaluates his own performance, looks at and seeks to modify his own behavior.[41]

The executive who would counsel a subordinate for these purposes automatically has to face certain expectations.[42] Consciously or unconsciously, the person being helped will expect the other person to treat his problem as important, and expect that the other will help to maintain the communication between them, not leave it all to him. He will anticipate that such assistance will open aspects of the problem which he has difficulty expressing himself. The superior is expected to be sensitive to the subordinate's tension in the counseling situation, and to help ease it by becoming the ally of the subordinate as he tries to organize his thoughts and feelings. How much the subordinate will welcome the interest and help of the superior depends on how helpful he thinks the superior intends to be.

When the subordinate is discouraged, confused, and her morale is low, she usually has a hopeless feeling. The tendency of the superior is to reassure her. The superior's quiet trust that the subordinate will surmount her problems is more helpful to the subordinate than reassurance. The superior personifies reality, the job to be done, competence, and strength.

Identifying with the superior, the subordinate acquires some of the superior's confidence in her and greater capacity to tolerate her own struggles. If she understands that the joint task of superior and subordinate is to help the latter become more capable, she will want to continue this process. Thus, a spiraling process is set in motion leading to greater mastery, enhanced self-image, and willingness to face more challenging problems.

Everyone has periods in their careers when their potential effectiveness increases enormously.[43] There are no instruments to help predict when the "blossoming" is apt to occur in individual cases. Psychologists who are studying learning processes, as well as many experienced executives, know that when the unfolding begins to occur under favorable circumstances, a person can make phenomenal contributions. Counseling, in effect, is the temporary "hothouse" that creates these circumstances. In microcosm, the counseling process is the model for the fulfillment of ministration needs.

CASE HISTORY 9

Not everyone needs the same kind of ministration: some people get along well with background guidance and can dispense with the explicit expressions of affection or support necessary to others. Some need more direct signs of appreciation if they are to do their best work. In a situation where people are poorly matched—when the needs of one person are not met by the personality style and behavior of another—how much accommodation can be expected? And who is to change? This case highlights the difficulties of a mismatch over ministration needs, and proposes some compromises.

"My boss is a top-level executive in our company. He's the kind of man people commonly refer to as 'brilliant,' is known for the highest standards of integrity, and has the degrees and knowledge to be known as 'highly-educated,' too. When he is with other executives who are his peers or his superiors or with company clients, Greg displays a bright and engaging personality, but on a day-to-day basis with the rest of us, Greg is sullen, contemptuous, and rarely even tells us what he wants us to do.

"I have a record of being a proven achiever. I report to Greg, but our relationship is, even on good days, strained. I never am able to be myself with him. I know, or at least I believe I know, that Greg respects my work, but I also know that I'm not the 'Ivy League' type that Greg prefers. My degree came from a small western university, known in its region for the quality of its education, but barely known here in the East. I know Greg would probably think of me in different terms if I held advanced degrees as he does, but, for me and at this stage of my career, I don't yet feel the need to take myself back to the classroom.

"I don't want to make Greg sound terrible. I respect him, and sometimes I feel that he has sincere affection for me. But he is so cold and aloof when we meet that the relationship is essentially quite impersonal. I've noticed that Greg, when I do attempt to break the ice with a small joke, will begin to laugh and then immediately suppress his laughter.

"More ribald forms of levity are met with an icy precision and a clinical impassivity that are positively chilling. Even so, our current relationship is a productive one, yet I feel that a more open, frank association would bring even better-quality results. I talked to Greg about what I felt was an 'imposed sterility' in our working relationship. I tried to indicate that my respect for him would be further enhanced by a warmer relationship. Greg apologized to me for seeming 'cold,' saying, that 'of course, we will keep the wall lowered' between us from now on. He had evidently forgotten the conversation by our next meeting, because he was as cold and impersonal as ever.

"I need Greg's support and need recognition of my efforts for the company from him. I need to know what track my career is going to take in the organization, and I particularly need to know when I've done an especially good or bad piece of work.

"I'm not the only one who has this trouble with Greg, but that fact doesn't help clear up the situation. As a matter of fact, it is getting more and more difficult to work with him. Is there any other way I can penetrate that icy reserve and get the feedback I need to do my work?"

Analysis

Where Is the Pain?   The pain is obviously in the narrator. While the behavior of the boss does reflect a certain kind of psychological pain, the boss is not disturbed by his behavior.

When Did It Begin?   We have no beginning date, but are led to believe that this is the way the boss characteristically is and behaves.

Ego Ideal   Obviously the boss is a perfectionist. He demands a great deal of himself, and this is reflected not only in his brilliance, but also in his standards, his degrees, and the kind of behavior he demonstrates toward those who are at a higher level than he.

Affection   Insecure people like Greg must be engaging to please clients and can be sociable with others who share the same value systems, goals, and attainments. However, with such insecurity they have difficulty interacting, fearing they will get too close to subordinates who will take advantage of them. They may have learned along the way that one must maintain appropriate distance from subordinates because familiarity may breed contempt, especially when a leader fears those from whom he wants respect. Distant people like Greg are often concerned with their own self-aggrandizement, their own position, their own trappings, and their own social network.

Aggression   People like Greg invest a great deal of aggression in themselves. They push themselves, demand a great deal of themselves, and overcontrol themselves to attain high goals. Striving so hard to acquire and maintain so demanding an ego ideal and feeling inadequate in the face of their own failure to be perfect, they tend to be condescending and contemptuous of those whom they regard as inferiors. People who strive in this perfectionist way are always judgmental. They tend to feel the same contempt for the imperfections of others as they do for their own. They invest a great deal in their work in order to attain perfectionist ego ideals and frequently are quite successful.

Dependency Obviously people who do not view themselves as adaquate cannot think others are adequate. They are unlikely to be able to depend on others well and will tend to keep them at a distance. This is reflected in Greg's coldness.

Is It Solvable? Probably not by the narrator. Greg is not going to change. While Greg's behavior is frustrating for the narrator, at least it tells him where his boundaries are. He can ask Greg, in all fairness, to give him reviews at reasonable intervals and to tell him in a straightforward manner how he is doing on the job. He can also ask Greg in a straightforward manner about his career potential, career opportunities, and career direction. But there is no way of penetrating Greg's reserve and keeping it penetrated. Since Greg doesn't wish to appear aloof and icy to his subordinates, no doubt he will respond to direct questions, requests for direct information, and appeals to his integrity. But he will not respond to efforts to get closer to him. The narrator will have to accept Greg as he is, understanding that his personality is not about to change, and will have to work with Greg as well as he can under the circumstances.

ELEVEN

Maturation Needs

In many respects, maturation needs are silent. They do not cry out to be met as do ministration and mastery needs. Maturation needs imply that a person has the potential for development and expansion. If circumstances are conducive—if there is a congenial climate, adequate psychological nourishment, and protection against inhibiting or destructive external forces—the process will occur naturally. If they are not, the person vegetates. Occasionally an observer may ask, for example, why some obviously intelligent person is in a lowly position. Otherwise it may never be apparent to the individual herself or to others that she might have been able to do better, that she has not grown as she might have, or even that she is stunted. Maturation needs act to prevent intellectual and competitive scrawniness. Fulfilled, they increase the potential of both the person and the organization. Unfulfilled, they deprive both the person and the organization.

Maturation is a process that begins at birth, and can continue indefinitely. Many people fear they have accomplished all they are going to by the time they are about thirty-five. But although many people do hit a plateau in their skills and performance when they reach middle age, others find that creativity blossoms late. A look at Nobel Prize laureates gives room for hope: most laureates in the sciences do their prize-winning work in early middle age. Some scientists are considerably older when they make their breakthroughs. Oswald Avery was sixty-seven when he demonstrated the genetic importance of DNA.[1]

Signs of maturation may emerge unexpectedly. Spontaneous leaders often step forward during crises after filling anonymous roles for years. Everyone around is surprised at the sudden transformation. In fact, this phenomenon may be more than the good fortune of being in the right place at the right time. Sociobiologists believe that it may actually be a form of biological growth, rooted in our genetic mechanisms. Biologist Richard Borowsky of New York University has found spontaneous maturity among male fish of the species *Xiphophorus variatus*. Young male fish remain small and sexually immature until the adult male population in their group is depleted. Then their growth and sexual maturing proceed at a greatly accelerated pace.[2] It is impossible to say for certain whether the fishes' sudden development is genetic. But it is clear that their biological and social systems are closely intertwined. And it is likely that the same is true of spontaneous leaders in human organizations. These people have innate capabilities that unfold when the time is ripe. External and internal changes together create a sudden and astonishing spurt of growth.

The human organism's natural tendency is toward growth, learning, and problem solving. Stimulating people to those activities calls for conditions that encourage creativity. Creativity is another name for fruitful spontaneity that can be used for personal, technical, organizational, or social problem solving.

Fostering Creativity

Recently at a professional meeting, a panel of psychologists and a playwright discussed the process of creativity. The gap between the statistics-laden sterility of the psychologists' comments and the rich imagery of the experience that the playwright reported were testimony to how little is yet known about creativity. When Alexander the Great visited Diogenes and asked whether he could do anything for the famed teacher, Diogenes replied, "Only stand out of my light." Perhaps, John Gardner notes, the best stimulant to creativity is to leave people free to do their work.[3]

What is meant by the term creative? In the conception of Abraham Maslow, to be creative is to be able to confront novelty and to improvise while enjoying change.[4] These are also the essential characteristics for flexibility in rapidly changing organizations. Creativity is not limited to artists. The survival of individuals and organizations hinges on their capacities to be inventive, to find ways of flowering despite seemingly adverse circumstances. Arguing that the past has become useless in many professions, Maslow calls for developing a race of improvisors. These are people who can divorce themselves from their past sufficiently to handle problems by improvisation if necessary. To do so, they must feel strong, courageous, and confident enough to trust themselves in their contemporary situations.

Psychologist Richard Crutchfield, suggests five obstacles to creativity: (1) inability to define the problem clearly or correctly, (2) insufficient knowledge, (3) rigidity and the inability to put aside popular assumptions, (4) lack of a period of incubation so that problems can sit in the mind for a while, and (5) fear of reaction to unconventional ideas.[5]

Reasons two and three are related in an interesting way. Knowledge itself can be one factor that inhibits creativity. While creativity is essentially a combination of previously unconnected ideas, this definition presupposes prior knowledge in the form of ideas derived from education and experience.[6] However, much of what is learned is taught as truth or dogma, whether it be in the field of arithmetic or sales technique. If the knowledge is solid in the sense that the possessor is certain of its validity, and if it is upheld tenaciously, there is no internal need for something new. Systematic learning often inhibits truly original creations.[7] One reason for such creativity-inducing efforts as "brainstorming" is that such attempts help surmount the barriers of traditional knowledge and customary ways of thinking.[8]

Reason five is a major one. Creativity in organizations is certainly inhibited by the knowledge that new ideas must be exposed to a hostile environment. A new idea may threaten the possessors of the now-obsolete one. It may mean that the person who generated it gains new power, or stimulates feelings of inadequacy in those who did not think of it. Whatever the case, a new idea generates hostility, attack, and rejection more often than enthusiastic acceptance, so protection must be offered to help foster creativity.

John Gardner observes that innovators have always been a threat to the status quo; even in an era in which innovation is highly valued, they still tend to be viewed as a disruptive force. ("If you don't like it here, why don't you go somewhere else?") But Gardner says that hostility toward innovators is no longer adaptive for the contemporary world, which both requires and thrives on innovation. To protect innovators, and simultaneously stimulate the innovative process, he calls for "a set of attitudes and specific social arrangements designed to ensure that points of view at odds with prevailing doctrine will not be rejected out of hand."[9]

Gardner advocates "a department of continuous renewal" that would view the whole organization as a system in need of constant innovation. This would entail bringing in new blood, and designing flexible personnel rotation; implementing far-reaching organizational restructuring; reducing excessive demands for coordination, administrative review, and endorsement; relying less on processed data and paying more attention to unprocessed reality (the feelings and attitudes of people experienced in personal contacts); and emphasizing flexibility rather than massive strength. Two of Gardner's suggestions are devoted to new people and different experiences for them. The others are concerned with alleviating the constricting pressures of the organization.

Stimulation is also necessary for encouraging improvisation. All people are creative to some degree because at least a sprinkling of innovation is required to survive. If the creative person is not different from other people, then his processes of creativity are an enlarged, more successful version of the same processes that occur in others.

Donald W. MacKinnon says, "Creativity is a process extended in time and characterized by originality, adaptiveness and realization. The more creative a person is, the more he reveals an openness to his own feelings and emotions, a sensitive intellect and understanding self-awareness, and wide-ranging interests, including many which in the American culture are thought of as feminine."[10] According to MacKinnon's studies of creativity in architects, people who are highly creative are inclined to have positive opinions of themselves. Their self-images include being inventive, determined, independent, individualistic, enthusiastic, and industrious. Less creative architects are more concerned with being virtuous, of good character, rational, and sympathetic to others. In psychological terms, it could be said that less creative people are more superego-oriented and self-controlling, and therefore more "on guard."

Gardner Murphy summarizes four stages in the creative process: (1) immersion "in some specific medium which gives delight and fulfillment"; (2) the acquisition of experiences which are then consolidated into an ordered pattern; (3) sudden inspiration or illumination; and (4) the "hammering out" and perfecting of the creative work.[11] The last two phases were perhaps the ones reported by Jacob W. Getzels and Mihaly Csikszentmihalyi, who observed a group of art students. The most original and artistically valuable drawings were produced by students who had handled the most objects, scrutinized the objects they handled, and selected the most unusual ones to work with during the predrawing period. The researchers describe this as "discovery oriented" behavior. "This concern with discovery," they report, "set apart those who were interested in formulating and solving new artistic problems from those who were content merely to apply their technical skill to familiar problems capable of more or less pat solutions."[12]

Finally, Dr. Silvano Arieti of New York Medical College suggests these conditions for fostering creativity: (1) aloneness; (2) inactivity; (3) daydreaming; (4) free thinking; (5) a state of readiness for perceiving similarities; (6) gullibility; (7) remembrance and inner replaying of past traumatic conflicts; (8) resolution of conflicts; (9) alertness; and (10) discipline.[13]

Since any creative act is a synthesis of primary and secondary process thinking—the primitive and nonlogical, which occurs in dreams and fantasies, and the logical, orderly and analytical—there must be conditions that allow the two to blend. The creative mind integrates them into something new, unexpected, and valuable.

Originality in the Organization

One thesis of this book is that an important way of developing "a race of improvisors" is to create organizational conditions that will foster this kind of behavior. Can an organization act in any direct ways, other than "standing out of the light"?

Traditional organizational hierarchy and its demands foster the personality traits that characterize less creative people. Even the most benevolent organizations reward virtuous behavior, not originality, and thus militate against their own perpetuation. True, every organization has to maintain its internal stability and can tolerate only a limited amount of internal dissension and turbulence (and, by definition, innovation is conducive to dissension and turbulence). The problem in industry is no different from the one in the public schools or in other organizations.

Paul Torrance, who has given much attention to creativity in the classroom, reports that creative students are estranged from their teachers and are not very well liked by them.[14] When teachers and parents were asked which of sixty-two personality characteristics should be most encouraged in children, they ranked "being most considerate of others" highest of all. Highly creative students often get so involved in the problems on which they are working that they give little time to social amenities. Teachers and parents ranked independence of thinking second, but independence of thinking requires independence of judgment. For the teachers, it was more important that the student be prompt, energetic, industrious, obedient, and well-liked among his peers. The teachers wanted the student to be receptive to the ideas of others, versatile, and willing to accept the judgments of authorities. While they rated determination as the third most desirable quality, it is apparent that a student resolved to do what he wants would not please them. For them, day-dreaming or fantasy which might produce ideas was no match for industriousness. Curiosity which might lead the student to the threshold of learning was not as highly valued as being studious.

Promptness is hard for creative students because they are likely to see their own thoughts as more important than an arbitrary deadline. Creative students are apt to be self-starters, but teachers tend to want them to follow instructions. Highly creative students are likely to regress occasionally, to be more childlike. Such regression is necessary if they are to draw creative fantasy from the preconscious and unconscious levels of thought, but it is irritating to teachers. Such students may seem emotional or even irrational to the teacher, particularly if they are bold in their ideas but shy in social relations. Their determination may make them seem negativistic, especially if they are unwilling to accept the teacher's answers or take "no" for an answer. Such students, Torrance notes, have an unusual talent for disturbing existing organizations and appear to be domineering when they are creating. The same kind of phenomenon has been reported in the relationship of university administrators to their faculties.[15]

Obviously, no organization can exist if each person strikes off in his or her own determined direction, however individually creative this may be. Nevertheless, exceptional executives can develop a better understanding of what creativity is. They can help individual employees improve their ability to improvise, use and go beyond accepted knowledge, think independently, and engage in discovery. From the MacKinnon studies it is apparent that the less defensive people are, the more they can be receptive to new ideas, experiences, and feelings, and the more creative they can be. They are able to tolerate more complexity, diffuseness of feelings, and the disorder of different thoughts and ideas in their confused, embryonic state. They are not impelled to have answers immediately. But why are these people less "on guard" psychologically?

MacKinnon reports that the parents of the creative architects showed an extraordinary respect for their children and confidence in their ability to do what was appropriate. The parents granted them unusual freedom to explore where their interests took them and to make decisions for themselves, expecting them to act independently but reasonably and responsibly. Apparently this expectation was vital for the children's sense of personal autonomy, which, in turn, became the hallmark of their creativity. However, personal autonomy, by definition, did not allow for intense closeness with the parents.

Despite the freedom granted the children, they had clear conceptions of right and wrong and of standards of conduct. Discipline was usually consistent and predictable, but rarely harsh or cruel. In half of the families there was no corporal punishment. Families of the creative architects engaged in frequent activities, thus providing greater opportunity for roaming, exploration, and varied experiences. As students, the creative architects tended to get mediocre grades unless the subject or the teacher caught their imagination. They were profound skeptics, accepting nothing on faith or authority. Containing so many varied and often conflicting ideas, they were not always pleasant people, and they frequently experienced much psychic turbulence.

These and other corroborating studies suggest certain generalizations that leader-teachers can use to promote creativity. Like Diogenes, leaders should present the task or challenge, indicate support in accomplishing it, and express confidence that the subordinate will succeed with it. They should expect relationships with the subordinate to be oriented around their joint task, and not be disappointed that subordinates. "didn't like them." They should establish and communicate the criteria for performance; penalties for failure would be self-evident. Varied experiences would provide the context for the subordinate's explorations. By encouraging a permissive atmosphere for "crazy" ideas to be expounded and examined, the leaders could hear more of them. Opportunity to choose among challenges and problems, when possible, would let people seize and develop the ones that most excited their curiosity.

Sometimes this opportunity can be provided by allowing the subordinate a portion of her working time to follow some problem that has aroused her interest. Although this interest may not at the moment be of major concern to the organization or the superior, the freedom to follow her interest would stimulate a flow of ideas. One consequence is that the superior would have to contend with the questioning, doubting, and restlessness that followed. Such an atmosphere can become the setting for what Murphy calls the "habit of creation." Creative insights come more frequently to those who work at them. "In every mind there are widening regions of creativity if once the spark has been allowed to generate the fire."[16]

This does not mean that the leader-teacher simply lets go of the managerial task or dismisses any person's unadaptive behavior because "creative people are that way." According to studies reported by Rensis Likert, a scientist in industry who is stimulated by frequent communication within the research organization performs more effectively than if he is isolated.[17] The number of patent applications and scientists' evaluations of colleagues' work is higher in laboratories where there is such communication, particularly if colleagues think differently from one another. Scientists and engineers who often see their administrative chief perform better than those who do not; their performance is even better when they can also set their own technical goals, or at least have some influence in setting those goals. Likert reports that the best performance is attained when the scientists have considerable self-determination about their work and when this is combined with free access to someone in authority.

Donald Pelz adds another dimension to the same findings.[18] He finds that increased communication means that the scientists allow their goals to be influenced by their colleagues. Thus, the most productive are the ones who allow their goals to be modified by others whose views they seek. In addition, talented persons prefer reliable situations when their talent is relevant to the situation.[19] Too much freedom may hamper creativity.

Generalizing from these studies, Likert suggests that the potentialities of younger subordinates are best developed by the superior who can maintain close interest in the young person's work without dominating it. He suggests further that if technical people's personal motivation is low, if they are not deeply involved in their work, it is not advisable to allow more than moderate self-determination. If motivation is high, then full self-determination leads to best results.

Using young management strategically is a strong step toward harnessing innovation. Those between the ages of twenty-one and thirty-five are in the most innovative and creative period of life. Not every person is dramatically creative, but all people at this stage possess a unique set of characteristics. They are fresh and naïve. They have not yet learned what cannot be done, and they are unencumbered with out-of-date habits and ways of thinking. Most will be armed with the latest consolidation of information and new conceptual tools. Almost all have great zeal to do things better than ever before, which means that they enjoy ferreting out practices that have not yet been proven effective. Forcing such people to stand in line and wait for opportunities wastes their best qualities. Even teams of business school students have made an excellent record as company consultants, backed up by experienced faculty members.[20] They are a great help for small companies with limited funds. Large companies have tackled otherwise neglected areas this way.

To be self-renewing, Gardner says, an organization must be interested in what it is going to become, not what it has been. Like a person, an organization runs on motivation, morale, and conviction. Development of the organizational ego, as well as the organizational ego ideal, is necessary for a climate of innovation.

Developing the organizational ego is a Herculean task. Raymond Miles correlates the success of such an effort directly to the importance of the tasks that the organization takes on.[21] The organizational ego is enhanced to the degree to which the organization discovers and uses the talents of its people to accomplish these tasks. Miles complains that the typical company wastes its human resources, sometimes because management does not know the resources exist and sometimes because it does not know how to create an environment in which they could be more fully used. These two reasons mask a third, less palatable reason: the process of unleashing talent is both challenging and threatening. Top management, Miles contends, is not at all certain how this talent could be guided or when, where, and if it should stop: "There appear to be real constraints on the amount of creativity, concern, and enthusiasm which the typical organization is equipped to handle."

Perhaps so. Perhaps executives who have to contend with renewing organizations by stimulating creativity are like parents who are simultaneously gratified and appalled by what their children are learning in school. Not only are the parents unfamiliar with new methods and systems, but in addition they are concerned with maintaining their own self-esteem in the face of precocious knowledge. Despite their own education, contemporary middle-class parents are often as alien to the intellectual world of their children as were immigrant parents of two generations ago. The older executive is in similar straits.

The conditions for creativity are also the conditions for personal flexibility and growth. They constitute the climate for effective supervision. A manager's effectiveness is reflected in the performance level of his subordinates.[22] Achieving effectiveness, however, is not just a matter of applying techniques, although they are an important component. Certainly, it is not a matter of gimmicks or styles; rather, it derives largely from the atmosphere of the workplace. How does it feel to be in a particular place, to work there?

It is a rare treat to walk into a company and find a whole group of people who obviously enjoy working together day after day. A big part of it is almost always the chief executive, who likes all the people and is liked in return. But this is not enough. The executive is also open with people. While trying to help them with plans and choices, the executive does not ask them to become completely dependent on the organization and thereby increase their vulnerability. They run their own lives. As a result, people are apt to come to work early and stay late. They have a spontaneous interest in work. It is a place where they feel a sense of continuous growth and increasing competence, as well as group solidarity. But it takes more than one person to achieve this, as Crawford Greenewalt describes.

> Differences in managerial competence are not due to one person, nor to the few geniuses that cross the stage from time to time, but arise out of the creation of an atmosphere which induces every man or woman connected with the enterprise, no matter what their position, to perform his or her task with a degree of competence and enthusiasm measurably greater than what could be called their normal expectations . . . Business success, then, can be measured by summing up the small increments of extra effort on the part of all the people who are joined together in a given enterprise.[23]

People, across many kinds of organizations, have no trouble expressing their expectations of how their superiors should behave. Stated in common-sense terms, they would like to see justice, courtesy, consideration, job competence, knowledge of subordinates' performance, control of the work group, straightforwardness and decisiveness, appropriate psychological distance, and reasonable assistance.[24] But if these expectations are universally held, they are far from being universally met. For example, a survey of 420 middle and junior executives disclosed that a majority of them feel severely handicapped by a lack of guidance from above: 58 percent said that their superiors had not told them—even in general terms—what was expected of them to qualify for promotion.[25] A majority stated or implied that their work suffered because of lack of communications. Almost half said that their superiors seldom or never commended them or otherwise rewarded them for outstanding work. Although they rated their bosses high on knowledge of and skill in traditional business principles, more than half rated their bosses as only fair or poor in the ability to motivate people.

Another study asked people in lower, middle, and upper levels of management whether the boss called meetings but failed to provide verbal or written information on what needed to be accomplished, or on who would be attending; it also asked whether the executive acknowledged work well done. The conclusion reached, after surveying 294 people, was that a level of "common discourtesy" is ingrained in executive work habits.[26] The cost—not only in deteriorating morale but also in loss of respect for the executive—can easily be imagined.

How do executives perceive themselves? Lyman W. Porter and Edwin E. Ghiselli contrasted the differences between a group of middle managers and a group of top managers. Top management perceived themselves as capable, determined, industrious, resourceful, sharpwitted, enterprising, sincere, sociable, pleasant, dignified, sympathetic. Middle managers saw themselves as discreet, courageous, practical, resourceful, deliberate, intelligent, calm, steady, modest, civilized, patient. Porter and Ghiselli observe:

> Top managers see themselves as the "dynamic brains" of the organization. Their role is one of thinking up new things to do, new areas to enter, new ways of doing things. They are action-oriented idea men. Middle management people, on the other hand, seem to see themselves as filling a role that could be called the "backbone" of the organization. Their chief forte is that they provide the careful, thorough investigation of ideas and plans that is necessary before these can be put into extensive use. They lend the stability to the organization that is necessary for it to function over an extended period of time.[27]

Such perceptions are typical of many young and middle managers.

According to another study, when senior executives rated themselves high in authority—that is, had a self-image of being powerful bosses—their juniors tended to characterize themselves as low or uncertain in responsibility.[28] When seniors rated themselves high in responsibility, their juniors tended to describe themselves as high in authority and also, except for small organizations, in responsibility. In other words, when the boss swings his weight, his subordinates run scared; when his concern with the work problems of the organization begins with consideration of the impact of his own behavior, subordinates feel more capable. What happened when seniors rated themselves high in both responsibility and authority? Juniors tended to delegate less to their subordinates. That is, when seniors tightened control, the juniors did also. In large organizations, when seniors delegated more, juniors also delegated more. In small organizations, this appeared to be less true because the senior was more likely to oscillate between delegating authority and revoking it. The leadership process, the researchers say, may be more smoothly maintained in a stratified organization where interactions are more formalized and less personal than in smaller organizations.

The less the subordinates trust their superior, the more they will evaluate her on the basis of her technical, administrative, or structuring ability.[29] On the other hand, they will also expect her to make more decisions and tell them what to do. Thus, the leader loses the initiative potential of her subordinates.

The issue of self-perception is made even more poignant when executives define the future in terms of the present. If the present is unfulfilling, the future in their eyes holds limited promise. In this situation, the "reservoir of talent" becomes endangered. Aspiration wanes. In a study by Hjalmar Rosen, executives saw the future as "more of the same" and did not tend to predict change in their situations.[30] They felt that they had to accept the status quo or find new jobs elsewhere. They had no sense of mastery, of reciprocation, of affecting the organization. Creativity in such a situation is stifled.

These perceptions are particularly important for several other reasons. Dero Saunders reports in *Fortune* that "the younger men swear it won't happen to them ... and have concluded that the concentration on work and achievement shown by today's senior executives is downright maladjustment." Saunders says further that they have deliberately tempered their business ambitions in order to enjoy more fully their families, their community life, and their recreation. In addition, they hope to modify the business environment. He quotes William E. Henry to the effect that change can occur in something as basic as the attitude toward the outside world: "Whereas the young [say, age thirty to thirty-five] executive looks upon the external environment as a thing to be manipulated or adjusted to, for the middle-aged executive the outer world begins to take on a kind of life of its own and to be seen as greatly more complex and full of unknowns—at times even *malign in influence.*"[31] John Howard reports that in a recent survey conducted among American corporations, one out of three managers were turning down promotions, "which suggests that those who are still writing about how to get to the top had better check to see if anyone still wants to get there."[32] What is clear is that there seems to be what Howard calls an "existential attitude." People recognize that they have the responsibility not only to make a living, but to make a life as well.

Saunders recommends letting middle managers know where they stand through some regular, impersonal assessment procedure. Such a process discourages the building of unfounded hopes for the future. It becomes a statement about reality. He also advocates decentralizing the company into the largest possible number of autonomous divisions to provide more top-management jobs; finding ways to bolster the egos of middle-rank executives whose upward movement is blocked; and capitalizing on what might appear to be personality defects in executives by building jobs around these qualities.

These are largely ego-supporting devices. Only one—creating more divisions—relates to stimulating activity. However, the task for the senior executive is to change the "dampening down" process, which limits horizons, to a stimulating process which expands them. To do this, the leader-teacher must remove artificial barriers and alter the perspectives of those who see themselves as circumscribed. No doubt there are as many ways to do this as there are executives. These recommendations compose a foundation upon which the executive may build.

First, executives must establish trust, largely by meeting the ministration needs that are appropriately fulfilled in the business situation. Trust will be further nurtured if executives look first to themselves and their behavior when problems occur, rather than seeking to blame others. Trust is not to be purchased by self-blame, nor should the executive maintain a constant attitude of *mea culpa*. But executives who continue to ask themselves about the influence of their behavior on their subordinates will be able to single out many such influences. Concomitantly, they will be viewed by subordinates as people who assume responsibility for their behavior. If they can initiate the pattern of being responsible for their own behavior, then their subordinates will be more likely to assume responsibility for theirs. And if executives cannot be responsible, then their subordinates will more likely scapegoat their juniors or cast about for other objects of blame.

The executive-teacher can also increase capacity by increasing responsibility. Too often this is interpreted as meaning promotion to higher jobs, and there are limited numbers of top-echelon jobs. However, there is no limitation on people thinking together about their joint tasks and problems and about the innovations that can be evolved. If the executive-teacher can create the circumstances in which subordinates are able to change their self-images, then many—though not all—can become more responsible in their relationships with the organization. They can shift their perceptions. Instead of feeling like the "backbone" of the organization, they may see themselves as part of its "dynamic brains." Conceivably such thinking could create alternative modes of organizing the business, which would make it possible for both organization and individual to advance to higher levels of functional responsibility.

Executive-teachers will have difficulty trying to ascertain their influence on the personal behavior and responsibility potential of their subordinates unless they are willing to ask these questions: "Why do I need to be powerful?" "Why do I need to patronize others?" "Why do I need to doubt the capacity of others?" Although these questions are not easy to answer, executives should ask them from time to time, particularly when they find themselves reluctant to trust subordinates or to increase subordinates' responsibility. They may be able to observe the self-defensive aspects of their reactions. To the extent that they must protect or promote themselves at the expense of others, they will be unable to build trust and to create conditions favorable for innovation.

Limited aspiration and pessimism about the future are fashioned out of defeat, however subtle the defeat process may be. Higher levels of aspiration and optimism are the product of demonstrated success. In this context, success means what Robert W. White calls "the feeling of efficacy." He defines this as emotions "which accompany the whole process of producing effects."[33] A sense of competence arises out of cumulated feelings of efficacy. Feelings of competence— feelings that one is able to have some effect on other people and the environment—are the foundation of self-respect and security. For the executive-teacher this means that the tasks and activities of subordinates must be structured in such a way that they can see the steps of success.

Success can also be gleaned from failure and from false steps. A department may fail to market one product successfully, but may learn from this failure new ways of marketing which can then be applied to the next effort. A successful research result may be economically useless, but the researcher has taken another step in personal development and in the development of the organization. "Destroying a painting, painting it out, is often important to the development of a painting," says Frank Lobdell of Stanford, who, with Keith Boyle, has been bringing students to their studios to watch them at work. Their purpose is to reveal the painterly process and demystify it. Boyle notes that Stanford students "are so goal-oriented that it's backbreaking to get them to destroy a drawing or painting, to wipe it clean, and start again and again if necessary."[34] A creative executive must also be able to plan a program, try it out, tear it apart, and then start over again before settling on a system that works. Many executives feel such pressure to get things done that few examine closely what they are actually doing. They do not see the implications of their actions and often prematurely close an incomplete system which later must be redone. Part of the responsibility of the superior is to point out the pattern of success when it is obscure, and also to point out that trial, error, change—"painting it out"—are part of the practice of management.

Self-Control

To be both creative and useful, organizational activity must have a counterweight: control. Without control, activity is merely random behavior. To create conditions for the flowering of ideas and innovations is a noble aspiration, but an aimless one unless the ideas and innovations are channeled in the common interest.

The cornerstone of Douglas McGregor's contributions to the psychology of leadership lies in one sentence: "In the recognition of the capacity of human beings to exercise self-control lies the only fruitful opportunity for industrial management to realize the full potential represented by professional resources."[35] This statement and the principles derived from it, which McGregor labeled "Theory Y," were powerful forces toward democratizing management. As with most innovations, the excitement of newer conceptions often overshadowed the lessons that had been learned from the old. In the eyes of some, all control other than self-control came to be viewed as bad, and executives who could not or would not be so democratic as to permit complete self-control by subordinates felt guilty. Attempts to be more democratic sometimes led to conflict, open hostility, panic, and failure.

To speak of authority and control today seems contrary to contemporary concepts of democratic management and to some of the practices previously advocated in these pages. However, one of the major functions of leadership is to control the system. "Regulation," says John Gardner, "need not involve the dead hand of conformity, the iron hand of authority, or the glad hand of conviviality ... Only when responsibility is neglected does enforcement in a punitive sense become necessary."[36]

Robert Dubin has expressed it differently: "We do not assume that men are exploited when led, or manipulated as puppets when supervised."[37] Leadership, teaching, and supervision are active roles. There is no necessary conflict between being active and supportive. In fact, to be inactive is often to be unsupportive, just as being too intrusive is unsupportive. The psychological distance is too close. Similarly, children do not want their father and mother to be pals. They want them to be a father and a mother and to act as people who are more mature, more experienced than they, and who can exercise *controls* that the children themselves have not yet developed.

In management, the difference between supportive and oppressive control has been demonstrated in a study of 656 salesmen in 36 branch offices of a national firm.[38] When the salesmen felt that they exercised some control over their manager, and when his control over them was a contribution to their efforts, high satisfaction and performance resulted. His supervision supported them when it rested heavily on his skill, expertise, and personal attractiveness. When the manager attempted to exercise formal control over the salesmen, by authority of his position, satisfaction and performance were low.

The issue of control is a delicate one. Freud's patients often could not function because they were too repressed, but today psychiatrists and psychologists are seeing more patients who cannot function because they do not have enough controls. These patients, says Christopher Lasch of the University of Rochester, are dissatisfied with life, have low self-esteem, and are unable to form solid relationships.[39] Roy Grinker of Northwestern University similarly notes that the children of the super-rich, who often suffer from parental rejection and material overcompensation, have inadequate identification models and no solid values.[40] Extreme examples of the "me generation," they are self-centered, unable to tolerate frustration, and emotionally empty.

More people will be coming to companies without clear identification with their parents. When the process of identification has been inconclusive and the people therefore lack clear identities, this will ensure weak ego ideals, little motivation, and little self-discipline. They will then need executives who can serve as identification models, filling as much as they can the gap left by the distant parents. Executives will need to "mother" such subordinates, establishing attachments that permit unhappy and unfocused people to become useful members of work groups.

Those who are comfortable with control, on the other

hand, may be uncomfortable in changing management situations. The higher people move in an organization, the less opportunity they have for "hands-on" control, and the more they are compelled to deal with ambiguity and high-level bargaining. This is one of the major changes in the managerial role. It is at this point that those who are heavily oriented to control have the greatest difficulty. They become terribly impatient with the extended negotiations that must take place among organizations (with, for example, government agencies) and within their own organization. As people move up into higher levels, this capacity for tolerating anxiety and less control of a situation needs to be tested. People should be put into situations in which they are compelled to engage in difficult and protracted negotiations, to see how well they can sustain this tension and ambiguity, to see if they can tolerate the rhythm of negotiations and the development of relationships that go along with hammering out a bargain. If they cannot easily do this, then perhaps there is serious question about the direction in which they should move in the organization.

In a study of randomly selected managers and first-level supervisors, it was found that while both groups said they believed in humanistic theories of motivation, they agreed that the managers overcontrolled the supervisors. Even when the managers saw the supervisors' painful dilemma, they could not relinquish control.[41]

When people try to maintain rigid controls, they indicate that they feel inadequate. They want to meet their own expectations of perfection but cannot, and they overcompensate for their failure by directing their energies into power struggles. But if overcontrolling bosses also tell their subordinates that they want them to have more autonomy and self-respect in their jobs, then they are creating a double bind, a no-win situation. The subordinates will fail no matter what they do, because they cannot meet the executives' contradictory requirements for success. They cannot offer the line people the carrot or the stick, because the bosses in theory do not want this; but neither can they use more flexible approaches when they are controlled by a firm system of reward and punishment from above. The result: frustration, anger, and cynicism. Executives need to ask how their behavior affects their subordinates' performances. What are their problems? How would they like to

operate? What gets in their way? Bosses may not be able to—
or want to—give subordinates as much flexibility as they wish,
but there is no need for the tensions that dissonance creates.
At least people can work under clear directives.

Organizations, like individuals, evolve through stages of
maturity. Management consultant Louis E. Allen makes the
point that at each stage a different style of leadership is required.[42] During the first evolutionary stage of any organized
undertaking, organizational requirements are not sharply defined or understood. People tend to put their own objectives
ahead of those of the organization. A leader who can exercise
positive, consistent authority by building a personalized organization is necessary at this stage. But, Allen says, when enterprises outgrow their early leaders, bureaucracy sets in. By following the early leader, the organization has established a
stable pattern, policies have been evolved and accepted, and
standard practices have become the organization's business.
There are well-defined roles and practices. Centralized control
is supported by sub-layers of authority. If the strong leader
does not "let go," the more capable people leave.

If the organization can move from an immature position in
which it is largely dependent upon the leader to a more mature level of functioning, organized groups evolve. "In a mature group," Allen observes, "the individuals have mastered
the skills required to work effectively with minimum supervision. They understand the nature of their own problems well
enough to be able to make most of their own decisions." The
members then put group objectives and requirements ahead
of personal ones. Such a group is ready for mature leadership,
which Allen defines as concentrating on efforts that get the
most effective results through others. "The mature leader
knows how to lead so that people will understand and accept
the limits of freedom within which they must work if they are
to remain a cohesive undertaking."

The disorganization that ensues when the leader fails to
exercise adequate controls is vividly illustrated by Moss Hart's
description of what happens on the stage.

> If [actors] cannot trust, or have lost faith in, the man who is
> to guide them and see them through that moment, they
> strike out in fear and hide their panic in bursts of temper

and impossible behavior ... the first necessity a director faces is the creation of a climate of security and peace, in which actors pass through the stage door on the first day of rehearsals until the curtain rises on opening night in New York.[43]

The organizational equivalent of Hart's experience is found in two studies of group processes. In one, it was found that "antagonism, tension, and absenteeism were determined in part by the failure of a group member to act as a 'leader' by providing orientations toward, evaluations of, and suggestions about the situation when these were demanded by other group members," if the group members expected that person to be the leader.[44] The more nondirective the group leadership, the more such disruptive behavior was likely to occur. According to the second study, when a group had a member who was uncontested as a self-confident decision maker, the group performed better at later stages in learning.[45]

If the senior executive is caught between the requirement that he exercise his power and his wish to be liked by his subordinates, he can easily get into difficulty.[46] If he tries to deny his power by acting the role of the "nice guy ," then, in Abraham Zaleznik's terms, he strips himself of status. Depreciating his power, he soon finds that the subordinates join him in this activity. Decision making becomes one continuous argument, and the subordinates become contemptuous of the superior. If this is the model offered them, then there is no point in wanting to achieve the boss's position: it promises nothing but futile argument.

A caution: the reader who misunderstands Hart's statement and sees these studies as a case for authoritarianism should reread the statement and review the studies to discern what directors control: the proceedings. They create and maintain an organized, supportive context in which people can work creatively. They act not as stars, but as facilitators.

Nor is the question group control versus leader control. Control may be viewed as a dimension on a continuum from complete group autonomy at one extreme to unquestioned dominance by the leader at the other. Optimum control on this axis will vary with the task and with the sophistication, competence, and maturity of the group, as well as the situation in which the group finds itself. Control of some kind is necessary. When the group has an adequate perspective on the task to be accomplished, and has the requisite skills for doing so, then it may have correspondingly more control over itself and will need less from the leader. When the leader has a perspective that others do not or cannot have, then the leader will have to exert correspondingly more control. In the latter case, the group will have to identify with the ego ideal and strength of the leader.

A simple case in point may be drawn from the Trist study of coal miners.[47] The miners knew their work and could spontaneously organize the most effective ways to accomplish it. However, they were unlikely to appreciate the complexities of marketing coal. They would have to depend on a leader who either did or could call upon someone who was knowledgeable. The miners would also have to trust that the leader's management of overall production would provide maximum income for them.

There is no need, therefore, to idealize democratic management. No democracy ever achieved anything without leadership. The leader has the task of welding together past ideals and present goals. This is a point that is often neglected by adherents of group dynamics, to whom a leader with strength is anathema. No organization can endure without leadership and none can endure for long without an ego ideal to hold it together. The leader must still lead. Leadership control and self-control need not be contradictory. Freedom never exists in a vacuum, but always within a framework of responsibility. Freedom within a context of responsibility means mutual control of leader and followers, of which self-control is but one integral part.

The Need to Test Reality

By stimulating activity under conditions that support its flowering into creativity and innovation, the executive creates, as Robert W. White puts it, a "constant connection between knowledge and action. We learn about the environment because we go out to it, seek response from it and find out what kind of response it can give."[48] By continuously testing reality, people learn what they can and cannot do; they learn what the environment will and will not do under various circumstances, and the costs of alternative behaviors. They provide continuous feedback on their own behavior.

There are two kinds of feedback: people's observations of the effects of their behavior, and reports from others. People learn best when they obtain direct feedback from the task itself, seeing how what they have learned affects their approach for solving problems.

If the worker does piecework, the feedback about quantity and quality is reasonably direct. Indirect feedback, or reports from others, is problematic: anything more than the simplest kind of direct feedback about a person's behavior is almost impossible to come by. If people's work is interrelated with that of others, it is more difficult for them to weigh their own efforts. Most men and women in managerial ranks must depend on the judgment of superiors to get a sense of the effectiveness of their performance.

When the leader has already established and maintains controls, the subordinate's need for the leader's judgment poses two problems. One is the need to avoid management that is so authoritarian that the subordinate winds up identifying with the aggressor. This kind of leadership behavior leads to simple imitation: the subordinate receives hostility from above, and in turn displaces it downward to his or her own subordinates. This practice leads to the antithesis of closeness, support, protection, guidance, and spontaneous activity. It is also self-perpetuating. Rigid control begets the need for more of the same. The second problem is to develop and reinforce self-control.

Performance appraisal is one important way of dealing with both problems at the same time. Next to direct feedback from the task itself, the most useful kind of feedback comes from someone whom the subordinate respects and who shares a mutual interest in the same problems.

A variety of appraisal systems have been formulated to provide feedback. Most have failed dismally. In a typical appraisal program, the superior analyzes the position description and the assigned duties of each subordinate and judges how well the subordinate has fulfilled the assigned tasks.[49] Although such an analysis seems simple, the fact that the superior is forced to judge performance makes the process painful and psychologically complex.

In many companies, the formal performance appraisal is an annual event. It becomes a theatrical confrontation between individuals and organizations. In such periodic appraisals, according to studies in General Electric, there is a tendency to store criticisms and complaints, and then to fire both barrels—the criticisms and the resulting anger—at the subordinate.[50] Praise on such occasions seems ineffective because the subordinate sees it as a wedge for censure. Criticism inevitably brings defensive denials of responsibility for poor performance.

Such mechanistic efforts are further impaired by the feelings that superiors have about appraising others. Anticipating the subordinate's denials and resistances, and afraid of their own aggression (which is inevitably a part of criticism) superiors become confused by their own guilt. Too often they feel they are destroying the other person, and therefore gloss over criticism or go to great lengths to deny their hostility. This, in turn, leads to "management by guilt."[51] Dishonest appraisal is destructive to both individual and organization; it undermines responsible leadership control.

People need abundant permission to speak up about basic emotional issues. Attention to feeling has been programmed out of most people in our society, and central emotional experiences have been so superimposed with habits of complicated rational discrimination that they are easily overlooked. When people express their feelings about somebody else or about a situation, they often act as if they have just revealed some terrible hostility. Yet once on the table, the issue does not look so remarkable at all.

Everyone is uncomfortable about negative judgments to some degree. This is because everyone has experienced in childhood the feeling that words are the same as actions. They can kill. The feeling hangs around in spite of rational knowledge to the contrary. Perfectly sensible people bend over backward not to say anything negative, or, if they absolutely must, they do it so obliquely that the message cannot be understood. The consequence is a breakdown of communication. The internal prohibition against direct expression of negative reactions is constantly in the way of many corporate functions. It especially cripples appraisal and supervision. This is why the best formulas for doing good evaluations still fail in practice.

The problems are not reason enough for abandoning the appraisal system. An appraisal system can provide a useful record of performance and a basis for individual development. It is necessary as part of the reality test that gives people data for making judgments and changing efforts. Superiors will be making appraisals and judgments anyway. The more candid the appraisals, the more they can serve as a basis for communication and trust.

There are three conditions for the constructive use of appraisal systems. First, appraisal must be continuous. The General Electric studies show that performances should be conducted not annually but on a day-to-day basis. Following an old education maxim, the more immediate the feedback on a given performance, the more useful and important it is. Furthermore, when suggestions for improved performance are given in less concentrated form, subordinates appear to accept them more readily. Besides, what basis for a relationship of trust is there, other than continuous honest interaction?

Second, superiors must have training for appraisal. People need a chance to rehearse the process. Groups of people who are going to be doing evaluations should sit down together and talk over the problems and their feelings about them. They can role-play, or practice what they are going to say and how they will say it. In a group they will get mutual support as well as feedback, so that they can make sure they are not dodging the issues. They must be helped to learn to convey their views to their subordinates without feeling guilty about offering criticism. They need to learn, too, that people are not destroyed by having to face a realistic picture of the world, even if it means they must give up their jobs. This abstract from a letter is a case in point:

> Several years ago, during one of our austerity programs, we were required to cut our research staff by 10%. This was greeted, of course, by anguished cries from supervisors. When it got down to cases, however, it turned out that we could let about 5% go with no loss of any significance.

> Clearly we had been carrying a number of employees with
> no real justification for them. A fair share of those involved
> were employees within a few years of retirement whom no
> one had the courage to let go. By forcing some early retire-
> ments, we cleaned our house a bit at the expense of bitter
> hostility on the part of those who were retired. I was some-
> what amazed that a little later, two of the younger men we
> got rid of came and thanked us! They said that they had
> realized for some time that they were not really doing a job
> but that since there was no pressure to get out, they just
> stayed on. When they were let go, they got new jobs for
> which they felt more qualified and seemed happier.[52]

This is not an argument for firing people indiscriminately, but
a plea for giving people the facts and letting them make their
own decisions, rather than deceiving them into thinking they
are doing well when they are not. In turn, it is a case for
teaching executives to carry out their part of the appraisal process honestly, without being devastating.

The third condition for constructive use of appraisal is that
it be a mutual evaluation process. There are two bases for this
condition. Young people are always appraising their elders—if
not formally, then by behavior. Abandoning the values of
elders, protests on college campuses, and the distance between
generations are examples of appraisals by behavior. A more
formal example is the contemporary effort to gauge the merit
of college faculties.[53]

Mutual evaluation can help address the problem of the
"cocoon factor," the natural capacity of executives to insulate
themselves from the realities of the external world and, particularly, their inability to sense and acknowledge other people's
feelings. Various polls show that executives are frequently out
of touch with the public at large and, in some companies, far
out of touch with the thinking of others in their own industries. Some read little—others not at all. Many executives pursue training for a working lifetime, unaware of the fact that
they have not become educated. That is the result of being involved in the daily details without having to think about the
implications. Others regard themselves as fighting a rearguard
action for the free enterprise system; they would do better to
think more creatively about sustaining its vitality. The "cocoon factor" refers to the skein of silvery threads that makes

for psychological comfort, economic warmth, and the illusion of achievement. It is not amenable to change in one-way evaluation schemes.

An important reason for making appraisal a mutual evaluation process is the fact that when two people work together, the most important common bond is their relationship. It must therefore be continually examined. In a superior-subordinate relationship, both parties influence each other and both have a responsibility for the task. In order to carry out the responsibility, each person must affect the other. If they are to carry out the joint responsibility in the most effective way, they must be able to talk freely with each other. The dialogue cannot be limited to what the subordinate alone is doing. Each party must have the sense of modifying the other. The talks must also include a joint setting of goals and the opportunity for each to express feelings about the working relationship. That mutual appraisal is no quixotic fantasy is reflected in the General Electric research cited earlier. Superior results were obtained when the appraisal process became one of mutual goal-setting for both superior and subordinate.

Money, too, is an important source of feedback on performance. It serves as a gross index of effectiveness and relative contribution to the organization. Salary discussion can be means for step-by-step improvement. Salary also serves as an index of comparative value: the higher they are in the hierarchy and the greater their education, the more likely people are to compare their pay with that of people outside the company. Someone may have good relative pay within an organization, but this will not compensate for what seems to be an inadequate pay level when seen industry-wide or community-wide. The higher the position the more value is attached to merit versus seniority, pay versus benefits. Furthermore, the stronger and less defensive the subordinates, the more they will approve of a performance-appraisal system.[54]

Performance appraisal as a method of testing reality has one other major advantage. The larger the number of followers who concur with the appraisal's results, the greater is the leader's authority by their consent.[55] Mutual consideration of both the results and the modes for achieving them—the joint confrontation of realities—strengthen the positions of both leaders and followers.

An organization needs creative thinkers. The creative thinkers need an organization to help make their ideas a reality. Yet often the characteristics of an organization—its need for structure, for order, and for a group of people who work together—are anathema to the spontaneous, sometimes erratic innovator. Working out these tensions in ways that are realistic and fair is a critical step in maturation for the innovator, for his or her superior, and for the whole working group.

"Mike Williams is the top chemist in our R&D unit. My problem is how to encourage and support his creativity. Mike, now thirty-eight, has been with our company for eight years—off and on. He's brilliant but unreliable, creative but impatient. To put my problem in a nutshell, I need the guy desperately, but I don't know if I can live with him. He is the stereotype of the erratic innovator, the imaginative eccentric.

"Our company, a plastics manufacturer, is deeply indebted to Mike. Six years ago he hit on the formula of what has become our most successful product. We wouldn't be where we are now—successful, profitable, and growing—without Mike's product.

"But the fact doesn't mean much to Mike. He doesn't care about the company or the people in this unit. He cares about one thing only: his work. He wants to work when he has a hot idea, and comes in late (or not at all) when he doesn't. In fact, after his star project was off and flying, Mike thought his next project was a turkey, so he walked out on the organization.

"I wooed Mike back after seeing my unit go through an eight-month decline. No one else had his drive or creativity. I felt he could do wonders for the company. And he has—his work is great. But he's tearing the department apart. Everyone else here is furious because Mike sets his own rules, runs them ragged when he's onto something, and yet never gives anyone the time of day. He's the classic star player who couldn't care less about anyone else on the team.

"I've talked to Mike repeatedly, but I just can't get him to see anything from my perspective. He says that I have a choice: either I let him work creatively, or I let him go. He says he can't produce the kind of work I say I want if I put him in a straightjacket.

"I want to reward Mike for all he's done for this company, but I've got a growing mutiny on my hands. Other people see him come and go at odd hours and say, 'What's fair for one is fair for all.' Mike says, 'I work hard. Why can't I work when I'm really working?' Last week he blew up, said this place was like a kindergarten, and threatened to quit.

"To make matters worse, my boss is putting lots of heat on me to keep Mike on. He's afraid that Mike will take his present project to a competitor, or set up a company of his own. But my boss doesn't want to hear about my problems—what it's like facing a string of bitter, complaining subordinates day after day.

"What are my chances of getting anyone in this situation to change? Am I the nice guy who's going to finish last? What can I do?"

Analysis

Where Is the Pain?   Obviously the pain is in the narrator. Mike deals with his pain by responding with erratic behavior to whatever moves him.

When Did it Begin?   Apparently Mike has always been this way because there is no indication that he ever was any different.

Ego ideal   Mike's ego ideal apparently has to do with the development of hot ideas and mastering complex and stimulating tasks. He says in his own words that he wants to be a creator.

Affection   His affection is channeled primarily into his work and into his creative achievement. He lavishes attention on his tasks and comes up with results. He is a self-centered person who wants to go his own way and does not have much investment in other people.

Aggression   His aggression is invested in his work and his pursuit of problem-solving activity. He drives other people in an effort to meet his own ego-ideal demands, but essentially all this is his way of attacking a problem.

Dependency   Unlike most employees, Mike doesn't feel dependent on the organization or on other people. For this reason he shouldn't be responsible for subordinates. He is dependent on what goes on in his head. However, he is also dependent on his boss to protect him from both the rigidities and the vagaries of the organization. Whether Mike knows it or not, he is dependent on his organization to maintain a climate in which he can create.

Is It Solvable?   Not completely, but it may well be manageable.

How?   This kind of situation is common when highly creative people work in large or tightly structured organizations. Creativity is a kind of controlled craziness, and it demands spontaneity—because without it, the unconscious thoughts and processes that lead to inventions and creations cannot bubble up to the surface. Creative and erratic people are bound to come into conflict with managerial, orderly types. Bosses who get caught in the crossfire must ask themselves, "How high a price can I pay for what I'm getting?" In this case, the narrator claims that the whole group is dependent on what comes out of Mike's head. If this is true, then he must protect Mike and clearly demarcate the responsibilities and expectations for Mike and the others.

The narrator can protect Mike by calling the others together and explaining how much they all have at stake in what comes out of Mike's head and why they cannot reasonably expect him to work creatively within rigid rules. So long as Mike is producing and the system is dependent on him, his boss needs to adapt the system to Mike's needs. And he can tell the others that everyone benefits if the system adapts and keeps Mike producing.

TWELVE

Mastery Needs

inistration needs require supportive and facilitative efforts that come from outside the person; maturation needs require conditions for the natural unfolding within the person. When both needs have been sufficiently met at each step of the person's development, the conditions are created for the next stage: the gratification of mastery needs. Each person must master enough of the world to survive in it.

Early on, children begin to differentiate themselves from the context of the world around them and to identify with figures who are more competent. These identifications become the bases for new ties to the world.[1] With every step in their own competence, they not only become more independent but also master more of the world and integrate this mastery into an ever widening relationship with the environment. The more psychosocial problems a child resolves early in life, the more stimulating his environment is; the more effectively the resolutions and stimulations are integrated, the wider will be the child's sense of mastery.

Every new maturational experience becomes integrated with others as the basis for further development. Each experience expands the ego and increases autonomy. But interference with this natural evolution slows the development of the ego and impairs its integration.

Imagine a child who is developing naturally. Her arms and

236

legs grow at comparable rates so that they can function together in running or playing ball. She develops smooth coordination; the more effective the integration, the better she is as
an athelete. Imagine the same child whose left leg grows more
slowly than her right, or even fails to grow beyond a certain
point. Coordination is more difficult, if not impossible to
achieve. She limps. She cannot be an athlete.

It is easy to understand what crippling or maldevelopment
means in physiological terms because the impairment can be
readily observed. If a study showed that a high proportion of a
sample of middle managers were physically handicapped,
readers would be astonished. It is much more difficult to understand psychological impairment. When studies demonstrate that significant proportions of middle managers have
limited perceptions of themselves and their roles, there is as-
tonishment.[2] Yet no one is aroused by the fact that a large
number of college-trained people with years of experience in
organizations view themselves as drudges and have little faith
in their capacity to improve their own lots and the effectiveness of their companies. But this is impairment, indeed.

The ego's failure to continue its natural development is
costly to both the individual and the organization. Limited in
one way or another, the individual's self-perception is distorted. With increased competence and power over the environment, on the other hand, the individual's self-confidence
and self-respect also increase.

H. Marshall McLuhan has argued that a wide range of
communications media will increase the input of stimuli, thus
enabling people to perceive the world differently and to be
more confident of mastering it.[3] From their covered wagons,
pioneers saw mountains as barriers. Distance was a great sepa-
rator. Enclaves of difference arose—North, East, South, West,
urban, rural. But with airplanes, television, and computers,
children of today are literally on top of the world. They can
look down on mountains; they can see news on television as it
is being made. They experience the world as being more amenable to fulfilling their own needs and aspirations. This is very
different from the way their parents experienced it.

An unlimited amount of new stimuli, on the other hand,
can overwhelm people, and the concept of "future shock,"
trauma caused by change that occurs too often and too fast, is

an idea that organizations must deal with as they try to design an environment where individuals—and hence the organization—can flourish.[4]

If development does not occur naturally in people, if there are psychological impairments, then compensatory mechanisms develop. Everyone knows people who are self-inflated, overweening, or exploitative—executives who attack their subordinates, undermine their superiors, or continually disagree with their peers. Organizations pay an astronomical price for such behaviors. Often, they represent people's efforts to prove to themselves and the environment that they are more adequate than they actually feel. Nor are these people able to change their behavior readily, because they are too absorbed with their own impairments to grasp fully the realities of the outside world. Impaired people become more concerned with themselves than with others or with society as a whole, and it is this relative lack of concern for outsiders that keeps them in continuous tension with their environment. Their preoccupations make it difficult for them to understand the past correctly and to anticipate the future accurately. Their orientation to the world is distorted.

At the same time, maldevelopment can lead to fear of failure that can, itself, be a roadblock to success. As John Howard points out, the new generation of executives may be particularly susceptible to fears of this kind because they grew up during a time when parents and teachers were doing their utmost to minimize suffering and disappointment. "If the individual has been uniquely successful in avoiding pain, he is also particularly vulnerable to the fear of encountering frustration and disappointment in the future ... Only those who come to terms with the fear of failure escape a nervous preoccupation with the future."[5]

The issue of individual development and mastery is of primary concern to organizations that seek to ensure their own survival. The greater the sense of mastery people have in the organization, the more flexible, the more uninhibited and innovative they are likely to be, and the less threatened by change. The less the sense of mastery, the greater the likelihood of organizational passivity.

Leo Cherne, capturing the executive's sense of concern, says that most organizational structures will be composed of second-best people and will experience a constant downward pull to mediocrity if counteracting actions are not taken. "When you get a case of excellence," he advises, "hang onto it, water and feed it with the best you have, protect it and don't let it die." He feels that the formula is to give it the one thing that it really demands—the chance to be itself.[6] Cherne's view concentrates on single individuals. The thesis of this book is that an environment that supports everyone permits particularly talented individuals to blossom more rapidly and abundantly than they would be able to otherwise.

John Gardner says that one of the dangers of modern society is that men and women will lose the experience of participating in meaningful decisions concerning their own life and work, that they will become cogs in the machine because they feel like cogs in the machine.[7] He contends that all too often people are inert components of groups, not participating in any significant way, but being carried along like grains of sand in a bucket.

The fact that people are frequently cogs in a hierarchical machine, and more often feel like it, has led some to condemn industrial society and its organizations. It is true that organizations constrain individuals, but it is equally true that organizations also contribute to their growth. A company may exercise controls over its employees. At the same time it may increase their freedom by raising their standard of living, their level of skill, and their occupational importance. The problem is not organizations per se, but how they are to be managed.

How can organizations further the experience of mastery and convert organizational shackles into links of strength? There are four components to mastery needs: the need for ambitious striving, for realistic achievement, for rivalry with affection, and for consolidation. The steps that executives take to further the fulfillment of these needs become links of strength, both for the individual and for the organization.

Ambitious Striving

The achievement motive, David McClelland notes, is stimulated by the mystic healer type of leader and is at the heart of a forward-moving society.[8] McClelland uses a hypothetical situation to distinguish achievement-oriented people from those who are affiliation-oriented and power-oriented. Given the task of building a boat, the achievement-oriented person would obtain gratification from making the boat. The affiliation-oriented person would have fun relaxing with others in the boat but would have little concern for the seaworthiness of the craft. The power-oriented person would focus on how to organize the production of the boat. Preoccupation with power or with affiliation usually interferes with accomplishing the basic task, although both of these motives are related to achievement.

People who are motivated to achieve set moderately difficult but potentially surmountable goals for themselves. They are always challenging themselves to stretch their capacities. "But," writes McClelland, "they behave like this only if they can influence the outcome by performing the work themselves. They prefer not to gamble at all ... They prefer to work at a problem rather than leaving the outcome to chance or to others.[9] They are concerned with personal achievement rather than with the rewards of success. Such people prefer situations in which they can obtain tangible information about their performance. They also habitually think about how to do things better. From years of study, McClelland concludes that those who have high achievement motive are not born with it. It evolves from a particular kind of family matrix. Their parents set moderately high achievement goals and were warm, encouraging and nonauthoritarian in helping their children attain these goals. The parallel between these findings and the previous discussion about family conditions that contribute to creativity is striking.

Just as in some people there appears to be an enduring disposition to achieve, there appears in others to be an enduring "fear of failure."[10] This behavior, too, seems to arise out of early relationships. The specific constellation in the relationship of child to mother seems to be as follows. The mother expects the child to become independent early and to achieve; unlike the mother of an achieving child, this kind of mother does not give much approval and recognition for independent behavior. However, she does punish if the child's behavior is unsatisfactory. Her neutrality toward satisfactory behavior and punishment for unsatisfactory behavior evoke a negative attitude toward achievement and a fear of the consequences of failure. If she reverses her behavior and rewards satisfactory behavior while maintaining neutrality about unsatisfactory behavior, the child is motivated by the positive consequences of success.

Any learning experience poses a difficult psychological task. At first, learning something new feels like losing something, because people lose the orientation on which they acted before. To find out suddenly that their approach was not sufficient and to have to tackle the world all over again differently is a blow to people's previously unchallenged sense of competence in some area.

Some settings give special permission or support for this experience. For instance, in childhood, most people can bear quite a lot of stumbling and fumbling because they know that no one expects them to have mastered everything yet. In adulthood, this becomes more difficult. A school setting makes the process comfortable for many. But some people can tolerate the experience only with a hobby, or some other activity that they do not have to take seriously. For adults who maintain high expectations of themselves, learning becomes steadily harder. The phrases "You're allowed only one mistake here" and "If you do something wrong, they'll tell you about it" reflect the tenor of typical managerial communication. Although some people carry these messages in their heads, in business situations they are frequently voiced by subordinates in response to supervision.

McClelland reports that people with a strong need to achieve, as differentiated from those with a need to acquire power over others, earn more raises and are promoted more rapidly than others.[11] They work more readily with people whose expertise helps them solve the problems they face, rather than with people who are their friends. Companies with many such people grow faster. Countries with such a dominant motive have higher rates of economic growth than others.

Some people wear high achievement motives more comfortably than do others. As a group, women have shown themselves to be quite uncomfortable with a strong drive to achieve. Many women associate achievement with aggression. Harvard psychiatrists Carol Nadelson, Malkah Notman, and Mona Bennett report that many of their patients seek help because they cannot assert themselves adequately or achieve their career goals: "Because women often view competitive activity as injurious to others, they may feel guilty about competing."[12]

In a landmark study, Matina Horner examined the attitudes and achievements of Radcliffe undergraduates and identified a similar obstacle: fear of success.[13] Against the research and publicity on fear of failure, the suggestion that women may fear success because it can conflict with their traditional views of femininity casts new light on working women and women in management.

Workaholics are another group in which individuals often are made to feel that their work habits are pathologically compulsive. In a therapeutic effort illustrating that not all compulsions are equally bad, psychiatrist Robert Custer has used workaholics as role models for compulsive gamblers. Employing the old psychiatric technique of symptom substitution, Custer has helped his patients redirect their energies and aggressions from gambling into work. Apparently half of his first one hundred patients have successfully made the change.[14]

The achievement motive can be taught, according to McClelland. There will be less success, however, if the environment does not support the person's desire to achieve. Training programs that have helped increase such motivation are based on four concepts: identification, expectation, people's assessment of their situation, and practice techniques. In McClelland's courses, participants were taught to think and talk like people who were achievers. They were encouraged to set realistic work goals for themselves over the next two years, and these were reviewed every six months. In playing various "experimental games," individuals could see the differences between their performance and that of others. They could examine some of the reasons why they differed and could calculate what these meant in terms of their life goals. Finally, they had the opportunity to discuss their experiences with others undertaking the same training and obtaining similar support.

Behind such a program are several psychological propositions.[15] The more reasons people find to believe that they can, will, or should develop a motive, the more the educational attempts to develop this motive are likely to succeed. If the development of such a motivation is consistent with the demands of reality, people are more likely to establish a "set" or attitude about the motive and relate it to actions; experiencing the new motive as an improvement in self-image and seeing it as an advancement on prevailing cultural values, they are more likely to accept it and act on it. Thus, people who commit themselves to achieving tangible goals, keep a record of their progress, are supported by others, and achieve membership in this supportive group are more likely to continue with it. The relationship between the achievement motive and performance appraisal is apparent: both relate to changes in ego structure and to the more effective mastery of reality.

From McClelland's various studies, the conditions for the achievement motive might be summarized as "expect, support, respect, leave them alone." Leaders should make demands on people, expect them to achieve reasonable goals as well as some that border on the unreasonable. They should respect their subordinates' capacity to chart their own course toward these goals, provide them with protection and support, acknowledge what they have to contribute toward reaching collective goals and, following Diogenes' dictum, "stand out of their light."

Realistic Achievement

The most important condition for fostering ambitious striving is the opportunity for people to face reality straightforwardly. Only then can they contribute directly to problem solving and have a sense of mastery over problems. Of course, this applies when people have the capacity to deal with the given problem. For example, a passenger in an airplane may be happier not knowing what struggles the pilot is having with the weather because he cannot do anything about the problem. A passenger on a ship, however, should know if the weather threatens the vessel because there are some efforts she can make toward her own survival. Much of the time, however, management makes the assumption that the first condition is true: there is no point sharing decision making with employees, as they do not know and would not care. Although employees cannot know everything or contribute with equal competence to all decisions, when they are not directly aware of reality they will construct their own to fit the facts as they see them.

To illustrate, a high-level executive encountered one of his company's employees and the employee's wife at a shopping center. During the casual conversation that followed, the employee was temporarily diverted by a passing friend. The officer and the man's wife continued their conversation, but there was an immediate shift in subject matter. The wife asked the officer if there was going to be a layoff at the plant. Astounded that there should be such a rumor when the company had orders for two years' work, the officer wanted to know why she asked. As both she and the officer knew, there had been a change from a hard-driving plant manager to an almost non-directive one. The employees were waiting for the new plant manager to demand work from them as the old one had. When he did not do so, they interpreted it to mean that management was trying to stretch the work. There were obviously limits to how far a small company could spread its work, the men knew. Ergo, a layoff would soon follow.

With the best of intentions, management had not kept the employees in touch with reality. From management's point of view, employees did not have to worry about such issues. They had only to do their work and draw their pay. But in fact management did the employees no favor, as the anxiety and rumors testified. The employees could only feel helpless, victimized by forces beyond their control. Furthermore, the employees could learn nothing about solving some of the problems with which the whole company was confronted, and to whose solution they might have contributed.

This is not a case for abandoning management to the group process, or for yieldiing the authority and responsibility of the executive. What is called for is an adaptation of the best qualities of the monarchical or priestly leader. Most important, the leader must always present reality as the focus of group efforts—the current and long-range problems that the organization faces. This reality must include the psychology of people as well as social and economic forces and trends. Leaders who would help people face reality communicate respect for and confidence in their followers. They do not limit themselves to cajolery with respect to part of reality—for example,

"Our market next year" or "We must do a better job of supervisory training." Nor do they make a black-and-white choice between good human relations and productivity.

Douglas McGregor has offered a four-point program for implementing such a conception:

1. An open presentation and discussion of management's view of the requirements for successful competition at any given point in time. This would include an analysis of the external forces and the internal problems reflected in the information on past performance and an examination of possible "restraining" forces that could prevent a realization of the organization's capability.

2. An analysis of changes in organizational performance necessary to meet the demands of external reality.

3. An analysis by each subunit, at every level, of the contribution it could make to the total organizational effort.

4. A statement from each unit of the goals and standards it could meet on the first two points, including help the unit would need in accomplishing these goals.[16]

Shared concern for organizational problems must evolve from shared concern with the immediate tasks to be accomplished. If the shared concern is with either level alone, no precise relationship is established between the two; people may have a sense of mastery over the task, but may still be uneasy because whatever effectiveness they achieve in their jobs brings them no closer to control over their fate. Or they may have some way of exercising control over organizational decisions but have no way to act on intermediate steps to achieve their purposes.

Focusing on the reality of task problems is an important first step. Virgil B. Day, vice-president of General Electric, reports that in his company's experience, the more the approach to employees can be problem-oriented and work-oriented the more likely it is to prove effective.[17] Local management and union officials, as well as employees, seem to be responsive to such an effort.

The concept of reality-testing can be applied to the individual as well as to the group. This means assigning a problem that is sufficiently challenging but not so massive as to be overwhelming. Most people want and seek such problems. Some companies are already providing them with the challenge they seek. At Koppers, newcomers act as understudies for top executives.[18] By doing so they establish both identification and a top-management view of the enterprise. They also obtain experience in analyzing "whole organization" problems. This prepares them to move into top-management roles early. At W. R. Grace and Company, this procedure has resulted in many executives in their twenties and thirties. Thiokol Corporation uses a project approach to manufacturing rocket motors. At one time there were thirty-five project teams within the company. Each had its own manager who was responsible for the delivery of the product and, in this respect, was comparable to the president of a small company.

Lyndall F. Urwick, a British authority on management, argues that business deprives itself of the opportunity to prepare young employees for managerial positions because it does not yet have an adequate conception of the role of the "assistant to."[19] Urwick notes that in the military, the commanding officer has a general staff—officers who assist him in carrying out his functions of command. "They help him think about the fighting and the main functions that contribute to fighting efficiency such as personnel, training, intelligence, tactics and logistics. They relieve him of much of the detail of coordinating these functions." In business, however, the "assistant to" position has not been effective because business has not yet defined "status, as distinguished from function, by the device of rank." Thus the "assistant to" is either an errand boy or a potential rival of those who have greater seniority. Without such a structure, business lacks the machinery to train men practically for the transition from specialist to generalist. Urwick describes the military provision for doing this: "After three or four years as a General Staff Officer, he is moved back into 'the line,' with a higher rank but in a lower echelon. It is a salutary experience because of the tendency of bureaucracies to become remote from reality. The former General Staff Officer finds himself at the receiving end of the damn-fool letters he has been writing for the previous three or four years."

Giving people a challenging problem to solve is only half of the reality-testing technique. The other half consists of supportive conditions under which they are expected to solve the problem. Supportive conditions include allowing employees room to maneuver, freedom to make mistakes, setting limits, and defining expectations.[20] Respectful treatment of their ideas gives them the opportunity to learn to treat others respectfully. Thus, extending the influence of support simultaneously strengthens mastery.

Task accomplishment and organizational survival, seen as the core of the relationship between employee and organization, avoids arguments about productivity versus human relations. In addition, it combines thinking and doing, a combination now compelled by two circumstances: the competence and expectations of younger people, and the need for organizational flexibility. Bernard Muller-Thym has advanced the thesis that new forms of organizational structure require such synthesis at every center organized for the performance of an integrated task. This integration cannot so easily be achieved in the older, more stratified organizational structure where so often thinking is separated from doing. He quotes E. P. Brooks, former dean of the Sloan School of Management at the Massachusetts Institute of Technology. Brooks's survey of executive development showed consistently that those managers who had functioned as members of a project team, had had the opportunity to run a small but integrated operation, or, in their managerial careers, had moved from one functional area to another had developed more rapidly than their associates who had progressed through the standard organizational structure. He summarizes the findings of those organizations that analyzed their own experiences in developing successful managerial personnel. First, managers are shaped in a context of work and experience. Such experience is most effective when it requires the developing manager to cross functional lines, to be the center of mobilization for diverse competences, and to make optimizing design and operational decisions. Second, the factors that foster the release of human energies and the development of people also encourage operating efficiency. Third, the organization or work structure is one of these basic factors.[21]

Another way to encourage reality-testing is to create conflict, not by playing people off against one another or inducing anxiety, but by posing unresolved problems and challenging people. This was one facet of McGregor's proposals. Arthur Schlesinger, Jr., describes John F. Kennedy as doing just this: "He had the effect on people, in short, of forcing them to fresh approaches—exciting them because of his great interest and his own brilliance, and forcing them to a higher, more imaginative performance than the bureaucracy would ordinarily produce or tolerate.[22]

Rivalry with Affection

Demand is a necessary part of achievement. McClelland reports that people with high achievement motives like a situation in which they can take personal responsibility for finding solutions to problems.[23] In this fashion, the reality situation makes demands on them. Gardner holds that the educational system provides young employees with a sense of what society expects of them in the way of performance.[24] If it is lax in its demands, they will believe that such are the expectations of society. If much is expected of them, they will probably require much of themselves.

The need for the realities of a situation to pull people out of themselves has long been a theme of poets. In "Considerations by the Way," Emerson wrote: "Our chief want in life is somebody who shall make us do what we can." Goethe expressed the same thought somewhat differently in *Poetry and Truth from My Own Life:* "If you treat a man as he is, he will stay as he is, but if you treat him as he *were* what he *ought* to be, and could be, he *will* become tht *bigger* and *better* man." Biologist Hudson Hoagland states it in terms of social obligation: "In all human relations, accountability is a necessity . . . I cannot see how a modern society . . . can function unless the individuals believe they are free and responsible for their actions, and unless society can hold them responsible."[25]

Demand for a high level of performance is an important part of challenge and dissonance, particularly when it occurs in the context of recognizing the realities of performance. A study of the experience of teachers shows that not only does the best-liked professor influence the decision to teach, and not only does she serve as a professional ideal for young teachers to follow, but also that her demands have an effect on the kind of people the teachers become.[26]

People learn faster when they understand the broader context of the system and how their training is a part of it. People do not learn skills or knowledge in isolation; there is always a network of prior knowledge into which the new information fits. Thus, the more people know about their work, particularly about the demands on the organization, the more likely they are to want to improve their performance.[27] A welder, for example, may demonstrate little concern for quality control or the number of pieces he produces until he learns that the pieces he is welding are vital components of an airplane and that people may die if his work is done carelessly.

One study of managerial success led researchers to conclude that when a company demands high standards of performance from its management trainees in their first year with the organization, the trainees develop positive attitudes toward their work and internalize the high standards.[28] Once this happens, the prospective managers turn in strong performances. They then experience success, which in turn leads them to promotion to a more demanding job. Thus, these people rise in competence in keeping with the company's expectations of them. This causes some friction with those who do not aspire, but this friction is one of the costs of survival.

Demand, here, is the specific expectation that arises from identification with the ego ideal of the leader—his aspirations, goals, and values. These become the shared goals of the organization, lifting people above their immediate horizons toward the broader aim of the common good. This is the kind of demand that people, particularly the contemporary generation of young adults, want when they ask that the business have goals beyond the immediate one of profit. It is particularly important because the social purposes of the corporation, unlike some other kinds of institutions, are not self-evident. They have to be clearly and publicly stated before anyone can identify with them.

When confronted with a role model who holds high expectations and makes important demands, the subordinate aspires both to emulate her—and to succeed her. College students should be motivated to pursue continuing scholarship throughout their lives, based on a sound value system and independent thought. Professors, therefore, do more than transmit information. The issues for teaching in the academic world are psychologically relevant for the leader in the business world; the meaning of aspiration is the same in both spheres.

The emphasis on the ego ideal of the leader brings the

question of values sharply into focus. The issue has been largely ignored in the world of commerce except for discussions of right and wrong in business practice.[29] The value issue is much deeper than this. William D. Guth and Renato Tagiuri illuminate this issue by considering the relationship of values to corporate strategy.[30] Both executives and employees, they hold, are often unaware of their values and tend to misjudge those of others. The researchers define a "value" as an explicit conception of what an individual or a group regards as desirable. People select alternative courses of action on the basis of these stable personality characteristics. The key point that Guth and Tagiuri make is that individuals are uncommitted until they apply their code of beliefs to judgments and choices of alternative strategies. If not clearly aware of personal values, executives will make choices on the basis of them but without being aware that they are doing so, which may lead to unexpected consequences. The researchers argue that executives should examine their behavior from time to time to clarify what they stand for, and take time to analyze the situation when they find themselves excusing behavior "because our values differ." By clarifying their own values, executives open the avenues to understanding the values of others and make commitment possible. Without commitment, corporate strategy will not be implemented: the goals of the business need to fit the values of those who are involved in it or there can be no commitment at all.

It is important to distinguish between striving and achievement, and between striving and destructive competition. From a psychoanalytic perspective, Robert Waelder observes,

> Historical experience as well as psychological considerations suggest that there are crucial issues which have a particularly high potential of violence. These are the issues which defy calculations of risks and costs, issues which by their very nature tend to be *non-negotiable*, goods which escape the calculation of costs because they are considesred to be priceless. They are the issues involving *self-preservation, narcissism,* and *moral principles* . . . The most critical issues seem to be those which imply threats of death, of castration, or of moral death—or their latter day modifications and symbolic representations.[31]

Competition that is destructive has two characteristics. First, it exists between *competing individuals*, of which one wins a dominant position and the other is thereafter submissive. A pecking order is established. There is something almost biologically accurate in the old adage that the devil will take the hindmost. Second, when defeated, a person is psychologically destroyed. The defeat may be a devastating blow to a woman's self-image. It may consign a man to the economic scrap heap. It may communicate to someone that he is "finished." He may judge himself to be worthless or irreparably injured. With respect to "moral death" or severe threats to the superego, recent studies show that conflicts of values and ethics, because of the severe guilt they produce, are particularly difficult ones in business. Here, however, the focus is not on destructive competition but on rivalry directed to vanquishing reality problems collectively. The problem can be overcome.

In addition, subordinates compete with their own ego ideals and with those of their leaders. They work to make themselves more competent, not merely winners in an economic life-and-death struggle. Their active striving serves to help them master reality and to become better than their mentors. In this kind of rivalry, most people can learn to become stronger even from failure. If they should fail, they can obtain feedback about their competence to use in altering their direction and strengthening their position. This contrasts with the contemporary practice of putting people who fail on an "executive shelf" and regarding them thereafter as defeated. The organization should be both realistic and supportive; it is not an economic ogre that grinds people up in the interest of making a dollar. Competition with mutually established goals toward solving reality problems rarely destroys people. They are destroyed when the business becomes a modern-day gladiatorial arena where colleagues, struggling with one another for power, daily stand to lose their innermost sense of competence and self-respect.

The way in which people handle rivalry makes a difference in an organization. F. W. Richardson, an anthropologist at the University of Virginia, comments that the primary advantage of humans over all other animals has been their ability to divert internal dissension.[32] Humans have not abandoned

their savage ways, he says. Although there is universal competitiveness to serve real needs, there is also rivalry. "Unique
to humans, however, are the aggressions that arise when con-
versants compete for talking time," though such competition
certainly seldom has drastic results. This is not to say that jab-
bering simians are not trying to outjabber each other, but simply to point out that during an average day, monkeys rarely
spend more than a few minutes socializing and harassing one
another. Bureaucrats, executives, and administrators commonly spend five to eight hours of every day at it!

In speaking about spatial and temporal relationships, the
give and take of power relationships, and the dynamics of
conversation, Richardson points out that the "superior individual who monopolizes talk and initiative runs multiple risks
of being poorly informed and escalating dissatisfaction."

Some people appear not to be able to tolerate rivalry, and
they cause problems in other ways, too. Here is a common situation. A subsidiary has been losing money, and top management has decided that it must be turned around—fast. The
perfect candidate is found for the job. He is young, welcomes
the challenge, does the job single-handedly, and finishes it in
half the time expected. Anticipating a promotion, he proudly
presents his team of successors. Everybody is disappointed
with the people he has chosen. And now some capable people
from the subsidiary are beginning to leave. The whiz kid has
become a liability. Charismatic, take-charge leaders are attractive in a pinch because they can perform badly needed res-
cues. But they leave a lot of aggravation in their wake. Among
other things, executives must deal with the weak people these
leaders have gathered to do their bidding. Most of these people do not perform well, and the capable ones tend to leave at
an early stage.

The organization's goal, then, is not to stimulate life-or-
death competition, or, at the other extreme, to do away with
all signs of rivalry. Rather, with accompanying support from
superiors and organizational resources, it is to direct competition to the solution of real problems.

Two sources of affection accompany this kind of rivalry.
The first lies in the intensification of the cooperative relationship between subordinates and superior, which occurs as a result of their common interest in their task, their complemen-

tary relationship with respect to it, and the superior's empathy for the subordinate. Empathy is the ability to put oneself in another's position, to understand what he feels or why he must act in a given way in a particular situation. Research indicates that superiors who can empathize with the subordinate are more considerate of his needs in accomplishing the task.[33] Superiors who demonstrate greater consideration engage in more reciprocal two-way communication with subordinates. Such communication is itself a mark of affection.

The second source of affection lies in the approval of the ego ideal. In the course of its development, the ego ideal ultimately incorporates norms, ethics, and social ideals which become part of the person's aspirations.[34] The ego ideal begins to develop when children discover that they are not as omnipotent as they imagined they were. Reacting to their disappointment at discovering how small and powerless they are, children idealize parents, who are obviously bigger and more powerful than they. It seems that parents know everything and can do anything. The child identifies with them, creating an image representing them, their values, aspirations, and competence. The parents' standards are higher than their achievements, and the child's picture of the parents transcends their actual behavior. In trying to fit this image, the child strives to become as competent as they appear to be. Subsequently, the child identifies with the ideals of heroes, saints, and gods, and by doing so attempts to recover earlier feelings of omnipotence.[35]

At the same time that the image represents the parents, it is also a substitute for them. When the child succeeds, the image approves and grants the love that the parents would have given for the same achievement. The two processes of idealizing oneself and idealizing the power gradually become integrated into one goal.[36] When people meet some of the expectations of their ego ideal, they experience the applause of the ego ideal with relief, satisfaction, and increased self-respect.[37] The consciousness of deserving this love is felt as pride.

Winning the affection of the ego ideal is a more significant factor in occupational satisfaction and achievement than is commonly recognized. Much contemporary management literature on motivation is based on the concept of self-actualization, derived from the work of biologist Kurt Goldstein and others who elaborated similar concepts. Goldstein held that organisms have an inherent growth force.[38] Put simply, they try to become what they are biologically capable of becoming. Abraham Maslow, in turn, placed the need for self-actualization at the top of his list of psychological needs: "It refers to a man's desire for self-fulfillment, namely to the tendency for him to become actualized in what he is potentially. This tendency might be phrased as the desire to become more and more what one is, to become everything that one is capable of becoming."[39]

This direct transition from biological theory to psychological theory has omitted one major facet of the human personality that distinguishes humans from other organisms: their psychological capacity for holding a self-image and for incorporating an ego ideal.

People strive to become what they are capable of becoming. Unlike animals, however, people are not content with this achievement; therefore, self-actualization or self-fulfillment are not the highest needs. Even these needs exist in the service of another force: the ego ideal. People seek to meet the expectations of the ego ideal even when they have "fulfilled" or "actualized" themselves.

Ernest Hemingway and James Forrestal, for example, achieved self-actualization and self-fulfillment. Hemingway lived a rich, exciting, varied life in which he became a recognized master at his craft. Forrestal was equally prominent and influential in financial and political life. Yet both men committed suicide. Neither, according to their biographers, could live up to his ego ideal.[40] Neither could love himself for what he was.

People strive toward their ego ideals even at the cost of self-actualization or self-fulfillment. Many a man who has the potential for becoming a company president prefers to operate a farm. One often sees people whose talents for other activities are evident between the lines of prosaic accomplishments. They prefer it this way. Their present activity meets the needs of their superego. Other achievements, however possible and at whatever heights, would not.

One problem for young women today is that they are not sure which they prefer—professional life or family life—and are increasingly disenchanted as they find they cannot all be superwomen who handle marriage, motherhood, and a career simultaneously. Sociologist Suzanne Keller of Princeton emphasizes that the image of a superwoman is no more helpful than the earlier image of the unworldly and dependent housewife.[41]

Managerial efforts to motivate people based on self-fulfillment will be only partially successful. Sometimes they will fail dismally. Unless they provide opportunities for people to act in the service of their ego ideals, people will be disillusioned in the organization regardless of their self-actualization.

The key phrase here is "to act." People cannot meet the expectations of their ego ideals by being rewarded. They can meet some ego expectations this way, but not all of the demands of the ego ideal. Their activity toward the latter goal is their major reward. Concepts of participative management are valuable precisely because they enable people to act toward the fulfillment of their ego ideals. They permit people to like their own images of themselves.

No amount of self-actualization will metamorphose a man into a superman. He will never match the talents of legendary heroes or of the man he imagined his father to be. Only as he acts as he believes they would act does he fit himself to their pattern. As Freud said, "There is always a feeling of triumph when something in the ego coincides with the ego ideal."[42]

Consolidation

No one operates as a series of disparate parts or personality traits. One major difficulty of most contemporary personality theories, and the managerial applications derived from them, is that they view people as bits and pieces of psychological traits added together—aggressive or passive, masculine or feminine, introvert or extrovert. At best, their picture of a person is a profile; the predictions about behavior derived from such thinking are merely statements of the statistical likelihood that more people will tend to behave in a general way than another.

Just as a person is physiologically integrated, so she is psychologically integrated. It is not a matter of being integrated or not integrated, but rather of levels of integration.[43] A highly intelligent, effective leader has integrated her life experiences into a pattern that is more effective for adaptation and survival than that of a person of similar age and equal intelligence who is demoralized and on welfare.

Effective adaptation requires someone to consolidate lifelong experiences into a composite that is internally consistent, made up of complementary identifications, harmonious values, and gratifying avenues for mastery. According to Erik H. Erikson, adaptation also requires a person to find "a niche in some section of his society, a niche which is firmly defined and yet seems to be uniquely made for him. In finding it, the young adult gains an assured sense of inner continuity and social sameness which will bridge what he *was* as a child and what he is *about to become*, and will reconcile his *conception of himself* and his *community's recognition* of him"[44] Three of the seven stages of development outlined by Erikson (see Chapter 2) take place during adulthood. As adults mature, they are likely to seek greater intimacy or closer relationships with others in the form of friendship, combat, leadership, love, and inspiration. If they cannot move psychologically closer to others, they become preoccupied with themselves and, as a result, may be stunted in their psychological growth.

Adults who are able to develop greater intimacy, on the other hand, lay the groundwork for the next stage of development: generativity, the interest in establishing and guiding the next generation. People who do not reach this level of development, says Erikson, often begin to indulge themselves as if they were their own only child. Only when a person has evolved through these stages is it possible to achieve the final, integrative stage. "Only he who in some way has taken care of things and people and has adapted himself to the triumphs and disappointments of being, by necessity, the originator of others and a generator of things and ideas—only he may gradually grow the fruit of the seven stages."[45] The person who achieves such integrity accepts himself, accepts his life as his own responsibility, has a sense of comradeship with people of diverse origins and customs, and is ready to defend the dignity of his own life against physical and environmental threats.

Erickson adds that the identity formation of young people is fostered when those whose activities are significant to them give them a function and a status, and treat them as people whose growth and transformation are important. As a feeling of identity increases, they have a sense of well-being, of direction and assuredness that they will be recognized by those whose recognition is valued.

When a person can judge her own accomplishments and recognize how well she is living up to her ideal, she provides herself with a reservoir of self-gratification. She meets her own standards with contentment. As a result, she acts as an integrated entity. Her actions are in harmony with her aspirations and she feels approved of by her ego ideal for what she has done. She is, then, self-approving. She likes herself; she is an important source of affection for herself. This is not the self-inflation of the egocentric person, which is a compensation for feelings of incompetence and inadequacy, but rather honest self-regard for one's own nature and activities. By providing such gratification, the ego ideal supports the ego in dealing with the inevitable disappointments and frustrations of living.[46]

There is another important consequence of the development of the ego ideal. When children internalize the "parental function" represented by the ego ideal, as psychoanalyst Roy Schafer indicates, they become parents to themselves. By doing so, they acquire the basic equipment for later becoming parents to their children (and executive-teachers to their subordinates). They have values, aspirations, and goals to transmit, and motivation "for learning and perfecting a certain moral, protective and comforting know-how. This know-how is part of being grown-up."[47]

Interest in establishing and guiding the next generation is important to the organization that wants each person to contribute to the development of new talent. It is also important to the individual, who must teach the next generation in order to achieve the personal strength of his own consolidation.

Mastery, "ascendency or victory in struggle or competition," as the dictionary defines it, is a major motivating force in all people. Yet it needs to be coupled with realistic self-assessment. Executives frequently have to provide reality tests for subordinates whose ambitious striving outpaces their sense of realistic achievement. Part of the executive task is to help them understand their strengths and limits alike in order to encourage them to make their best efforts. Sometimes, in the process, they are faced with an awkward situation, as is the executive in this case.

"I am the vice-president in charge of real-estate operations in a $300 million corporation. I report to the senior vice-president of finance. I moved into my new role recently, having moved up steadily in the same organization. I have inherited Monte Forsythe, a likable, intelligent, kind, and unaggressive manager. Monte is about my own age (forty-nine), appears to be happily married, and has three children. At work he is a slow, methodical plodder, but he and I have gotten along well because we can talk quite openly about matters of mutual concern. He has been reporting directly to me for the past three months. During this time I have been aware of no friction between us.

"Some years ago, top management saw Monte as their 'fair-haired boy.' In fact, ten years ago the company sent him to the Amos Tuck school to earn his M.S. in management at company expense. As Monte already held a B.S. in civil engineering and had a number of years of excellent experience in our regional offices, he seemed to be headed directly toward one of the top spots in the organization. He seemed to be advancing nicely until about four months ago when he was transferred permanently to the home office.

"Monte has told me that the job he held before he came to work under me was an unhappy experience for him. Although he admits he may have been partly to blame for the experience, Monte basically feels he was assigned to do an impossible job, and that the company prevented him from accomplishing the goals he wanted. The job required a self-starter—someone with the talent and drive to accomplish tasks without much direct supervision. When I spoke with others who worked with Monte during this period, they implied through guarded responses that he seemed to lose his drive while he held this position.

"All Monte's experience has been in staff work, and until recently he had supervised only technical people. He now wants to move into a higher-management position with line responsibilities. Monte feels that his superiors don't think he can fill a line manager's job, but he says he 'won't buy' this attitude until he's given the opportunity to prove himself in one of these slots.

"Competition is really fierce in our organization. Top management positions do not open up with any frequency, and when they do, a lot of good people within the organization as well as a number of top-notch outsiders compete for these jobs. It seems to me that Monte is a perfect example of a corporate employee who functions well where he is, but who can't quite cut the mustard to make it to the top.

"How do I, as Monte's immediate superior, help him accept the fact that he may never attain the high goals that he—and perhaps the organization—expected? How specific should I be when I counsel him? How can I motivate him to work toward more realistic goals?"

Analysis

Where Is the Pain?   Obviously both Monte and the narrator are in pain.

When Did It Begin?   Apparently when Monte was in his previous job, although it would seem from the way the narrator describes Monte that he is hardly of top-management material.

Ego Ideal   Monte aspires to a top-management role with line responsibilities. Apparently he wants to please and to achieve.

Affection   Monte seems to be able to relate well to people and to invest a good deal of himself in his task.

Aggression   The narrator tells us that Monte is not particularly aggressive. Indeed, he seems not to have been competitive at all, but to achieve by mechanical plodding. Apparently he cannot be a self-starter. Apparently, too, he feels ill-at-ease directing the work of others.

Dependency   Apparently Monte is heavily dependent on his superiors for guidance and direction. He did very well until he got into a job requiring that he accomplish without much supervision.

Is It Solvable?   Possibly, but with a good deal of careful effort on the narrator's part.

How?   A likable but mechanical plodder certainly has no place in higher-level management. It is difficult for people who have executive aspirations to accept the fact that they are not the competitive and aggressive people they think they are. And, as the narrator indicates, it is equally difficult for a boss to confront such a person with the realities of his performance and opportunities.

One useful way to approach this problem would be for the narrator to ask Monte what he has accomplished in his jobs, with particular emphasis on the performances and achievements he takes particular pride in. What specific actions did he take in those roles that gave him satisfaction? What specific behaviors on his part demonstrated his competence? The boss can then ask the same questions about those roles in which Monte feels he did not perform as well as he would have liked. What did he have difficulty with? How did he go about solving problems? Why did these solutions not work?

The narrator may then point out that line executives are people who are comfortable putting forth ideas, initiating programs, and spontaneously attacking problems and directing others as may be necessary. By pointing out the difference between the kind of behavior required in a line job and particularly in a higher-level position, and the kind of behavior that Monte has described, he may help Monte form a more realistic ego ideal.

Just how does a line manager have to behave? What does he do day in and day out? Based on Monte's own assessment of his past work, does he or does he not characteristically behave in those ways? When the gap is clear between what Monte does well and what he expects, they can talk further about where Monte's career path should be headed and how his talents could best be used. If Monte needs supervision, the narrator can help him appreciate the fine work he can produce under those circumstances.

If the narrator cannot help Monte form a more realistic ego ideal and accept his psychological reality, and if Monte is terribly hard on himself, demanding a role that is impossible for him, the narrator should suggest that he seek professional help. He can vent some of his anger and frustration with himself for his failures, and then be in a better position to appreciate his strengths and successes.

PART 4

Moving with Change

Riding with change, managing change, is the organization's underlying mandate and the executive's primary task. Part Four, in addition to addressing some major changes, illuminates some of the mistakes that executives are likely to make in carrying out their task. These errors and conflicts, when recognized and enumerated, are like shoals marked on a map; though unseen they can be navigated more safely for having been located. The task thus becomes opportunity, and the shoals the demarcation of a route rather than a threat to survival.

THIRTEEN

Change:
The One Constant

mbiguity confronts business and industry today at every turn. Situations change so fast that stability cannot be guaranteed to anyone. The future is difficult to predict. Not only is this instability destructive to morale, it is threatening to the mental and physical health of people who have to tolerate these conditions.

In the animal world this is illustrated clearly. Chickens in a flock develop a pecking order. Each animal finds its place, and once this is established there is a certain equanimity in the group. A veterinarian experimented with repeatedly transferring chickens from one flock to another so that the pecking orders were constantly being disrupted, which kept the flocks in turmoil because no chicken could maintain a stable position. He found a much higher incidence of a virus-caused cancer in the experimental chickens than in the control group.[1] In a similar way, rotating work shifts upset people's biological rhythms and create many symptoms of stress, including digestive problems, menstrual disorders, colds, nervousness, fatigue, and insomnia, according to a government study.[2] Thomas Holmes and Richard Rahe, working with a social readjustment rating scale found that significant life changes—even those that bring happiness and prosperity—have a stress-producing potential.[3]

Managers who must assign people to shift work will probably find that the workers perform more efficiently and with better morale when shifts are regular, not rotating. But what is the implication for executives, faced with all the dimensions on which change may occur?

In the face of the uncertainties and even the physical side-effects generated by too much change, it is easy to develop a very change-resistant posture. In fact, there is evidence that American society has moved very far from the age of eager change agents. We have gone from a presidential cabinet of entrepreneurs to one of bureaucrats, according to Nicholas Lemann, editor of *The Washington Monthly*.[4] In Theodore Roosevelt's day the entrepreneur was widely respected. In the intervening years, the great organizations that were founded under Roosevelt have grown, prospered, and come to dominate our national life so that now the energies of ambitious people are channeled through them. As the economy has shifted from production toward providing services, it has come to reward expertise and universal skills more than innovation—hence the success of the bureaucrat. Bureaucrats acquire vested interests in the status quo and perform before an audience of potential employers. This, Lemann argues, is seen today as an absolute precondition of success.

In turn, this system produces a sluggish, change-resistant nation. Lack of change is stultifying, just as too much change is disruptive. The longer someone works in one company, the less likely it is that he will adapt well when he moves.

Seeing change solely as a threat, and not an opportunity, people attempt to deal with it by exercising control. They often try to cope with greater pressure from the inside by increasing tightness on the outside—working especially hard, controlling their emotions, fulfilling a rigorous schedule. But when control means keeping a lid on troublesome feelings, the pressure will build and break out. This approach hurts individuals and reduces their chances of adaptation. There is a limit to the extent to which controls can be applied to the process of change without doing damage to the idea of managing—not denying—change.

Managers, for instance, are taught to plan ahead and prepare for change. Whether they are developing new product lines, marketing strategies, or organizational development efforts, they think they ought to be able to forecast the effect of their initiatives. It is commonly believed that a manager's job is to implement change smoothly and see that it does not bring any rude surprises. James Brian Quinn of the Amos Tuck School at Dartmouth points out, however, that real change is not easily blueprinted. It "tends to *evolve* as internal decisions and external events flow together to create a new, widely shared consensus for action."[5] Too many executives browbeat themselves for neglecting to consider every aspect of a situation before they act. They feel inadequate and ashamed when something unexpected happens and they need to change course. Certainly, it is important to plan well enough to avoid unnecessary surprises. But no one can take every small detail into account or get a bird's-eye view of every situation. Psychologists often use a method called "successive approximation." Executives must often do the same. To paraphrase the poet Robert Burns, the best-laid plans of mice and men often bear last-minute revisions.

Because organizations change so rapidly that it is hard to know how long anyone will be in an organization, another question arises: to what do employees commit themselves? In the past, people often committed themselves to an organization, saying in effect, "I'll be whatever you want me to be and put my career in your hands." People used to be able to identify with a product, a function, or a service. But organizations can no longer accept responsibility for the length of a person's career, nor can a person trust an organization to do so, if only because of the inadequacy of most organizational records and the transiency of the men and women in managerial and executive roles.

Changes in Middle Management

Change is a feature of life at every stage in management. It may be actual change, keenly experienced, or change dimly perceived as a cloud on the horizon. It may even be camouflaged by a situation apparently so stable and static that a significant alteration is all but unthinkable. Important actors may delude themselves into believing that the unthinkable will never happen.

Nevertheless, some developmental phases in executive progress—as in adult progress—are more conspicuously marked by changes than others: the long period of middle-management is one. The various demands and ambiguities of the middle-management role cause their own brand of stress. For many, this phase coincides with important personal demands of midlife. Executives who are motivated to support those under their supervision during this time can profit by developing a clearer picture of what the stresses are and where they come from, in order to provide the understanding and direction that will be most constructive.

Some of the stresses are felt by men and women as they first move into middle management. Vaguely uncertain about which skills and abilities they are transferring to their new roles and which they must leave behind, they need time and counsel to learn how to behave in their new positions.

One can sense a growing disquiet among executives promoted to higher-level administrative roles. Previously highly successful operators, and now in roles in which operators report to them, they miss the excitement of hands-on operation. They are frequently uneasy because they cannot get direct feedback on their performance as they did when they were operators. These "doers" are capable of the higher-level abstractions they are now called upon to work with, but they are less comfortable with the ambiguity they must now face. Their dependence on others has increased. They must spend more time in planning, in looking ahead, in public-relations responsibilities, and in showing the corporate flag to its many constituencies. They are not content with accepting their success as an indication of their capability. They seem to need to continue to confirm themselves, but this has become more difficult.

People who are moving into such roles should have the opportunity to talk over the loss of their operating images. They could well use help establishing their own benchmarks and defining modes of penetrating the ambiguity. Unfortunately, because of their success, nobody thinks of this need.

There is a particular problem when the man or woman moving into middle management has a dual loyalty to the profession as well as to the organization: it often seems as if the profession comes first. This is because professional people tend to move up first through the profession. Consequently, they are less likely to consider management as seriously as they might, especially if they are not immediately involved in the problems the organization faces and are left isolated in their professional activities—a problem that is increased by the large turnover of professional and technical people.

Helping professionals make this shift calls for a great deal of group discussion. They need to be able to identify with common purposes and strategies. They may need transitional counseling to enable them to give up some of their technical identification and identify with managerial roles. They need greater knowledge and understanding about people's behavior and about the motivational issues involved in leadership and supervision, and they need help with the specific problems of adaptation, whether at the entry level or the transitional level.

People entering middle management would have an easier time adapting their previous skills, and synthesizing from their past experience the abilities they should bring with them, if the roles they were moving into were clearly defined. Often, however, there is considerable ambiguity about the new role. "Executive vice-president" may sound convincing, but how does the title translate into tasks? Five managers, like five blind men trying to describe an elephant by touch, will write five different descriptions. And the larger the organization, the more room there is for ambiguity. The executive vice-president is not in charge of long-range planning and strategies: this is the chairman's job. He is not in charge of running any of the lower divisions (much as he may long for the days when he did): this is the job of the lower division heads who report to him. Unclear about what they should or shouldn't be doing, executives in this dilemma are likely to intrude too much. Or else, feeling helpless, they retreat into their offices, occasionally emerging to deal with some crisis. Their profile of activity begins to look like that of a transatlantic jet pilot: eight hours of boredom followed by ninety seconds of terror. They can only respond to the crisis if (1) it is brought to their attention in time, (2) they are familiar with the situation that produced it and the possible resources to be mastered or strategies to be implemented, and (3) they can act quickly. Otherwise, they are likely to be in the position of the Red Sox coach who is criticized for not pulling people out and replacing them fast enough.

"How to use human resources" is the core question during transitions of this kind. The main problem is structural: determining what the task of this middle-management post should be. How well the transitions are carried out after that (in other words, how well the person fits with the job) can be affected by the way in which the job is described.

At the other end of middle management are the problems felt by people leaving to move on to the rarefied aeries of top management. They, too, are concerned about what they are leaving behind, especially for the people. Miles Shore, director of the Massachusetts Mental Health Center, underscores the importance of those concerns. He reports the reactions of young psychiatrists who were leaving as chiefs of their respective sections after completing their professional training.[6] The topic under discussion was "How are your people and staffs taking your imminent departure?" The young psychiatrists talked about a wide range of reactions. Chief among them was their own guilt about not having done well enough in their roles, about leaving behind "unprotected" people whom they felt they should have served better and left better fortified against institutional and societal forces. They regretted that they did not know at the beginning of their administrative careers what they now knew upon leaving them. They talked about their initial urge to impose order on an organizational system. Some kept trying, but others soon decided the system was too big for them. In effect, with very powerful ego ideals, they themselves inevitably were dissatisfied with a system that could not be perfect.

For those presently in middle-management posts, there is the pervasive problem of alienation. Men and women are no longer in the more communal line of technical positions and may be subtly excluded from the informal communication networks at that level. At the same time, they really do not want to be: they look up to and identify with top management. But top management frequently fails to recall what it was like along the way. It is very remote in most cases from the day-to-day operations, from the front-line context of marketing, sales, service, or production. The distancing factor is an important one, because it impedes understanding. One study found that top executives proved harsher disciplinarians than lower-level managers.[7] The investigators asked seven levels of management from five electric companies to rate cases involving infractions of rules by hourly workers. The greatest variability of decisions appeared at the lowest level, where supervisors could take *context* into account. Management is generally permeated with a reward-and-punishment philosophy of motivation. The less in touch a manager is with his people, the stronger the assumption that people are basically motivated by the desire to obtain rewards and avoid punishment. When upper-level management generates policy after policy based on such an assumption, its fulfillment is practically ensured. People respond to these expectations in kind. Thus, by underestimating their own influence on their subordinates, managers often waste their most valuable resource.

Not surprisingly, differences in assumptions and expectations exist among people at different levels of middle management, as well as between them and top management. An informal study conducted by some corporate graduate students revealed that upper- and lower-level middle managers see isues of career development in different lights. Upper middle managers think that operating experience is an important asset for continued advancement in a large organization, while lower middle managers think that it is overrated and that fewer opportunities for advancement exist than the upper-level managers believe. The lower-level people also think bosses overestimate how much time they need to learn a rotational assignment, and they want the assignments to be better defined. Lower-level managers think that they would be best prepared for rotational assignments if they were briefed on the new jobs by their predecessors, but the upper-level managers think they should brief the new people.

These findings indicate that there is not enough communication between upper and lower middle management. The result is that grossly different perceptions of reality are operating at each level. This informal study suggests that middle managers (as well as those at the top) should talk more with people two levels below them. Even more important, they should listen to people below them and find out what they are feeling. People who move up a few notches are in much the same position with regard to subordinates as parents who have forgotten what it is like to be an adolescent. Unless they are willing to inform themselves about the situation, they are not going to understand what is going on.

In most companies there is a two-generation gap between the top and the bottom. The middle-management layer, which should be the communication link, rarely serves this purpose.

Middle managers are generally so preoccupied with not making waves, for fear of jeopardizing a possible promotion, that they neglect interaction with subordinates. Those below the middle, assuming that top management is busy with more important matters, muddle along by themselves. To counteract this gap, top management must model the behavior they expect of middle management by continually questioning middle managers about the problems their subordinates are up against and what these subordinates need from higher management to help them cope. In addition, top management should assess how the organizational structure and reward system encourage middle managers to focus upward rather than on the problems at hand.

And yet, there *is* real power at the middle level of organizations. *Washington Monthly* editor Charles Peters calls it "subordinate power" and says that subordinates who point out errors, make suggestions, or protect their bosses from embarrassing mistakes wield great influence. Subordinates also have great power to do ill—as when they pad expenses, drag their feet, or pass carelessly performed work on to the next department.[8]

Why is the middle level so powerful in organizations? Because this is where the heart of their functioning is and where the changes that affect entire organizations can be initiated. A middle manager who initiates new performance-appraisal standards can sometimes affect the productivity and atmosphere of a company more significantly than the CEO can. And even when CEOs take actions that ripple throughout their organizations, they are largely dependent on the people lower down—the specialists and speechwriters and consultants who often have significant influence on what CEOs say and do. To make the most of this organizational resource, however, executives need to understand more about the middle-management situation and the pressures it engenders, stay in closer touch with these subordinates, and give them support based on a realistic knowledge of the challenges they face.

Midlife and Middle Management

Men and women may move into middle management at any time. Because of talent, chance, the particular requirements of an organization, exquisite mentoring, or some combination of any of these, individuals may find themselves in middle-management roles in their twenties or early thirties. Often, however, because the rate of personal growth and development usually coincides with the rate of progress through an organization's hierarchy, people are surrounded by the demands and difficulties of middle management at around the same time that they are feeling the strains of midlife.

Today the stages of adult life are no longer treated as minor phases in a development that has already reached its peak at eighteen or twenty. Investigators are now able to look differently at life events that were acknowledged as important and troubling long before adult development earned status as a legitimate field of inquiry. In midlife, family changes occur. Marriages, not infrequently, cool. Adults see their children enter adolescence (with all that this entails—primarily, forcing parents to confront the unfinished business of their own adolescent years) and then leave home. The children's departure may also remove an easy role definition for some parents, and the glue for some marriages. Or it may remove an important source of conflict between parents and—if conflict over children was not their only bond of communication—leave them better able to explore the other bonds.

If changes in the balance among members of a family group seem to dominate, they may not, after all, be the most salient. It is the questions that adults in midlife have about themselves that ultimately cause the greatest shifts in balance. There are three in particular that encompass the individual both as a private person and as a professional; their rumblings, often barely felt at forty, can come to drown out much of the sound of daily private and work life by the time the individual reaches fifty or fifty-five.

"What haven't you achieved that you had expected to?" is the first question people in midlife ask themselves. They ask it no matter what they have achieved. The plant foreman asks it. The neurosurgeon earning $200,000 a year asks it. No matter how "well" people have done on some counts, they know that on other dimensions they have not lived up to their promise. People have multiple expectations of themselves, not just one. Even if someone seems to have pursued one line of expectation relentlessly and successfully, this does not mean that no other hopes have been lurking on the sidelines. On the contrary: the more single-minded someone has been in pursuing one avenue of endeavor throughout early working years, the more likely it is that other dreams will stir when that person reaches forty or forty-five. Highly educated people are under greater pressure to accomplish more in their lifetimes than others, perhaps because they demand more and expect more of themselves. The result is that they are more easily frustrated.

A survey of middle managers in Bell Telephone reveals interesting insights about careers after twenty years. New managers entering the Bell system at the bottom rung were recruited into a "management progress study" in the 1950s (so the sample includes only white males and no women or minorities). Twenty years later "successful" managers—those who reached the fourth or fifth rungs of management in the organization—shared common characteristics. They had important managerial abilities and were highly motivated to use them; they were deeply involved in work; their personalities emphasized achievement and leadership along with a wish to be independent and free from the demands of others. Those who were most successful were likely to give work first place in their lives. And (this was one surprise) they were somewhat indifferent to friendships and, in spite of their success, aggressively hostile.[9]

A second problem in midlife concerns the organization's ability to give life meaning. It is articulated in a question that the individual poses (usually in silence) to the organization: "What did I have that I do not have now?" The earlier excitement of challenge, mastery, and promotion fades. In addition, when the economy is slowing, prospects for promotion, with or without excitement on the part of the middle manager, are far less frequent. On top of disillusionment and a dull sense of disappointment, managers may feel a keener resentment: betrayal. This turns into active dissatisfaction with the organization which was supposed to fight city hall and which—like parents before—turns out to be not nearly as protective and powerful as once thought. Dealing with these feelings in subordinates requires understanding and skill on the part of executives, and often a degree of second sight. The feelings are unlikely to be voiced directly but only acted out in behavior that is negative, withdrawn, disruptive, cynical, even irresponsible.

Too many managements try to "motivate" middle-aged middle managers by holding out prospects for promotion, but the managers are not fooled. They know there are not enough places for most people to move up. One study of a major organization showed that many managers respond to the midlife crisis by withdrawing into their own narrow work worlds and investing themselves only in their immediate tasks. They also withdraw from friends and community activities, becoming more dependent on the company and their families.

As they reach middle age, these managers want more autonomy. It is harder for them to accept being told what to do. They often become hostile toward others, usually as a displacement of their disappointment in themselves. Their career paths have narrowed to the point where they can no longer succeed by conforming. As a result, they use their talents less fully than they used to.

Middle-aged middle managers who can no longer move up should not be offered false promises. They are fortunate when they find satisfaction in their work, and bosses should support these positive feelings. Executives who want to motivate midlife managers further should look at their personality needs. Dependent people respond to nurturance and guidance. Others respond to social relationships, or to the chance to teach and guide others, earning the respect and gratitude of young protégés. But some middle-aged middle managers will not respond to these or any other motivations. When this happens, bosses have no choice but to spell out the options for these people. They need to talk over the import, impact, and implications of the situation and their feelings about them. These people need to vent their anger and disappointment. Executives can then help them think through what they have learned and how they feel about it, so they can make choices in their own best interests.

A third problem is one that has troubled thoughtful aging people throughout human history: coming to terms with their own mortality. It is articulated in silence, in pantomime, and aloud to oneself ("What? Not here forever?") and to the family, organization, and world at large ("What—is *this* all there is?"). This is an important reason why surveys about people's work satisfaction are contradictory and will continue to be so: they miss the fundamental psychological question behind people's dissatisfaction—their fear of death.

Many surveys report that 80 percent of people questioned say that they are happy with their jobs. But in response to other surveys, which ask if they would change occupations if they could, 60 percent of the people questioned say they would. When we ask people if they are satisfied with their work, we are, in fact, asking them to evaluate how they feel about themselves at that moment (self-image) and how they see themselves at their ideal best (ego ideal). We are implicitly asking what they expect, how they compare themselves with others, what they hoped for in life, and about many other feelings. Few people are satisfied with themselves. Most are highly self-critical.

When they are angry with themselves, as happens when the gap between the ego ideal and self-image widens, they are likely to spill this aggression over onto their work, which is a major source of self-esteem. Organizations foster this kind of dissatisfaction. They do so when they make people feel helpless or demeaned by moving them arbitrarily, reducing their status; when the organizational pyramidal structure, with its emphasis on winners and losers, leaves people feeling defeated and useless; and when they do not effectively take into account, in assignment, the behavioral consequences of aging.

"What—is this all?" is really the other side of the question "What—not here forever?" Too many people assume that after they "make it" in middle age, they are going to die; when they discover they have not died, they wonder, "Now what?" This is what James I. Adams of Stanford calls the "delayed death syndrome."[10] These people, he says, are not quite sure what to do after they arrive, and it is at this point that they become driven to change their fields of interest. Adams thinks that they have to change their style of thought as well as their interests. He asks his students to do three things: write a poem, design a lamp, and solve a mathematical problem. He notes that people can do one, but not the other two, indicating that we all have intellectual specialities and get involved in rutted thinking. We can change, when we are compelled to, by some sudden awakening.

Writing about work, aging, and social change, Seymour Sarason notes that someone can be alienated from work but still be satisfied with the job because it is better than other jobs—it has a certain kind of social anchoring and gratification, even if it is no longer stimulating.[11] Other people, perceiving the work as good, view the person who withdraws from it as neurotic. Most would ask these professionals, "How can you be so dissatisfied when you have so much?" These attitudes make it difficult for people to make changes (quite aside from the economic considerations they must take into account) and help account for the increase in depression among professional people. These people cannot proclaim their dissatisfactions or doubts because to do so is tantamount to questioning the significance of their life and future, to appear to others as "deviant," and to raise questions about their own personal stability.

Realizing the complex issues faced by midlife managers in middle-management roles, executives will more easily understand that in some cases the managers' way of handling the problems, stresses, and changes is by undertaking yet another major change—a change not just in jobs but in careers. That changing careers is a profound wrench is aptly illustrated in interviews with William Damroth, cofounder of Lexington Research and Management Corporation, and with Wheelock Whitney, former CEO of Dain, Kalman & Quail.[12] The interviews show that people making changes must expect severe psychological upheaval, a period of despondency and depression, and a long period of self-doubt before they regain their upward momentum. Psychological help, in the cases of both Damroth and Whitney, was instrumental in enabling them to make their career changes.

Executives who leave high-paying jobs in midlife and mid-career to go on to other things have been highly publicized by both the press and television. One of the reasons for all this publicity is that so few really make these changes, despite the impression that many executives do. Those who have made this choice usually have been successful executives who have other things they want to do and who have the monetary resources to do them. David Krantz studied people in Santa Fe who had changed their careers.[13] He found that the majority of respondents came from reasonably secure middle-class backgrounds. People with such backgrounds are more comfortable in changing careers or less fearful of the consequences, which is why there is unlikely to be much change in this direction except among people who have, in some fashion, already made it and can afford to either reduce their standard of living or live on what they have earned, saved, or inherited.

Krantz does argue that the imperative of one career is less potent than before and that changes in career directions will occur much before mid-career. Obviously, the more preparation and planning there has been, the more likely it is that a career change will be successful. Management consultants advise people to start thinking about developing second careers in midlife so they may leave organizations when they wish and not run the risk of being pushed out early or being unprepared for transitions in the economy. They often ask, "Well, what shall I do? All I know is management."

People thinking of alternative careers might seriously consider service organizations. These are organizations, such as consulting firms and hospitals, that perform personal services. Even restaurants are primarily service organizations. Theodore Leavitt of Harvard cites McDonald's as an example. McDonald's, in developing its fast-food approach, applied the same systematic modes of analysis, design, organization, and control as those used in the manufacturing process, to make use of unskilled machine tenders and to produce a reliable product at great speed and very low cost.[14]

When considering a second career, executives can ask what service they would like to render. How would they go about organizing it? How would they define the advantage of what they are going to do as against what is presently available? What kind of gap would they fill? Who needs it? And at what level of sophistication are their skills required?

It is the practical art of management—identifying problems and opportunities, defining goals and purposes, selecting the means, marshaling resources, motivating, energizing, directing, measuring, controlling and rewarding worker performance—that makes all economic progress possible, says Leavitt. Management skills are useful everywhere, but it is necessary to choose the right plan to use them fully.

Helping Subordinates Plan for Retirement

There are changes that require counsel and accommodation when people enter an organization, when they change positions, and when they assume middle-management roles. All of these transitions can be managed more smoothly by executives who are aware of the difficulties that their subordinates face and who are sensitive to feelings that the subordinates experience but may not be able to express directly. In the same way executives can make the most of the human resources available to them by skillful management, rather than studied evasion or mismanagement of older subordinates who are looking ahead to retirement.

Strategies designed to use fully the best talents in the organization arise from taking into account the specifics of personalities and situation, and this may mean working to counteract cultural prejudice against older executives. Older executives sometimes do become less flexible, it is true, although it may not be for the reason commonly given. Everyone has encountered the aging person who cannot remember what happened last week, but recalls with vivid clarity an experience of many years ago. While brain damage due to the aging process has often been cited as the cause of this behavior, Dr. Tobias Brocher offers another explanation. He suggests that as a person ages he is increasingly surrounded by young people with whom he has little in common. He also experiences the loss of friends, social contacts, and other cues that reaffirm his identity. As a result, he begins to lose his identity and retreats to his previous world, acting as if his environment had not changed.[15]

Aging leaders who continue in their leadership roles may become quite rigid and may insist that their younger subordinates do things the way they have always been done. This withdrawal from younger people means that those in older age ranges become increasingly obsolete and go off in directions that are less and less relevant to the organization.

There is also the question of whether decision-making performance is related to age or to experience. Ronald N. Taylor studied a group of male line managers ranging in age from 23 to 57 to seek an answer to this question.[16] He found that older managers tended to gather more information and to diagnose the value of the information more accurately and quickly than younger managers, regardless of previous experience. They did have some difficulty in coming to a decision, showing less confidence in their decisions and more flexibility in altering them.

The studies of Brocher and Taylor suggest that differences in life stages, rather than processing abilities, are the significant factor. Young managers can successfully deny both their dependency on others and their mortality. They are growing and doing things. As people grow older and noticeably less capable physically, they become more dependent on higher authority to be kept and not discarded.

All executives who have reached the integrity phase of life (fifty-five and older) need to make special efforts to be engaged with younger people, to hear what they have to say, and to learn about the new techniques and skills they bring to the organization. The heavy emphasis on youth in our culture constantly threatens older executives and acts as a damper on their potential contribution to an organization. Mutual reinforcement can counteract this cultural emphasis and bring out the benefits of their greater depth of experience.

An approach that expects more is likely to get more, and efforts to use older executives in varied and productive ways are likely to reap greater benefits for the organization than an approach that belittles or discourages their contributions. One well-known company, for instance, has a "target age" of fifty-five for helping executives toward retirement. At this point, when many men and women feel that they are still highly productive, the company puts them to work as both internal and external consultants to begin to wean them away from the company.[17]

Although fifty-five is the theoretical beginning of the integrity phase, all people are not ready for such roles at this age. And organizations are becoming increasingly guilty of forcing early retirements without adequate performance appraisal or consideration for the possible effects of managerial action on the employee's mental health. An example is the decision of the U.S. District Court of New Jersey in the case of *Rogers et al.* v. *Exxon Research and Engineering Company.*[18] Rogers, who had been employed by the company since 1938, was retired at age sixty by Exxon. Rogers experienced severe abdominal pain, vomiting, and impotency as a result of the emotional stress following his compulsory retirement. He died three and a half years later. The jury awarded Rogers' family $750,000 plus court costs, which the court found to be excessive, reducing the final award to $260,000 and costs. Perhaps the most important part of the case lies in the court's reasoning as enunciated by U.S. District Court Judge Herbert J. Stern:

> It is difficult enough for anyone to encounter and to surmount the psychological and physiological problems of the aging process. Simultaneously to find oneself arbitrarily discharged because the clock has struck a certain hour adds sustantially, as the evidence demonstrated here, to these already formidable stresses. The cumulative effect of an arbitrary and illegal termination of the useful and productive older employee is a cruel blow to the dignity and self-respect of one who has devoted his life to productive work and can take a dramatic toll . . . The court is aware that the most pernicious effect of age discrimination is not to the pocketbook, but to the victim's self-respect. In this case, the out-of-pocket loss occasioned by such discrimination is often negligible in comparison to the physiological and psychological damage caused by the employer's unlawful conduct.

What this says, in short, is that organizations are going to have to be more sophisticated and sensitive to psychological issues for subordinates encountering change at all levels and stages.

Organizations never stop changing—expanding to supply new markets, introducing new technologies, increasing efficiency, outmaneuvering the competition. But it seems that no matter how or why managements go about effecting change, they fail to take into account the two factors—their human resources and the damaging psychological effects of change—that disrupt their forward motion and prevent them from achieving desired goals. Only after mourning a loss does the reconstitution process begin.

The impact of change, whenever it occurs, is widely felt and frequently disruptive, as illustrated by the case below. Senior officers are ultimately responsible for helping their subordinates settle down and perform effectively. How they do it, and how well, will depend on the situation, the personalities, and the insights and resources they can bring to bear on the changed environment. Some of the strategies outlined here can be useful in other situations, as well.

"My company, a manufacturer of consumer goods, operates throughout a five-state region and has thirty-two thousand employees. We have always been organized into these five geographical areas, with only loose direction from our corporate offices in Chicago. Each division was headed by a vice-president, with a general manager who ran the various departments within the division. Because of the differences in state work practices, culture, and climatic conditions, there was no standard procedure for getting things done. The result was that the vice-presidents, the general managers, and the people who worked in the plants were able to run their own shows. One of the problems with this, of course, was that the staff people felt they had little or no impact on the corporation and little chance of advancement to the upper echelons of the company.

"About three years ago, our entire organization was reorganized by a new CEO, who decided to implement a 'hands-on' type of management. Rather than have five units operating nearly autonomously, he retained the facilities but changed their functions. Consolidation of effort was the byword, with the result that, for example, the soap and detergent plant, instead of handling its own customer complaints, would now just manufacture products. The sole and glove-leather unit would concentrate on production, but its sales force would be integrated with the sales forces of the other divisions, where control and market forecasting could be handled by people more expert in the field.

"The new CEO also set up a staff to give directives to the other units. They prepare policies, procedures, and training manuals, and keep in constant communication with the plants.

"This new, centrally controlled company, based on uniform methods of operation, has created a group of unhappy and nearly rebellious vice-presidents and general managers, who feel they have lost their authority and with it the imeptus to be innovative.

"I am the senior officer over these people, and I'm committed to the new CEO's concept of a directive staff. I've noticed, however, that the staff members, who felt so out of things prior to the reorganization, have, on more than one occasion, been overdirecting. They are young people with excellent training, but they really haven't been with the company long. The older people resent these 'mavericks' and are pressuring me to give them back their old authority and autonomy. The young staff people are full of vitality—innovative and 'busting' to do their jobs, while the others seem to be sitting tight, hoping we'll 'get back to doing things the right way.' What can I do to make the reorganization work, keep our older people happy, and not lose any of the good, albeit unseasoned, new staff people?"

Analysis

Where Is the Pain?   Apparently everybody has pain, including the narrator who is responsible for making the organization work.

When Did It Begin?   With the advent of a new CEO.

Ego Ideal   The ego ideals of the line and operating people involved are significantly related to their freedom to function and to run their own shows. The ego ideals of the staff people usually have more to do with the operation of their particular technical expertise, as well as advancement based on demonstration of this expertise.

Affection   Apparently people were previously able to work together in a relatively informal, mutually supportive way, although there was hostility between line and staff. At the moment, there does not seem to be much affection, but rather a group of unhappy, rebellious line operators.

Aggression   Much of the aggression seems to be channeled into resistance to change, resentment and hostility to the mavericks, and the attack by the mavericks on those people who needed to be shown all along how to manage.

Dependency   Under such conditions there are no adequate interdependent relationships, although the mavericks are now compelling the line people to depend upon them. There is little indication of interdependence among the operating units, and certainly not between line and staff.

Is It Solvable?   Yes.

How?   Whatever the changes in an organization, some people are going to win and some are going to lose. These problems are likely to be more acute when those who lose are in line operations. The line always looks on staff as a nuisance, partly because people in staff roles rarely have had much in the way of training for leadership, or supervisory and consultation experience. Staff functions tend to be more intellectual than action-oriented, and staff people have a tendency to look down on line people if the latter are more limited in education or more set in their behavior patterns because of age or experience.

In an organizational change of this type, it is critically important for the CEO to meet with the managers and executives as a group. He should outline the history of the organization for them, explaining what has come about and why, the particular problems presently being faced, and what the future holds. People can then talk over what he has said, make sure that they understand exactly what he intended, question him, and look at how they might cope with the issues being raised. This provides an opportunity to come to terms with the present reality. The group can then talk about who should do what about the problems they are facing and how they need to deal with them. Everyone in the organization should recognize the four steps in managing crisis: (1) impact, (2) recoil-turmoil, (3) adjustment, and (4) reconstruction. This allows people to plot where they are and to see that their reactions are normal.

Essentially, since all change is loss, the narrator must deal with loss—loss of power as well as loss of self-image.

It is also vitally important to examine what the historic psychological contract has been and what are perceived to be violations of it. The contract must be renegotiated on the basis of the new realities within the organization.

If the CEO cannot be prevailed upon to conduct such a two- or three-day meeting, the narrator might gather his own people to explain what has happened and why, answer as many questions as he can, hear people out, and then convey their feelings to higher management.

FOURTEEN

You Can't Win Them All

What should executives do with the "jet" who asks sharp and incisive questions, unerringly gets to the heart of the problem and solves it, but intimidates peers with tactless remarks, antagonizes superiors by showing little patience with elementary questions, and bullies subordinates? Such abrasive people stubbornly resist change because their passion for excellence masks a desperate need to be perfect.

What should executives do with a rigidly meticulous manager who performs excellently, who understands every detail of the work, and who is impeccably dependable and thorough—but who refuses to teach subordinates anything? There is no point in telling such managers to delegate responsibility. Reasoning, persuading, urging, and cajoling will not work. These people withhold from others because they fear losing their jobs if others know what they do.

What should executives do with insensitive but technically competent managers who make life miserable for the people who work for them? Their bosses think that somehow they have failed as leaders, and want to find the right thing to say to make these managers change. But rigid, insensitive people are not going to change. The executive can talk to such people again and again, but they will refuse to hear and will not accept advice to change their behavior. The executive must then decide whether to put up with them the way they are or to get rid of them.

Executives frequently hold themselves responsible for subordinates' personality problems that cannot be solved, if at all, by managerial efforts. At the same time, they fail to see what they are doing that contributes to organizational malfunction. Executives try to help people by pounding them into shape as if they were loosening the fibers in a steak, or by trying to soak them in a psychological marinade to soften them up. But when psychological problems are deeply ingrained, they will not go away. These people have always been and will always be the way they are, and the sooner executives recognize this fact, the better it will be all around. But bosses must be more willing to face the hard decisions that follow.

This kind of situation is common—in fact, it is practically a managerial plague. The widespread use of management consultants for every conceivable purpose and the consequent recurrent reorganization of businesses testify to the extent of the problem, reflecting the chronic pain of management, enormous dissipation of human energy, and the palliative nature of the attempted cures. Karl Menninger coined the term "polysurgical addiction" to describe people who repeatedly demand operations to cure their multiple, repetitive complaints.[1] It would not stretch the analogy to speak of "polyconsultative addiction" to describe this common mode of solving managerial problems.

If some problems defy solution within the organization, others are amenable to change—given a changed perspective on the dynamics of interaction among the people in the organization. Psychotherapists Augustus Napier and Carl Whitaker speak of the process of family therapy as the "family crucible" in which patterns of behavior can be changed and the family, functioning as a system, can be recast.[2] In a similar way, management consultants can provide an "organization crucible" by making visible to the group the existing patterns of behavior and pointing out options for change. The irony is that the executive often already has the power to cope with managerial problems without individuals or the organization undergoing "therapy," especially if the main problems are of the executive's own, if inadvertent, making.

Managing Aggression

Three common managerial failures—encouragement of power-seeking, failure to exercise controls, and stimulation of rivalry—derive from the executive's inability or reluctance to recognize and manage aggression. It is easy to understand how executives can fall into the pattern of encouraging power-seeking. No single kind of subordinate pleases superiors as much as the person who is able to assume responsibility during a crisis, plunge into the task with zest, and accomplish it successfully. Usually these are talented, energetic managers who have considerable ability and even more promise. They become the "jets" of industry. Sometimes they rescue part of the organization from failure or produce outstanding results in resolving difficult problems almost single-handed.

Higher management naturally rewards such men and women for their capacity to attack and solve problems, and encourages them in their wide-ranging pursuit of personal power. But then, at a certain point, management abruptly changes the signals: from that moment on further advancement hinges not on what they can do individually but on their ability to lead others.

It is at this juncture that highly important, talented people become problems. As "hard drivers" they have dominated their staffs, concentrating decision making in their own hands while exerting heavy pressure on subordinates. They have been authoritarian.[3] Their individual achievements have resulted in promotion. For a while, their track record obscures the fact that they are now destroying some part of the organization, or at best failing to build it, since they are unable to coach and develop subordinates. "They could be outstandingly successful if only they could work with people," others observe. But since they cannot, ultimately they have to leave their companies or are doomed to the continued frustration of their ambitions. Do they have trouble working well with others because of the kind of people they are or because of organizational pressures to produce? Usually both.

Senior executives have several alternatives. If they are primarily concerned with building an organization and making it possible for managers to assume greater responsibility, then, contrary to popular conceptions, the leaders must provide for close supervision, directed toward helping managers support their subordinates and reward them, rather than toward individual productivity. Some of the jets may not be able to work in harness and will have to leave, but at least they will leave before they have come to believe that they can succeed in the organization by vigor alone, and before management develops unrealistic expectations about their future careers.

A second problem is the failure to exercise controls. Senior executives often seem to condone behavior that grossly exceeds the bounds of common courtesy. The result is devastating to those on the receiving end and detrimental to the organization. Out-of-bounds behavior is more hostile than creative, although an inventive person may also be antagonistic. People who are so hostile as to be destructive vent their anger all around them—at colleagues, subordinates, and superiors. Unnecessarily critical, they argue too long and too much. They are rude to others and flay at their working environment.

It is sometimes difficult to determine how much of this behavior is triggered by conflicts in the organization. The senior executive's failure to exercise adequate control is particularly evident when self-centeredness is the offender's most conspicuous trait. Self-centeredness takes the form of exploiting and attacking others as the managers try to maintain and increase their status. These people are different from others who are authoritarian and directive: they are more manipulative and more obviously concerned with their own aggrandizement. Often they seem not to care what they do to others in the process. Authoritarian executives, more frequently, are sympathetic to others in a paternalistic way.

The astonishing aspect of both the angry and the self-centered executives is the way in which they are able to intimidate others with impunity. Sometimes these problems are permitted to go on for years, especially when the executive has some particular skill or talent that the organization needs. Even when senior executives know that such behavior is destructive to the organization, the subordinates, and the person, they often permit it to continue, excusing it as "temperament" or explaining it as "the problem he has with creative people."

People vent their spleen or exhibit their self-centeredness for varying reasons. It may be a way of demonstrating power or of getting attention (since for some people, any attention is better than none). Anger or self-centeredness can express in-security and anxiety, particularly if job burdens are felt to be onerous and failure threatens. As long as the senior executive condones or tolerates such behavior, the problem is swept beneath the rug. A pattern recurs: the superior is startled by the aggressive outbursts or the chronic hostility of the subordinate. The superior may fear the subordinate's anger and, cowed by it, retreat from confrontation or control for fear of precipitating even more anger. All this hostility may arouse the superior's wrath to the point where she feels guilty for her anger toward her subordinate. If she feels inordinately guilty about her own fury, and doubts her ability to control her feelings once they are unleashed, she may be paralyzed into inactivity as a way of coping with them.

The abrasive personality, while less volatile, can also intimidate superiors and also needs controls. The tendency to lash out in anger is most often a product of poorly contained, fuming hostility, which usually accompanies a perfectionist outlook. Usually a person's irrational anger with himself spills over onto others. Frequently criticizing others, often to the bruising point, he has little capacity for diplomacy and rarely is able to sense other people's feelings. Although abrasive personalities are usually intelligent, keenly analytical, perfectionist, self-starting people, their behavior often undermines the organization. It certainly undermines their own career advancement because bosses and subordinates want to avoid them.[4]

To control such behavior, the first step is to define the problem. (As long as others endure the behavior, the offending managers have no reason to stop it, since for them there is no problem.) Once the superior has defined which facets of the subordinate's behavior are unacceptable and has confronted the subordinate with a statement of the problem, the two must look at their own relationship. Are there features of the superior's behavior that provoke and sustain the anger of the subordinate? Are role conflicts among superiors tearing at the subordinate psychologically?[5] Work stresses may take their toll. The subordinate may be unconsciously asking for more support, or acting out the conflicts apparent between two superiors. Whatever the case, the two of them must examine the situation for possible causal influences. Superiors must be alert to possible fears and anxieties that the subordinate cannot express, such as the fear of failure or a sense of inadequacy in supervising others.

Regardless of mitigating circumstances, the superior still has to draw the line at destructive behavior, being careful to distinguish between destructiveness and a healthy—that is, creative and constructive—conflict of ideas. If environmental circumstances that precipitate anger cannot be altered, if there seem to be no problems of such magnitude as to induce fury, then it is reasonable to assume that the problem is primarily within the individual, and he must take the responsibility for correcting it. This may mean seeking professional help. Even if the problem is an intrapersonal one, the organization does not have to suffer such behavior until the problem is solved. If the person still cannot control these outbursts after the limits have been drawn, then he should be removed from the job.

However, there is a danger in assuming that the problem belongs only to the subordinate. Senior executives do sometimes fail to recognize how much pressure they exert upon subordinates, which may precipitate or exacerbate such behavior. They may assume that the undesirable behavior can be stamped out by forbidding it. Discussing problems means just that: self-critical examination of the working relationship by *both* parties. The superior's responsibility does not end after telling the subordinate to stop the hostile behavior; this should be just the beginning of the conversation.

The third recurring problem results from rivalry between subordinates. Sometimes the senior executive recognizes the rivalry aspects of the problem, but more often fails to, concentrating instead on the hostility between two subordinates. Without recognizing why they have become antagonistic to each other, the senior executive is likely to try to resolve such problems by exhortation, compulsion, or wishful thinking. These are all equally effective approaches, which is to say, not very.

More subtle aspects of rivalry, particularly their own rivalry with the subordinate, tend to escape the notice of senior executives. For instance, a production-minded president may see the need for a strong sales effort and employ a competent sales executive, only to resent his success. He may then reject or sabotage the sales executive without understanding the reasons behind his actions. It is no surprise, for instance, that Henry Ford fired Lee Iacocca in 1978. When he fired Semeon Knudsen and then Iacocca, Ford, an entrepreneurial personality, showed that he wanted no real rivals for power. Iacocca probably lost his job, in other words, because he was too good at it. Rising quickly through the ranks after starting as an engineer and then a salesman, Iacocca proved an invaluable executive when his Mustang and Maverick helped Ford recover from the Edsel fiasco. But Ford's action indicated that he could not tolerate a manager with such initiative and ambition, especially when the company's fortunes depended so much on the successful rival. Strong entrepreneurs are often people in conflict. As much as they want their businesses to succeed and are grateful to successful executives, they can also hate good executives for undermining their own sense of importance. As Iacocca's departure shows, entrepreneurs will even threaten to undermine their businesses to save face.

Executive emphasis on selecting and promoting people who will do what they are told, and do it with a smile, has a predictable consequence in the behavior of young executives: they go all out to sell themselves, to put themselves across, and to be liked by those who are more powerful. But adapting to external demands often occurs at the expense of *being*. Young executives follow another's decisions about where they will live and what they will do rather than doing what they and their families want.

In turn, behaving in ways that are marketable impairs relationships with colleagues and subordinates. People must look out for themselves first rather than for the interests that they and the organization share. They must compete with their peers, although in the long run this very competition may be injurious to the organization because competitive circumstances make it more difficult for people to cooperate toward common goals. This phenomenon, it should be noted, is not limited to business organizations. David Halberstam's book *The Best and the Brightest* portrays the same situation in a political system.[6]

Senior executives rarely recognize the destructive effects of rivalry. Usually unaware of the deep-seated psychological roots of rivalry and the guilt feelings that immediate personal competition can arouse in people, they often consciously encourage rivalry on the assumption that all competition is good. When a forceful competitor suddenly stops competing, they cannot understand why, let alone see the psychological trap set for the subordinate.

Young executives who are promoted rapidly over the heads of older people may have guilt feelings about preempting these opportunities. Such feelings are rarely recognized by superiors. As a result, they do little to prevent or ameliorate frictions that inhibit the effectiveness of the parties concerned. The issue of rivalry is almost never confronted in discussions about promotion, either by the prospective opponents or by their superiors, as a preparation for dealing with their new jobs.

By definition, rivalry is the essence of competitive enterprise. In an enterprise where the primary outcome is the result produced by the organization, however, all effort should be focused on its collective attainment. The superior who plays subordinates off against one another, overstimulates rivalry, or acts competitively with subordinates forces them to divert energies from competition with other organizations and into interpersonal antagonism. Misdirected rivalry drains collective energy that could be applied to resolving organizational problems. Subordinates become defensive, destroy cooperative possibilities by attacking each other, or maneuver for the favor of the boss. The more intraorganizational rivalry is stimulated, the more acute the problem of the company becomes.[7]

Applying Pressure

In the problems above, subordinates' behavior got out of hand because executives did not exercise enough controls of the right kind. But executives face a different challenge in dealing with people of more limited ability. They must know when not to apply pressure.

Any senior executive will acknowledge that there is, somewhere in the organization, a typical trio: someone who is too rigid, someone else who is too dependent, and a third who is too impulsive. As a rule, executives try to "shape up" these managers by frontal assault. They attempt to persuade a rigid person to become flexible, to exhort a dependent person to become independent, and to cajole an impulsive person into better self-control. Although often the executives know that people are inflexible or unable to accept responsibility or assume initiative, they tend to act as if they could compel or stimulate the subordinates to do so. But this will not work. In spite of their efforts, the rigid, the dependent, and the impulsive only become more so.

Rigidity in high places is a very real danger. Looking at military history, Norman Dixon, a former British army officer, describes classic examples of incompetence among military leaders in the Crimean War, in the Boer War, in India, and in the battles for Singapore and Arnheim in World War II in an attempt to discover why the various lords and generals who organized these defeats behaved as they did.[8] Dixon concludes that incompetent militarists have certain personality traits: rigidity, conformity, traditionalism, anti-intellectualism, indecisiveness, and stubbornness.

Such people as business leaders get companies, too, into difficulty. Inflexibility may be a personal characteristic or the product of environmental factors. Some people resist change not because they are personally inflexible, but because the organization has prepared them poorly and they are angry. One company in the United States today is so rigid that the best man available for any given post will not be promoted if he does not believe in God! Rigid people find their self-protection in well-ordered lives. Often they have high standards for themselves. Those who become more rigid under stress build a protective shell for themselves. Executives can make things more difficult or facilitate efforts to achieve.

Task responsibilities should be *delimited* in such a way that the person can confine herself to standardized, detailed work with definite policy guidance. It should be made clear to her what her responsibilities do not include. Senior executives should review what demands have made her more anxious and defensive. Change always requires support from superiors if it is to take place with a minimum amount of stress. Much of the time senior executives take it for granted that people can and will change. Actually, few can do so without stress. The most effective kind of support lies in joint problem solving, so that people can be master of themselves and their fate instead of being arbitrarily buffeted about by anonymous forces over which they have no control.

A second kind of personality presents different challenges for an executive—the type of personality that is simply unable to assume responsibility for others or to act on management problems. Often such men and women are described as dependent, but this rubric does not do justice to the complexity of their problems. Frequently, they have been suppressed in an extremely authoritarian structure for years. Some function reasonably well as long as they have the close support of their superiors. Some cannot make decisions themselves.

Undoing dependent behavior is no easy task, particularly if the organization continues to demand conformity. Where conformity is the first rule of survival, no amount of exhortation will produce initiative; where mistakes are vigorously hunted out and prejudice a person's career thereafter, few people will risk making a mistake. In addition to supporting the individual step-by-step toward assuming greater responsibility, senior executives must examine the costs of doing so. The effort often causes great conflict among senior executives, who may be caught between the wish that subordinates demonstrate initiative and the wish to be in complete control. It is difficult for executives to understand that grown men can be frightened and dependent. Sometimes, in a misguided effort to stimulate the subordinate, they offer the possibility of greater responsibility and more active participation in decision making, sometimes even promoting such a person in the vain hope that the subordinate will change when handed more responsibility or when returning from a management-development course.

This will not work. As H. R. Trevor-Roper, the British historian, said about a particular author, "It would be like urging a jellyfish to grit its teeth and dig in its heels. The poor creature lacks the rudimentary organs for such an operation."[9]

Since even middle-management ranks will soon be too lean to absorb passive, "nonmanagerial" people, companies have a greater obligation to prepare them for organizational realities. Executives must take the initiative (1) to determine the degree of dependency at an early stage, (2) to spell out to them specifically what they do well and what they do badly, and (3) tell them what they can reasonably expect to achieve within the company. This could be the first step in developing alternate career tracks. In addition, it is a necessary step in making it clear that management is an *active* role, not to be acquired simply by waiting in line.

A third problem is presented by impulsive people, who act erratically and without adequate thought. Some can do their jobs well "when they want to." They are frequently absent, often embroiled in multiple family difficulties, and sometimes irresponsible about completing their work or doing it thoroughly. In this category are the people who, though not alcoholic, drink too much in front of their superiors and those whose worst behavior occurs when they are with highest-level superiors.

If in some respects impulsive people are competent, even gifted, superiors are reluctant to face the problems of their behavior realistically. Too often their "mistakes" or "slips" are attributed to youthfulness with the expectation that they will mature. Poor impulse control and low frustration tolerance usually reflect considerable anxiety and insecurity. More often than not, such behavior indicates a need for professional counseling. Repeated admonitions usually serve little purpose.

Senior executives usually do not understand that putting pressure on people who are already devoting great effort to controlling or protecting themselves (which is what the aberrant behavior means), only increases the intensity of the undesirable behavior. If someone is characteristically rigid, dependent, or impulsive, he is likely to become more so under increasing stress, which is what the pressure of the boss becomes.

Right Person, Wrong Job

Fully 80 percent of all American workers in every job category may have jobs for which they are unsuited.[10] Many employees find that over the years their jobs have changed. Others have built up pension rights or acquired certain skills, and cannot readily shift career directions. They are simply stuck.

Much too often people are placed in the wrong job. Half of the time the job is wrong for them because it has outgrown them. Either way, the executive in charge perpetuates the problem by failing to act.

Despite the plethora of psychological consultants, assessment and rating scales, and literature on promotion, there is little *careful* assessment of people's capacities and limitations. Personnel people think they are doing an adequate selection job by using tests that they do not understand for jobs that are poorly defined. Important personality characteristics are dealt with glibly by reference to norms or profiles. The psychological climate of the organization and the personality of the superior with whom a person will have to work rarely enter into consideration. Little wonder that many people are trapped in roles that they cannot perform well.

At the same time, senior management rarely anticipates that people *will* outgrow their jobs. As a result, in most companies there is no continuing discussion of the problem to help people become aware of what they should do to maintain or sustain their jobs. Neither is there support for them in facing their feelings about becoming less competent to do the job or about having to relinquish it.

Often people who are unable to function adequately when given larger responsibilities do well in less demanding jobs, showing promise of being able to assume a more responsible post. Others, however, are placed in managerial positions despite the fact that their limitations—particularly their inability to supervise others—are known. Still others move up through the ranks because of their technical knowledge, only to flounder as executives.

The most common example, and one that is most trying for the executive, is the subordinate who cannot keep pace with the continuing growth of the organization and the particular job he has. He simply lacks the knowledge or skills for the expanding responsibility. This problem is even more poignant when the subordinate has long service in the position or has made significant contributions to organizing and developing an activity, sometimes even the company itself. In these situations the executive feels considerable pain because she feels compelled to take action against someone who has contributed to the organization. The executive's anger toward the person who "forces" her into such a situation arouses severe guilt feelings.

The subordinate may fail to keep up with the growth of the company as a gesture of silent protest. Often rigidity and plateaus in performance are products of passive aggression.

One way of being covertly aggressive is by not changing, not doing what is expected of one, letting the boss down in one way or another. Passive aggression is a widespread phenomenon.

What is the answer to the question of job fit? One suggestion is an internal job-posting and bidding system. Its advocates believe that individual self-selection into jobs is more likely to produce a good fit—taking into account an employee's motivation, needs, and value patterns—than a policy that gives him little choice.[11] While job bidding is an excellent idea, it certainly does not cover all the problems. (What about a boss's subtle loss of interest in developing a subordinate who has bid for other jobs?) Companies need to encourage many approaches to fitting people with jobs. A personnel office operating in confidence could be another route. A comprehensive skill bank in which are recorded the interests, skills and experiences of everyone in the company would be another. A company's continuing relationship with a psychological consultant is still another.[12] Psychological testing and evaluation is no better than the person who performs it. The judgments and predictions depend on a knowledge of the individual, the position, and the company. To serve all three, the psychologist must develop a "feel" for the company, knowledge of specific jobs and the people who supervise them, and some understanding of the candidate. Where good upward appraisal systems and good communication between superiors and subordinates exist, superiors can help. Unless a range of avenues are open and unless people know about them, some careers will always remain blocked.

Executives often get angry and frustrated trying to motivate disgruntled, bored, or badly placed employees. When this problem arises, it is wise to let people air their feelings. What is the nature of their dissatisfaction? What tasks have given them most satisfaction? What skills do people want to develop? How do they feel their talents are misdirected? Can they use their skills in new ways? No job, not even the CEO's, is gratifying for many years on end. Managers cannot endlessly enrich jobs, but when they let their people air their feelings, managers help employees accept the reality of their job limitations. It is often very difficult for executives to face a dilemma squarely or to accept the consequences of necessary actions. Executives, like their subordinates, want to live up to their ego ideals, and they experience great anguish and guilt when they cannot see how to solve a thorny management problem short of firing the subordinate. But when bad attitudes undermine job performance, people must be told this, and when dissatisfied employees cannot shape up, they must go.

Quite a different story is presented when the problem is situational rather than characterological, when a subordinate's behavior changes for the worse because he is going through some kind of crisis. It may not feel any easier for the executive. The same reactions of guilt and anguish arise when the subordinate is clearly in a crisis, needs help, and may even—directly or indirectly—threaten suicide. Easy solutions are in short supply. Nevertheless, executives faced with the choice of continuing to live with a "failure" or resolving it, even if it means termination, will make clearer decisions if they have a more thorough understanding of the dimensions of a crisis.

Understanding Crisis

The precipitating event in a crisis may occur in any of the arenas of a person's life—the break-up of a marriage, an adolescent in serious trouble, the death of a family member, the loss or threatened loss of a job. Not infrequently, several events occur together like chain lightning. Sometimes the precipitating event, to outside observers, may seem "too minor" to be causing such upheaval in the individual. Yet the death of an aged parent or a move to a new town may trigger deep and unsuspected feelings or may be the final straw that topples a person's sense of balance. It is not what the event looks like from the outside that is significant, but how the person experiences it.[13]

First, there is the impact of change. People tend to underestimate how disruptive change itself, apart from the implications of the change, can be. Second, there is a high degree of uncertainty. "What *are* the implications?" "What does this change mean for what I will do?" "What does it mean for the way I will feel?" The latter question especially is linked to the third, and perhaps most critical aspect of a crisis: it threatens the tenuous bridge between what people want to be (ego ideal) and how they really are.

Executives are ambitious men and women with high aspirations. Most seek power, prestige, and money and compete intensely with other executives and businesses. These are conscious manifestations of even deeper, unconscious wishes. Executives have extremely high ego ideals—that is, they carry inside them a compelling vision of what they will be like at their future best. Because they demand so much of themselves, they always feel a long way from their goal. This gap between their self-image, or view of themselves at the moment, and their ego ideal, or secret hope for themselves, is discomforting. The narrower the gap, the better people feel about themselves. Each failure, on the other hand, lowers self-image, thereby increasing self-criticism and anger. It is the self-directed anger, often experienced as depression, that leads to suicide.

Depression is probably the most widespread of all symptoms. Its roots in high expectations of oneself and low self-image are laid early in childhood. Some infants experience the early frustrations of life as evidence of a hostile world and therefore take a fighting stance toward it. Others interpret the pain and the frustration as a product of their own inadequacies. They are ready always to blame themselves. This is the depressive position. It becomes a contest for self-flagellation when later frustrations or failures confirm this already established belief. Regardless of their achievements, such people see themselves as deficient and, according to their internal logic, deserve self-punishment. When achievement is a cherished dream, the threat of failure, real or imagined, is a constant companion.

It is against this background that executives must see the effect of an important life crisis on colleagues or subordinates. Although the precipitating events are dissimilar, and individual coping strategies moderate in varying ways, Dr. Ralph Hirschowitz of the Harvard Medical School outlines a pattern of reactions through which individuals tend to pass.[14] The first phase is characterized by shock and numbness. It is followed by anger, distraught distress, flight and avoidance, dependence and holding on, denial, a period of bargaining, and identity disruption. As Hirschowitz describes it, after the onset of the crisis, there is a period of life disorganization. Then, depending on individual coping strategies combined with outside interventions, comes a period of life reorganization: dependence will shift to independence, denial to realization, and identity disruption will come to a halt, and identity consolidation, in a new form, will occur.

This "grief sequence" can apply to the loss of a job, the loss of a marriage, or some other important change. There is always the possibility that people will conclude mourning and move to a new consolidation. There is also the possibility that the downward spiral will continue, uninterrupted and without a resolution; the end will be serious, long-term disorientation or death. Death by suicide is an obvious possibility. Less obvious is another possibility: that depression, followed by a sudden, usually pleasant development, precipitates death. One study found that such a development preceded the unexpected deaths of twenty-six industrial workers in Rochester, New York.[15] Children leaving home or deeply disappointing their parents were the most common precipitating events. Investigator Dr. William Greene suggests that being made angry when already depressed, or shifting back and forth from being depressed to being angry may disrupt body chemistry catastrophically.

Stepping In

How can executives recognize and cope with threats to self-image that may precipitate depression in subordinates and potentially lead to self-destructive behavior?

First, they can recognize the universality of the phenomenon of self-directed aggression. Second, since people need perspective in order to temper their self-demands and their demands on others, executives can provide accurate, honest, and frequent performance appraisal. While there may be temporary lowering of self-esteem if a person is not doing well, alternatives to failure can be opened up before failures become too large to manage.

Third, when a problem seems massive and insurmountable, executives can suggest that the subordinate break it down into components and tackle them one at a time. Talking with spouses, good friends, or colleagues in trade associations helps people do this. When these resources are not available, professional outsiders can help.

Fourth, in reporting relationships, superiors should try to relieve people's irrational pressures of guilt. One constructive way to do this is by making clear what is the subordinate's responsibility and *what is not*. Job descriptions usually include the former but not the latter. Sometimes recounting their past problems and failures will help subordinates more easily accept the human quality of imperfection in themselves and others.

Fifth, executives can be alert to signs of depression, noticing when people stop eating and lose weight, when they are sleepless or excessively fatigued, begin drinking too much, start overdosing themselves with tranquilizers or energizers, are unable to get their work done because they are lost in paralysis and reverie, become increasingly irritable, develop frequent physical symptoms, sigh deeply and often—and, in the extreme, when they talk of suicide.

Sixth, where individual executives or executive groups are enduring a particularly stressful business situation, someone from outside the organization can be called in to serve as a point of orientation.

Emotional problems can beset any person at any time, yet seen globally, certain patterns occur. Statistics compiled by the Metropolitan Life Insurance Company show that emotional problems are increasing for young people of both sexes and for middle-aged women, but have stabilized for middle-aged men and eased for older people.[16] The study points out that middle-aged males (forty to sixty-four), portrayed as being so harried in much of contemporary literature, have shown an unchanged or even slightly declining suicide rate for the last two decades, whereas women in the younger and middle-aged group (under forty and forty to sixty-four) have shown sharply upward trends for the same period. The authors of the study suggest that this reflects more women entering the employment market with all its stresses, more women becoming heads of single-parent families, and the role confusion and conflicting emotions relating to women's liberation.

Occasionally executives must acknowledge that, for whatever reasons, someone in the organization is disturbed, that it is not just temporary, and that it is serious. It is helpful for the executive to realize (1) that executives do have a constructive role to play, and (2) that this role has limits. As a rule, the executive can take on one or more of three roles: a firm parent figure, a friend in need, or a lifeline to professional help. Executives are acting the part of a firm parent when they help people anticipate problems before they become too large to manage, or help them focus on the nature of the problem. In one study, for instance, the researchers found that employees in a closing plant did not anticipate future problems, and tended to seek help only after potential problems had grown into full-blown crises. Moreover, they say, the social services designed to help these people were too problem-oriented. To use the services successfully, a person had to diagnose the problem correctly and then find the correct agency for this specialized help.[17] By contrast, many far-sighted organizations call in firms that specialize in out-placement, and make a good job of helping employees find new work before the plant or division is closed.[18]

Executives also act like firm parents when they give realistic, perhaps unwelcome, but nevertheless necessary feedback on the subordinate's performance or personal behavior. They will have to act eventually, and it is best to let the subordinate know, *in advance* of any ultimatum, just what the organization will tolerate and what it cannot. At least then, in a crisis, subordinates do not also have to deal with unrealistic and value-less delusions about their ability.

When a subordinate has been told two or three times (certainly not more than that) that her performance is not satisfactory, then the executive must decide what the options are, tell the subordinate what they are, and ask what she would like to do. The big problem in such situations is that often executives think that they must do something to the subordinate—fire, demote, or transfer laterally. They then think it is all their fault and that they are destroying the subordinate. However, if superiors recognize that the subordinate is also responsible for her own behavior and should be making choices, then they will establish the parameters within which decisions and choices can be made. The subordinate can then assume responsibility for what she wants to do, including leaving the organization. This way the superior is not left in an impossible situation and the subordinate is deciding how to cope with the problem within the framework possible in that organization.

Often subordinates unwittingly put a load on their superior's back for denying promotions or for unfair treatment by others when, as a matter of fact, the superior has nothing to do with these problems, and cannot do anything about them. Frequently this is done in such a subtle fashion that the superior does not know he is being used and merely feels responsible for whatever is happening to the subordinate. Executives in turmoil about a problem of a subordinate should ask, "Why should I be in such turmoil? Whose problem is it? To what extent am I being used as a receptacle for somebody else's problems?" It is surprising how often they discover that they have been put in the middle.

Second, the executive can agree to be a friend in need and hear out the problem. Being such a friend helps in three ways: (1) it relieves anxiety by putting another person's resources at the subordinate's disposal; (2) it gets the problem outside the troubled person and helps him gain a new perspective on it, easing the decision of what to do next; and (3) it prepares the troubled person to seek additional help if necessary.

At this point, however, the executive's own anxiety is often aroused. The behavior of the troubled person may be frightening; the problem may touch the helper's own conflicts; the helper may be asked or required to take burdensome or unpleasant action. At this point executives must *listen* to discover just what the problem is, and they must *limit* their role in terms of their particular business situation.

Listening is the key to emergency relief for emotional distress. Listening to someone express painful feelings demonstrates a willingness to help. It shows respect for the troubled person as a fellow human being, and it acknowledges that we all need to feel as we do. Good listeners are sounding boards who allow others to talk, explore their feelings, and come to their own conclusions. They do not impose their own logic or reason on the other person's revelations. They give a sympathetic hearing and ask open-ended questions that help the troubled person gain fresh perspectives.

But executives offering emotional first aid should remember that the more ill and less in control a person is, the more active the helper's role will be. An executive cannot tell a forty-year-old woman what to do if she is accidentally pregnant. But if a hysterical employee sees visions in the office, the executive must get him to a doctor immediately.

Listening fails when listeners cannot control their anxiety and impatience. Impatient listeners often want to escape. They may suddenly find pressing business elsewhere or become coldly businesslike and aloof. They may close the conversation quickly with a piece of advice. No executive who feels uncomfortable with the listening role *must* offer emotional first aid. But those who do should listen long enough to get the troubled employee's basic message. They will at least understand the problem well enough to make sound managerial decisions.

Third, executives can be a lifeline to professional help. Setting limits of emotional first aid is as important as taking action. An executive is not a professional psychotherapist. He can therefore perform only a relief function. The executive must remain within his professional role. Relief counseling is to psychiatric treatment as first aid is to medical treatment. Emotional first aid helps most when problems arise from sudden external stresses, like immediate family or job difficulties. It does not much help inflexible people with little awareness of their problems or sensitivity to their feelings. People with chronic problems, those in acute panic, and those threatening themselves or others need professional help.

A business situation imposes its own limits on what an executive can do. An executive with heavy responsibilities and time commitments simply cannot meet frequently with a disturbed employee. Someone who cannot be helped in one or two interviews must be referred. In addition, executives must take care not to hear too much of a personal nature. Allowing a subordinate to talk on and on about marital and extramarital relations, for instance, can permanently disrupt a business relationship. Instead, the executive should refer the subordinate to professional help once the nature of the problem is clear.

Finally, in setting limits the executive must keep the troubled employee's revelations and distress confidential. When people seek help for emotional distress, they remove some of the protective layers of personality to reveal what is troubling them. Their behavior—which may include bursting into tears or an angry tirade—is an act of confidence. If listeners violate this trust, they debase the dignity of the troubled person and discredit their own reputation for integrity.

Executives want to be able to resolve all the problems, personal and organizational, that impede the smooth flow of work. They want to solve them within the management context, and often without assistance. They cannot. Their efforts to "try harder," frequently a response to feelings of futility, irritation, boredom, or guilt, often signal increased stress but not necessarily greater productivity.[19]

Executives cannot win them all. Some personality problems and organizational dilemmas are recalcitrant, and after making the best efforts possible, the only proper choice may be to fire a subordinate or alter the organizational situation. Executives do not experience such events as successes. Sometimes, however, it is necessary to acknowledge and tolerate a degree of failure in the present in order to avoid a grand harvest of failures in the future.

CASE HISTORY 13

Not all organizational problems can be resolved to everyone's satisfaction—nor should they be. Executives know that there are limits to what will work in a group. Understanding people's behavior and seeking to motivate them in the most positive ways, executives still run into situations or personalities so potentially damaging to the organization that someone has to go. When this person has also made a real contribution, it is an especially taxing problem, as this case illustrates.

"A situation has developed in a department that falls under my supervision. Dick, the department head, was seriously ill for eight months last year. The only person who was really capable of replacing him was on leave of absence, with the result that Michael, whom you might call the number three man, was elevated to department head on a temporary basis. This temporary status was made clear to him. Michael set about his work with a determination that surprised even those who had known him for some years. He wanted to do well and he did, reorganizing work routines, establishing communication between people in the department who had previously had little access to a department head, and generally building up a small personal empire before anyone, including myself, had noticed.

"When Dick returned to work after his illness he received a cool reception from employees who had formerly been quite happy with his supervision. Although Michael relinquished the outward signs of his temporary role, his fellow workers continued to seek out his advice and reactions to problems instead of going to Dick.

"It is only fair to say that prior to his illness, Dick had been somewhat inaccessible to his subordinates, but his close brush with death seems to have changed him considerably. He is more open now, able to joke, tackling his old responsibilities with a renewed enthusiasm and employing good innovative thinking.

"I had thought the problem would iron itself out until I overheard a conversation telling of a meeting Michael had called among the departmental employees to discuss the hiring of a new employee. Since Dick usually includes me in final hiring decisions, I called him to ask about the meeting. He didn't know anything about it. Dick told me he had interviewed a candidate two days before, but had decided to interview further. In the course of our conversation it was revealed that the man Dick interviewed was a friend of Michael's.

"I called Michael and told him that Dick and I did not like his attempting to pressure Dick into hiring Michael's friend. He said, 'We need new people in the department who are young and ambitious. Each time we get a good candidate who meets these criteria, Dick turns him down. I called the meeting to see if we would have a base upon which to at least talk with Dick about it. I was waiting to get consensus.'

"As you can see, Michael has nearly taken over the department while Dick sits as titular head trying to reestablish his authority. Michael is too hot-headed and too underhanded for me to consider him for Dick's job when we move Dick up in a year or so. How can we break down the little empire Michael has built, maintain morale, and con-

tinue to give Dick support when the subordinates are listening to Michael?"

Analysis

Where Is the Pain?   Obviously the narrator has the pain,
having to deal with a subordinate who has done a good job
and at the same time with the return of a loyal subordinate
whose work has improved but apparently still does not encourage the employment of young, lively, aggressive candidates.

When Did It Begin?   With the illness of the department
head.

Ego Ideal   Michael obviously wants to be the head of a
well-managed department of spirited, innovative people.
Dick's ego ideal has now changed somewhat inasmuch as
he seems to have enthusiastic, innovative ideas. The narrator's ego ideal includes integrity of both person and organization.

Affection   Apparently Michael's people like him and, because he is more openly accessible, find him a congenial
leader. While Dick's affection was previously constrained
and is now more openly expressed, he is apparently still
not as close to his subordinates as Michael is.

Aggression   Michael is intensely competitive and manipulative. He works both in an underhanded way and on the
surface. That is, he is apparently capable of reorganizing
routines well, establishing communications, and restructuring the work group's efforts with some considerable
success. At the same time he maneuvers around the legitimate authority, including the narrator.

Dependency   The narrator cannot depend on Michael because of his manipulative mode, nor can Dick, who is his
boss.

Is It Solvable?   Perhaps, but maybe it shouldn't be solved.

How?   The narrator's role in all of this is to take charge. Michael, taking advantage of a previously unfavorable situation, has manipulated himself into a position of power at the expense of his boss. Though his subordinates may like him better, and indeed may even now turn to him for leadership, he cannot be allowed to undercut his boss or to act impulsively (even contemptuously) toward his boss and toward the narrator by continuing to do what he is doing.

The narrator must call him on his behavior, point out that it is manipulative and destructive and that he will no longer tolerate it. He must then transfer Michael to another area after having told him that he is ineligible for promotion because of this manipulative behavior. The other alternative the narrator has is to terminate Michael's employment.

After the narrator has taken one of these steps, it is up to him to meet with Dick and Dick's group and indicate that the kind of manipulative behavior displayed by Michael will not be tolerated from any employee. He must then take time to coach Dick in his effort to act more warmly and supportively toward his subordinates while keeping close tabs on how things are going in Dick's department. He should be prepared to continue this until Dick gradually can feel more comfortable as the person who is fully in charge of the department.

Manipulative people like Michael are destructive. They cannot be allowed to continue their kind of behavior for, if they are highly skilled at manipulating others, they can create divisiveness among others which undermines work relationships and which can cut into productivity levels. In more extreme cases, these people can actually foment office revolts. Unless they are tightly constrained and closely supervised, they usually will not abide by any agreement with superiors. They cannot be expected to respond to rational performance-appraisal feedback with significant change in behavior because of their ingrained propensity for manipulating rules, policies, practices, and people. Only tight control will demonstrate to what extent they are manipulating.

While it might be argued that Michael had done a good

job, the fact that he built an empire and the manner in which he did it make his work unacceptable. The method used is even more critical than the end attained. In the final analysis, if Michael cannot be trusted, what good is he?

FIFTEEN

Strengthening the Organization

An organization depends on its resources—raw materials, technology, market outlets, and the capabilities of its members. The most important of these resources are the human ones, necessary to make sense of the rest and to oversee the process of production or service with insight, competence, and a sure hand.

Just how well human resources are used varies from organization to organization. Problems of fit and effectiveness derive from management's inability to elicit the best talents and efforts of employees, either because management is unaware of these talents, does not know how to tap them, or cannot motivate the people. Psychologist Robert Guion argues that there has been "long term neglect in developing a major part of the practical technology needed to achieve better individual-to-the-job fits. It is an obvious logical point that it takes two sides to make a good fit."[1]

The same problems are reflected in the employee's reluctance to become fully involved. Absenteeism, in American industry, is one barometer that shows how productively an organization functions (that is, how well the fit and effectiveness of its human resources have been achieved). United States Bureau of Labor statistics suggest that work hours lost through absenteeism come to about 3.5 percent and cost about $20 billion a year in lost pay alone. Sick pay and fringe benefits are extra.[2] Keeping people on the job is one problem. Low pro-

311

ductivity among those who make it to work is another, and absenteeism figures, which do not relate to this issue, can only hint at what the cost to industry of low productivity may be.

It has been almost a personnel axiom that 10 percent of a group of employees are responsible for 90 percent of absenteeism. New evidence suggests that although absentee rates may remain the same, the core of employees who contribute to absences changes from period to period. In a study of 195 employees who worked in an accounting department of a large public utility, Kathleen R. Garrison and Paul M. Muchinsky found that between 50 percent and 58 percent of the employees were responsible for 90 percent of paid and unpaid absences, respectively. According to the authors, studying absences during a quarter, a month, or a week will show that a small percentage of employees are responsible for a large percentage of absenteeism, but using an expanded time of a year or more the distribution of absences changes.[3] This means not only that more people are involved in absenteeism than has been suspected, but that a broader range of reasons may be the cause. Clearly, life-change events may play a large part. Unquestionably, what goes on in an employee's family affects what happens at work. Jean Renshaw describes it well: "Work organizations and families are independent social systems. But the two systems intersect at crucial points, and the interactions deeply affect both. Families and organizations have large stakes in finding creative and mutually satisfactory solutions to the problems in that relationship."[4]

For reasons that begin inside or outside the organization, executives feel unable to "reach" the people who work for their organization—to know them well enough to put their various talents to the best use, and to relate to them as individuals in such a way that they are motivated to contribute what they can to the organization's progress and well-being. Feeling out of touch with what is going on is as much a problem for the employee as it is for the executive. The executive feels the pain in terms of productivity and profit; the employee feels a loss of effectiveness and a sense of detachment. The carrot (in the form of pay, benefits, and status) can offset some of the employee's dissatisfactions, but not—over time—nearly enough. Even the threat of the stick (termination) is not sufficiently galvanizing to push a potentially productive but poorly functioning manager into a new and more effective mode of behavior.

There are limits to what an executive should do, or can be expected to do, to change the behavior of particular subordinates. At the same time, some organizational approaches are likely to have productive results by offering subordinates a greater sense of involvement. It must be emphasized that there are no magic recipes. Management by cookbook has not yet been successful, and is unlikely ever to be because it fails to take into account the role of unconscious motivation. Nor can it specify the nature of the relationship between two specific people or among a collection of people working together in a particular group. For the same reasons, a number of promising management innovations have failed (that is, failed to live up to the unrealistically high expectations generated by some early encouraging results) because they were adopted in isolation from the underlying facts of human interactions and asked to carry more freight than they could. Then, when obstacles arose, they were discarded before enough time and thought had gone into working on them so that they could be developed into useful approaches.

Dr. Rene Dubos of Rockefeller University, a widely respected medical leader, notes that an important aspect of recovery is faith. "Faith in the gods or in the saints, cures one; faith in little pills, another; hypnotic suggestion, a third; faith in a common doctor, a fourth."[5] Much of what is now being written about success with organizational development activity parallels Dubos' observations: the power of suggestion combined with faith in the consultant brings immediate but not necessarily long-term results. This is why any new fad gains nearly immediate adherence, and why many do not work after a while. This phenomenon has long been called the "Hawthorne effect" after the fifty-year-old Hawthorne experiments at Western Electric, which inspired many of the subsequent "quality of work life programs." It turns out, however, that the social scientists who analyzed these experiments have until recently overlooked one crucial fact. Richard Franke of the Worcester Polytechnic Institute and James Kaul of the Environmental Protection Agency point out that during the period studied, two workers who "exhibited undue independence from management . . . were replaced by two more agreeable workers."[6] Production rose after the insubordinate workers were fired. Employees were undoubtedly motivated as much by fear as by the enrichment process.

Three approaches to the best use of human resources are commonly presented. Each has some inherent difficulties, yet at the same time contains the principles of an idea which, with the right tests and modifications, could be adapted to good use in work settings. These are work innovations, participation in management, and organizational communication.

Work Innovations

Instituting democratic procedures even at the plant-floor level has met with considerable success at the Hunsfos mill in Norway.[7] Workers have learned each other's jobs and have dispensed with foremen altogether. Their program is part of a far-reaching reform effort underway throughout Norway and Sweden to make work more challenging and more satisfying for workers of all kinds.

Before rushing off to follow suit, however, executives should note that the results of similar programs elsewhere in Norway have varied, and progress at the Hunsfos mill has been slow. Even democracy is not an easy answer.

Judging the success of various work innovations, writes Richard E. Walton of the Harvard Business School, is a complicated business because efforts often are measured against standards other than the ones relevant to the innovations at hand.[8] Walton uses three categories to classify the planned changes, called at various times "work improvements," "work reform," or "quality of work life programs."

Design techniques address the way in which work is organized and managed. For example, auto plants in the United States and Scandinavia have assigned related tasks to work teams, let them decide among themselves how to divide up the work, and created buffer inventories between adjacent work teams so that they can have more control over the pace of their work. Intended results differ. Some of these techniques have an economic goal and are intended to benefit the organization through labor efficiency, materials usage, and machine capacity utilization. Some have human goals and are intended to benefit the employees in the form of real income, security, challenge, dignity, or a sense of community. As Walton points out, human gains need to be closely coupled with improved competitive performance in the present business environment.

Work culture includes the combination of attitudes, relationships, developed capabilities, habits, and other behavioral patterns that characterize the dynamics of an organization. He emphasizes that in the most successful work improvements, the culture simultaneously enhances business performance and the quality of human experience. In one food plant, where management sought to promote the employees' identification with work goals, such identification increased not only the workers' motivation to work, but also their sense of belonging in the workplace and pride in the plant's achievements.

There is widespread interest in modifying organizational patterns, in spite of the difficulties encountered. Work patterns should reflect life stages and not rigid schedules, says Fred Best of the National Commission for Manpower Policy.[9] Our present linear life plan, with progression from school to work to retirement is unproductive and debilitating, says Best. He hopes to see greater social flexibility, with shorter work-weeks for students, parents of young children, and the elderly. People at the peak of their powers should work longer hours, says Best, and all employees should be able to choose between more time off or more pay.

Job sharing, especially in academic settings, is one innovation that has developed out of a tight job market and increased affirmative-action requirements. Two-in-one jobs may suit individual personal needs and permit the organization to accommodate more candidates.[10]

Although flexibility is likely to increase in many kinds of work, the apparent futuristic look of such proposals may be deceiving. There is a limit to what people can do with part-time work. Where cohesion and investment are important, businesses need full-time employees. Part-time people have gaps in their relationships, with too little time for staff meetings or for building the network of social and political relationships that are the context in which work gets done. Proposals for part-time and flex-time work ignore or slight what is fundamental to work organizations: organization. These innovations have some value. They allow some work to be done more efficiently, and they bring new people into the work force. But managers should be cautious about their benefits.

Work innovations, if not uniformly successful, are widespread. Walton estimates that an "important minority" are attempting some significant work-improvement projects, often in the context of new plant start-ups. This minority includes General Motors, Procter and Gamble, Exxon, General Foods, TRW, Cummins Engine, Citibank, and Prudential. Although projects such as those tried in the Volvo and Topeka General Foods plants have been highly publicized, others may be more extensive. The GM assembly plant project in Tarrytown, New York, for example, involved workers and the union in redesigning the hard- and soft-trim department facilities and evolved into a plant-wide quality of work life program that included some 3,500 people. Not all companies publicize or boast about their efforts. One leading nondurable consumer goods company sees its track record in implementing innovative work systems as part of the experience that gives it a competitive edge, and is not about to disclose its work improvement efforts.[11]

Not only do work innovations seem to be expanding, but there is also increased upper-management interest. Whereas a few years ago it was largely plant- or division-level managers who looked for consulting help in setting up programs, today top corporate executives are as likely to be making inquiries.

Do work innovation programs work? It is important to assess how well a particular program has succeeded when measured against its goals. Clearly the sponsor's motives make a difference. It is also important that they be sincerely stated; that the expectations of the program's results be realistic to begin with; and that the managers behave as if both economic *and* human values count.

If efforts to improve the quality of work life succeed, it may well be because they help distract workers from the boring routines of their jobs. Irmtraud Seeborg of Ball State University reports that, in a simulation, people with repetitive, uninteresting jobs seemed to value the social aspects of a job redesign program more than the vertical loading. Seeborg hypothesizes that employees who find satisfactions in the *process* of redesigning their jobs may in turn find more satisfaction in the jobs themselves.[12]

Executives trying quality of work life programs should realize that it is important not to overpromise what they can accomplish. Good feelings can be generated in any organization when people put their heads together to improve a procedure, a product, or a program. And many employees can make valuable contributions and improve the ways tasks are done. But wise managers expect—and help their subordinates anticipate—the inevitable return to the daily grind. The new ways may be better, but even they may become familiar and dull in time. And the enriching process cannot go on endlessly. There are only so many ways to make a product *and* make money. Many employees will mourn the past glory days when efforts to improve the quality of work life were new. Others will find satisfaction in maintaining feed-back on the work process. J. Kenneth White of Michigan State University points out that "enriching a job may involve different psychological phenomena than just having or not having a 'rich' job."[13] But an enriched job will always be a poor relative to a rich job, and no one should be told differently.

Participation in Management

A vice-president participating in a recent executive seminar reported the following experience. He made a practice of meeting regularly with all of the department heads who reported to him. One day he decided to try a less authoritarian style. Instead of taking his usual seat at the head of the conference table, he joined those on one side. His regular seat remained conspicuously vacant until every other chair was filled. The last department head to enter the room was forced to take it. The meeting was slow in getting started. As it progressed, the vice-president found himself increasingly uncomfortable. Everyone seemed to be responding to the head chair, not to him. He and the department head in his seat began to bicker over picayune points. Nothing the vice-president tried helped the situation. Finally he had to stand to command enough attention to adjourn the meeting.

Unfortunately, many experiments with participative management end abruptly because people forget that any change in a power relationship requires the consent and preparation of all parties. A person never knows how comfortable an established role is until he tries to give it up. Dr. Don R. Lipsitt, chief of psychiatry at Mount Auburn Hospital in Cambridge, Massachusetts, has studied this phenomenon in doctors who become patients.[14] He points out that even when one doctor is willing to become temporarily submissive and dependent, a colleague may not be willing to risk a supportive professional relationship by really taking charge. As a result, he or she may not do adequate testing or relay unpleasant or complicated information. The biggest mistake of the doctor is to assume too much of the patient and fail to clarify adequately or give clear directions to someone who is not used to following them. The doctor being treated is equally vulnerable to distortion of role. His situation is "not only a threat to his autonomy, authority, sense of omnipotence and control, but also an experience which forces him to think of himself like all those patients he has treated, mistreated, abandoned, deceived, neglected, ridiculed, and so on. He is loath to be 'one of them' and is certainly fearful that he will now be in for a dose of his own medicine."

There is an additional hazard with bosses who pretend they do not have power over others. In trying to be one of the gang, they create a "web of dependence and resentment" that enmeshes their subordinates, says Richard Sennett of the State University of New York at Stony Brook. People do not know where they stand with a boss "who has power . . . but doesn't want to be dictatorial."[15]

Bosses who pose as peers are like wolves in sheep's clothing. Even when they mean well—and when the last thing they want is to be wolves—the disguise frightens people and throws them off balance. Subordinates know that when bosses want or need to use power, they will, so they are never comfortable pretending that the power does not exist. Even when the boss seems to want familiarity and group decision making, subordinates fear that he or she will snatch off the lambskin at any moment and reclaim the boss's power and prerogatives.

There are, of course, executives who really do let go of the reins—completely. Management by abdication is spreading fast. It occurs whenever a manager assumes that delegation or participation simply means leaving things to subordinates. The result is usually no management at all, and the manager wonders why. The reason is that few people can assume increasing responsibility without explicit permission from the boss, for doing so is usually experienced as usurping the boss's role. Before increasing their areas of responsibility, subordinates need to be able to consult their boss and get general support, opportunity to review alternatives and weigh risks, and a clear idea of what is expected. Sometimes a mere nod will be enough, but more often considerable rehearsal of coming events will be necessary. A manager instituting participative management does not have less work to do, just a different kind of work, especially initially.

Delegation and participation do not mean abdication. The contributions that people can make in participatory management programs are limited by their capacity to abstract, to think conceptually, and to project into the future. Employees in any organization can contribute significantly within the range of their knowledge and experience. But participation does not mean abandoning traditional roles entirely.

A major problem with democratic management is that people are not willing to work hard at it. Democracy in any form requires a great deal of work—issues must be discussed, all opinions heard, and solutions thrashed out. It is this hard work that most proponents of democratic management will not take into account. The other is that organizations—democracies included—need leaders. Employees participate by raising issues, ideas, and suggestions. But someone has to shape these suggestions and ideas into programs for action. The job of a boss always has been, and always will be, to make decisions. In the words of Minneapolis *Star* editor Stephen Isaacs, who introduced a participatory management program to improve his paper's performance, "Participatory management means having an input into management . . . It doesn't mean reporters making decisions. They are only paid $460 a week, and that's not enough to make the kinds of decisions I have to make."[16]

Organizational Communication

Participative management, as it is practiced, may have some pitfalls and unrecognized limitations. But certainly it is best to involve people in the issues, in varying ways. It is important for executives to know what people can contribute and—if they invite participation—what they themselves are prepared to do about it. Organizations, like social groups, do best for themselves and for their constituents when they build a sense of community, which by definition is based on shared interests. The Belvidere Mountain Quarry and Mill in Lowell, Vermont, is a good illustration. This asbestos quarry was owned by the GAF Corporation, which decided to close the quarry rather than spend over a million dollars for antipollution equipment. The employees bought the quarry from GAF in March 1975. A year later, they were making a good profit. Those employees who had invested in the new company got back in dividends all they had invested, the new company paid off its debts and complied fully with the government's pollution rules, and the new owners were looking to future expansion.

The ambiguous track record of employee ownership is worth mining for insights and information. Actual ownership—what James O'Toole of the University of Southern California calls "having a key to the plant"—may work out successfully only in some situations.[17] But in any group, it is as a result of common purpose, the gratification of ego ideals, and striving for self-respect that members are held together. It is psychologically sound for a community or organization to develop a sense of common purpose, and the kinds of communication that take place within an organization are central to its development.

There is a growing shift to in-house management development and educational activities. More and more companies are setting up their own programs which provide people with an opportunity to talk together about common problems and to become more closely identified with one another while sharing common views. Powerful things can be done with these programs. However, their effectiveness will depend on whether management sends clear messages to subordinates and whether it communicates accurately with the people at the top.

Young people in management training programs recognize that top management often has no awareness of the effects of its decisions on people lower down, and, what is more, does not care enough to ask for their opinions about these decisions once they have been made. They also express resentment about the irrationally imposed stressful demands being placed upon those in lower echelons. When people are moved from building to building, for instance, they not only change offices but they also change social arrangements, social networks, communications patterns, support systems, and access to resources. Only rarely is the impact of these changes taken into account. It is simply assumed that people will manage somehow and that everything will be all right soon.

It is better if building changes can be carefully anticipated. People should be walked through a mock-up or blueprint of the new facilities, encouraged to ask questions about the kinds of problems that the new setup will pose for them, and asked to give thought to any issues that may have to be resolved because of the move. They particularly need to remain in touch with people they have been associated with for a long time. They should have the opportunity to learn in advance where their friends are to be located by being given maps or charts that have their own new locations marked.

When a company is considering cutbacks in response to a tight economic situation (another common change), it can be helpful to give people the opportunity to decide for themselves how to handle the problem. They may come up with imaginative solutions. For instance, employees in some companies have chosen a three- or four-day work week to ensure that everybody in the work group could remain employed, rather then let some people be dismissed arbitrarily.

Managements that try to take the burden of difficult decisions off other people's backs are overlooking possible serious consequences. Unilateral decisions from the top often leave the seemingly lucky ones with a tremendous burden of guilt, which drains their productive energy, whereas when an entire group works out a solution together, people are likely to draw closer and renew their dedication to work. To accomplish this, however, they need thorough and honest information about the realities that have to be accommodated. They also need strong leadership—someone who can help ease their fears and guilt while they explore solutions.

Every important change should be discussed with each person involved before it occurs, giving these people the opportunity to express their feelings without embarrassment or fear. When they can tell their superior how they feel about an organizational decision, and the superior listens, the receptiveness to their views conveys to them that they are accepted and respected as individuals. This supports feelings of self-esteem and makes it possible for them to deal with the change and with their feelings more reasonably. No amount of sugar-coated praise will substitute for being heard.

Many executives do conscientiously take time to explain to their subordinates why decisions have been made or will have to be made that are counter to the recommendations or wishes of the subordinates. The executives try only to give information, but also to convey respect for the subordinates. This consideration for the other is frequently helpful, but sometimes it goes awry. If people's recommendations are not followed, they are usually disappointed and sometimes angry. When superiors go to great lengths to soothe ruffled feelings and give reasons for decisions, they run the risk of unwittingly trying to keep these ruffled feelings from being expressed. The boss may need to be liked too much or may find it unpleasant to incur the disappointment, hostility, frustration, or dismay of the subordinate. Trying to get the subordinate to agree to a decision, or at least accept it, can be perceived as seduction and coercion, and may increase the subordinate's anger.

It is far better to tell subordinates the facts and to let them react with all their disappointment and hostility. A simple explanation of the facts is enough. If superiors can allow subordinates to express disappointment, they will have constructed a psychological arena within which it is safe for subordinates to express negative feelings.

Executives should follow a fairly simple rule. Before they change anything, they should ask; after the change has been made, they should ask again. Between the "before" and the "after" they should set up a mechanism for coping with the changes, a mechanism that will allow for the anger, depression, and mourning so necessary for adaptation. Obviously this requires a capacity to listen—an executive skill often in short supply. The Royal Bank of Canada's "Monthly Letter" says, "No one in his thirties can ever do too much listening; the best leaders know that people prosper not in proportion as they inform, but as they elicit . . . It is more important to know people's thoughts and to anticipate their reactions and to draw up a systematically correct manifesto of the firm's aims and regulations. Able managers and supervisors, whose skill in working with people has been called uncanny, merely are careful to watch for bits of evidence which others ignore . . . Workers must understand what management is trying to do before they can be counted upon for enthusiastic support."[18]

One of the striking things in management meetings is the degree to which many executives delude themselves about how open their organization is. Higher-level management usually dominates the conversation. When a manager's tendency is to take control of the situation, nobody else is going to speak up.

These managers often deny their need to control by assuming the attitude of "I'm a nice guy; therefore, everyone and everything else is fine." Such an executive does not see that failing to examine a problem allows it to continue to be disruptive. Furthermore, this kind of orientation becomes a model of subordinate behavior.

In another way, too, executives are less than open: they hide their mistakes, setting an example that percolates downward. Executives often worry that subordinates will lose faith in them if they let on when they have made a mistake. Nobody's ideal self-image includes making mistakes, so everyone is ashamed of them. Yet good managers want their people to learn how to look at mistakes and benefit from them, and the best thing to offer is a model. By acknowledging their own mistakes, executives convey to their subordinates that they know that risk-taking is necessary in a competitive society and that mistakes are inevitable. This will help counterbalance subordinates' natural tendency to judge themselves harshly for mistakes, to try to hide them, and in the end to become reluctant to venture into risky territory.

In addition to modeling some tolerance for mistakes, executives can keep people from being disappointed in themselves and in their managerial roles by helping them keep up-to-date on trends both inside and outside the company. This can be done by holding periodic one-day refresher sessions with outside speakers, by conducting workshops and reading groups, or by having specialists from within the organization summarize the latest developments in their fields. People can use themselves best when they are abreast of changing expectations and when they are helped to become more proficient in meeting these expectations.

Studies continue to suggest that managers are far happier at work than clericals or hourly employees, and the gap is widening.[19] Yet most of these job-satisfaction studies focus too much on peripheral issues. Pay, benefits, scheduling—even autonomy, responsibility, and creativity—are not the heart of a work experience. The real problem is not that much work is mechanized and routinized: it is that working relationships are often dehumanized. Employees are dissatisfied because their organizations are not coming alive for them. Bosses often do not respond to their people as people. And they do not represent their organizations in a personalized way to their subordinates.

Not even a huge corporation must be impersonal. Small internal units are like families. And good managers, like good parents, do not focus only on their subordinates' achievements and measurable skills. They enjoy responding to their people's individual styles and inclinations, needs and abilities. They know that no two people will respond alike to the same stimulus. They take pleasure in the personal interactions that inspire good work and create good feeling. An executive who wants to see this happen throughout the organization has to set the pattern. High-level executives *must* make the rounds, touch people, make their presence felt, let people size up who they are and how they think. This is the only way to be a leader, not just a decision maker with a title. General James Gavin has remarked that General Dwight Eisenhower was too far removed from his military operations to run them, and attributes much of his own success to his closeness to men in combat. Gavin was visible and available, an organizing point for his subordinates.[20]

There is an important lesson here for executives who think that they belong in their offices. In meetings with top-management groups in recent years, people complain again and again that they need to meet more frequently with their top-management colleagues and with CEOs. They have a deep, fundamental need for personal contact. It is their only way to affect the power source in their organizations.

If two-way communication with subordinates is often a

problem for executives within an organization, they may understand better the difficulties subordinates face when they reflect on a problem that they themselves face: speaking up to the boss.[21] The people at the top often do not hear all that they should, partly because they do not listen but also because they are not told enough. Top management often seeks recommendation from its upper middle-management infrastructure. Middle management then makes policy recommendations and often evolves procedures and practices to implement them. However, people who undertake such tasks and suggest to higher-level management what it should do rarely suggest to top management what it should *not* do or what the hazards of alternative courses of action may be. As a result, top management is often poorly served by middle management, which offers programs and practices whose consequences top management must bear without being absolutely aware of the ramifications of the actions. This is especially true with respect to personnel programs, particularly those related to performance appraisal, compensation, management by objectives, and sometimes organizational development. It then becomes the top executives' responsibility to seek out both the positive and negative possibilities before putting new programs into effect.

Many managers underestimate their bosses and then wonder why their bosses do not think better of them. For example, many Levinson Seminar participants claim that while they are interested in what is taught, their bosses are too narrow, too stupid, too critical, or too insensitive to pay any attention to these new ideas. These subordinates, prejudging what their bosses are willing or able to understand, block the flow of information.

It is true that many bosses fail to share their subordinates' interests. Many are not as smart as their subordinates, or perhaps are less abstract in their thinking. But it is also true that subordinates err in underestimating their bosses. Too many times they are wrong (as was the person who did not want to discuss the critical-incident method of performance appraisal with a boss whom he knew to be disenchanted with traditional methods). People in personnel functions are often fearful of discussing various kinds of counseling with their bosses, fearful of having "shrink talk" rejected, and unaware that these same bosses are in psychotherapy themselves.

How to speak up to the boss becomes an increasingly important issue as organizations become more flexible and as more leaders seek to involve their followers. Few are comfortable speaking up, even when invited to do so. Before dealing with the specifics, it is necessary to answer two questions: What is the organizational climate? And what is the nature of the political structure above the boss?

Any subordinate's action, as well as that of any boss, occurs in an organizational context. In many organizations, the unwritten motto is "Don't make waves." These are usually highly structured companies where superiors do not encourage differences and reward passive acquiescence. In such an organization, any approach to the boss will have to be tactfully indirect. It is important for subordinates to know the political structure in which their superiors work and, as much as possible, what forces are operating on them.

Having considered the organizational climate and the political structure, subordinates must take into account the kind of person the boss is and under what circumstances they might wish to speak up. The basic question to ask when trying to understand the boss is: "What is the boss's ego ideal?" What is he striving toward? What does it take for the boss to like himself? People may not be able to put their ego ideals into words, but others usually can infer from their behavior what they are trying to look like and where they are aiming. Everyone is always striving toward an ego ideal. Therefore, each one tends to see others in terms of whether they are helpful to his striving or are going to create disappointment.

Subordinates should ask additional questions. How does this boss handle aggression? What about affection—does she need many approving people around, or prefer to work in a more isolated way? Finally, how does she handle dependency? Does she lean heavily on organizational structure, or rely on flexibility?

Having sized up the boss and the boss's environment, the subordinate is now in a position to take up specific problems with the boss. There are essentially two kinds: those that have to do with the boss's behavior, and those that have to do with the organization.

Issues may center on what seems to be "unfair," highly critical, or idiosyncratic behavior on the part of the boss. Or

they may arise from decisions made in the course of performance appraisal, promotion or career options, or conflicts involving others. What is critical is the manner in which subordinates speak up to their boss, and their intentions in doing so.
A wise editor once said, "Never underestimate the intelligence
of your audience or overestimate the amount of informtion
they have." The same applies to the boss. Subordinates should
always seek to inform.

In speaking up to superiors it is important to maintain
some personal dignity and psychological distance—not overly
friendly, but not too cold and distant. There *are* times when it
is appropriate to be angry. When a subordinate has been repeatedly attacked unfairly or manipulated, it is entirely appropriate to express anger. To fail to do so—to smile when
enraged—is to send two messages that contradict each other
and that result in no communication at all.

Working with a superior is similar to being married. Each
member of the relationship has a lot of expectations of the
other that are not clearly specified. Subordinates need to let
the boss know what they think and feel—not in a hostile, ar-
gumentative way, but in an informal way. This means that
they can continually renegotiate the psychological contract, re-
defining mutual expectations as time passes. It is this continual
renegotiation of the psychological contract that is the basis for
effective superior-subordinate relationships.

Finally, it is important to remember that communication
can only be as constructive as the message that is communi-
cated. In an effort to improve morale, a common device is to
"improve communications" when actually the problem is not
that communications are unclear—much of the time they are
all too clear—but that the messages themselves are not supportive. Messages that convey avoidance of issues and manipulation of employees often destroy morale. In the same way,
companies with autocratic leadership and many internal political conflicts often keep on with their team-building and other
organizational development efforts because these give managers the opportunity to size up the weaknesses of their opponents and to arrange their strategies accordingly.

It is important to pay attention to two aspects of communication: the lyrics and the melody. The lyrics are the
words people say; the melodies are the feelings that are fre-

quently masked by the words and that sometimes must be read between the lines. Communication is incomplete until one has assessed both these elements, just as a Beethoven sonata is incomplete unless one uses both hands to play it. When hearing the lyrics, one must always ask, "What is the melody?" and then try to uncover it. If the message is constructive, supportive, direct—even if it is also critical or carries bad news—it can be useful. If it is indirect, ambiguous, or deceptive, the act of communication alone cannot solve many problems.

An organization is made up of many parts. Different units may have different working styles as well as different functions. Sometimes the right hand does not know what the left hand is doing, or knows but does not know what to do about it. In the case below, some principles are suggested that will make the demanding yet sensitive job of one personnel officer easier. They can be extrapolated to apply to other situations as well, and used to make the whole stronger than its parts.

"I am employed by a large airline as corporate director of training, reporting to the vice-president of personnel. I was hired to accomplish certain personnel objectives over a two-year period. The corporation maintains two separate training units. One unit trains middle-management people to work in the legal, financial, administrative, and other functional areas. The other trains those more directly involved with the actual flight service, including such people as flight attendants and reservation clerks. Both units fall under my charge.

"The first group does not require as much attention and effort as the second. The second group views itself as privileged, beyond rules and conformity. Most of these trainees are young, eager-to-fly people, ebullient about their forthcoming world travel. They see their jobs as 'romantic.' The staff who train them seem also to have adopted some of these attitudes. As a result, the trainees are not being prepared adequately for their jobs. Customer complaints are increasing, and I was charged to get to the root of the problem.

"I decided to use the MBO [management by objective] approach while also tightening discipline in the second unit. When I approached my superior for permission to inaugurate the program, he was cautiously enthusiastic, telling me to talk to the corporate attorney and other executives for their reaction and input. That was eleven months ago, and I have no final word yet.

"When it looked like I wouldn't complete my assignment on time, I asked my superior for some kind of answer within a week. He then told me the attorney had reacted negatively to an MBO program, and had in fact undermined a similar program in the past. I don't know why he didn't tell me this earlier, but I have discovered that the corporate personnel office and legal offices have had strained relations for years now. My supervisor asked me to sit tight, and to wait until after the next planning session—months away.

"To have some effect, I went (without a clear charge) to the people in the training areas, and instituted a watered-down version of part of my proposal. Under a new performance-appraisal system, the training units have begun to turn around after thirty days. The trainees are grumbling, particularly the maverick types, but generally the unit is more efficient. In the meantime I'm working for small successes with other projects that are sure to be better received.

"I am still very frustrated because I am not doing the things I feel I can do best. I now the problem predates my arrival and involves politicking. But I worry that I'll be blamed for any failures. My superiors have said nothing about the changes I've slipped through. But I believe we need a clear-cut method for operating both units, and I would prefer to make those changes in the open. What should I do now?"

Analysis

Where Is the Pain?   Obviously the pain is in the narrator who cannot get the job done (which he feels needs to be done) in the way that it should be done.

When Did It Begin?   When he took over this new role.

Ego Ideal   The narrator's ego ideal is to produce a well-trained staff who can render effective service with such reliability that customers will not complain.

Affection   Apparently the second group, which views itself as privileged, is engaged in a kind of occupational party. They conceive of their roles as "romantic" and, it woud seem, are engaged in a kind of juvenile fantasy.

Aggression   Aggression in this organization is apparently handled by constraint. The narrator's superior is cautious; the attorney is resistant; people are expected to "sit tight," which speaks of control. When the narrator appropriately institutes control, there is some grumbling, but obviously greater efficiency. The narrator expresses his aggression through his role in ways that are at variance with those in the rest of the organization.

Dependency   The narrator is heavily dependent on the success of this program in order to survive. And the company is dependent on his efforts if customers are not to complain.

Is It Solvable?   Apparently the situation can be improved because his superiors have said nothing about the changes that he has slipped through. If he can continue to make improvements in slow steps that allow his superiors to feel that they are still in control and sitting tight, then he probably will be able to make a good deal of progress. However, there are certain steps he can take that will make his job easier and avoid possible threat.

How?   Organizational change is slow and necessarily political, especially personnel changes. Sometimes personnel functions specifically under the authority of a strong chief executive officer. But in organizations where personnel is a staff function, it must always do a gradual selling job and slowly gain acceptance for the programs and policies it has to offer. In many organizations, line executives have been sold a bill of goods by personnel people who all too frequently pick up one fad idea after another and seek to impose them on the work routines of others. Among the new games and gimmicks that over-zealous personnel managers have grabbed at are MBO programs and various performance-appraisal forms. Many executives distrust personnel programs that have been oversold, and are therefore appropriately cautious about new personnel recommendations, wanting to avoid other gimmicks.

Before the narrator prescribes a solution, he has to gain a deeper understanding of the problems he is trying to resolve. He must go to the people in the departments concerned and find out what problems they perceive, what issues they see themselves and their people up against, how they understand the problems to have come about, and what methods they could comfortably use to resolve the problems. Apparently, the narrator has not done anything like this, but has merely made a recommendation for a program that, predictably, has run into resistance from above. In other words, the narrator suggested a therapy without having done an adequate diagnosis of the political situation, and defined the political steps to be taken before creating a context for any program he wanted to implement. The narrator reflects his disdain for the necessary building, maintaining, and entrenching of political support in the organization by using the word "politicking."

Though he may get temporary results by tightening up the two units, he does not have organizational support, and sooner or later is likely to get clobbered. He does well to wonder when and where the attack will fail. He needs to go back and talk with the respective people whose permission is essential to his survival and success. He should meet them with the attitude that it is more important for him to listen and learn than to talk. After he has gained a thorough understanding of what the problems are, he will be able to formulate an appropriate program rather than simply instituting a previously designed package, whether MBO or something else. If the higher-level people are not coming through with their assent, and if there has been a previous history of difference and difficulty with the personnel department, then obviously the narrator must patch up these problems before getting permission to go further.

Epilogue

anagement has come of age. Every social institution now recognizes the need to make best use of its resources. The techniques of management have long since grown beyond simply keeping accounts and setting up an industrially engineered assembly line. Management requires conceptual thinking and mathematical models, research and reorganization, strategy and tactics. It also requires leadership.

If you pick up a handful of sand and grip it tightly, the sand will stay together as long as you sustain your grip. Open your hand and the sand falls away. The sand remains loose and inert, merely a pile of tiny stones. There is nothing to hold them together. If you are to use this sand—to make concrete, for instance—there will have to be some agent to make it cohere, something to give it shape and form and to put it into a useful context.

So it is with organizations. Techniques, strategies, products, or methods are by themselves inert. Like a surgeon's scalpel, they are no more than instruments. In the hands of a skilled person, however, they can be devices for solving problems and attaining ends.

Organizations are made up of all kinds of people. Each, like a grain of sand, is an individual. They may be piled up together, like sand held in an open palm, or they may be held to one another and to the whole by some form of psychological glue. This glue is leadership. Leadership gives purpose, direction, and meaning to action, helping to evolve internally consistent adaptive strategies and flexible tactics. Leadership creates organizational structures and processes that enhance the strength and momentum of the individual organizational particles. People cohere around, and adhere to, leadership.

Leadership transcends and subsumes management. Leaders these days deal with the conflicting forces of multiple constituencies outside the organization and similarly conflicting forces within the organization. Organizations cannot readily adapt without internal conflicting forces, since these enable people to examine the multifaceted nature of problems and their possible solutions. Organizations without loyal opposition become stultified bureaucracies; without external opposition they are unable to realize their contributions to society as a whole. This can be seen in cases where business organizations have tried to act in a more socially responsible way, to combat discrimination against women and minority groups, and to develop more efficient and imaginative products.

In addition to opposition from the outside, leaders are troubled by their own feelings of hostility. Most people fear their aggressive impulses, because they are afraid of their potential destructiveness and because they fear retaliation by others more powerful than they. Aggressive feelings are always unruly. They become even more so when exacerbated in conflict and competition. This is one reason why there is so much conflict between the responsibility to exercise power and the wish to be liked. Another facet of the same issue is the loneliness of the leader, who must make decisions for which he or she is then vulnerable to criticism. Even more than others, leaders fear failure because success is crucial to them and so many people depend upon them. Yet success, too, is something to be feared. Each successful step opens new vistas of opportunity—and possible failure.

The executive confronts other anxieties. One is the fear of not being needed. The better he does his job, the more successfully his organization can operate itself and the more he will feel himself to be superfluous. If anything is more forlorn than a cause without a leader, it is a leader without a cause and without a sense of purpose.

Beneath the prospective feelings of uselessness is a more

subtle fear. Men pursue power because, among other rewards, it provides an illusion of invincibility. If a man engages his power with that of others, some will oppose him and thereby threaten the illusion. He will therefore be under inexorable pressure to assert his leadership role in ways that demonstrate his potency and defeat his rivals. The executive will always be navigating the psychological shoals of his internal struggles.

Struggles and problems notwithstanding, this book has tried to present another meaning of leadership. Implicit in the discussion has been the concept that the relationship between superior and subordinates is a dialogue. The superior speaks to subordinates with every action. Every policy, every project, every failure or achievement is a phrase in that dialogue. When leaders speak or fail to speak, act or fail to act, they reveal what they think of themselves and how they regard their subordinates. Those who respond to leadership, though often verbally silent, nevertheless reply in kind when they produce or fail to produce, when they develop symptoms of emotional distress, when they stay or when they go.

As the work of organizations becomes more abstract and intellectual, the demand for leadership grows at all levels of the organization. Even at low levels of the organization, people with high intellectual competence require equally competent leaders so that independent judgment and conceptualization are possible.

The higher the level of aspiration and the more people become concerned with achieving the personal ends that give meaning to their lives, the greater the importance of leadership. It is the task of leadership to establish this meaning. By establishing common elements, it creates a collective meaning that imparts a cohesive momentum to the organization's tasks. The greater the need for mutual support deriving from organizational relationships, the greater the need for leadership—a key element in that support.

The sociopolitical ethos and the contemporary business scene cry out for leadership. There is a demand for figures whom we can trust, who will speak out and act to achieve our goals. Institutions with social power must recognize and use this power to combat the problems that affect us all and that individuals and communities are incapable of solving alone.

Business leaders, however, are not trusted by the public. It is imperative that the business leadership community build for itself a basis of trust. This requires working to solve the problems within the organization and between the organization and its environment, as well as the collective problems faced by organizations and communities. Today's executives by and large are a well-educated, well-to-do, politically conservative group whose concerns are primarily focused on economic issues and whose social and business contacts tend to be limited to those of similar status and interests. By virtue of their background and training, they have little capacity for interacting with and understanding larger segments of the population. It is precisely this kind of pattern that must change if trust and cooperation are to develop.

If I were to rewrite this book ten years from now, I would expect little of its substance to change. Ideally, I would like to be able to say that American business leadership had earned for itself greater respect and trust than its forebears. I would like to say that it had made efforts to improve the quality of work life and of life in general—that it had become an agent of the continued development of individuals and communities.

Notes
Index

Notes

1. Tomorrow's Executive

1. Chester I. Barnard, *Organization and Management* (Cambridge, Mass.: Harvard University Press, 1956), p. 112.

2. Harry Levinson, *Emotional Health: In the World of Work* (New York: Harper & Row, 1964).

3. "Labor Relations: A Thorn in Corporate Mergers," and "Courts Rule on Thorny Question of Sub-Contracting," *Industrial Relations News*, April 11, 1964, p. 2, and October 2, 1965, p. 1.

4. Leslie M. Dawson, "The Human Concept: New Philosophy for Business," *Business Horizons*, December 1969, pp. 29–38.

5. Carl Menk, "America's Chief Executive Officers: An Endangered Species?" *SKY*, November 1979, pp. 82–84.

6. Robert Heilbroner, a review of *America and the World Political Economy*, by David T. Calleo and Benjamin Roland, *New York Review of Books* 20.19 (November 29, 1973): 31.

7. "The Bonanza in Econometrics," *Newsweek*, July 30, 1979, p. 60.

8. "Vanishing Vigor," *Time*, June 26, 1978, p. 51.

9. Philip Shabecoff, "A Fast Aging Population," *New York Times*, July 30, 1978, p. 16.

10. "Conversation with Fletcher Byrom," *Organizational Dynamics*, Summer 1978, p. 41.

11. B. Inhelder and J. Piaget, *The Growth of Logical Thinking from Childhood to Adolescence* (New York: Basic Books, 1958).

12. Abraham Zaleznik and Manfred Kets de Vries, *Power and the Corporate Mind* (Boston: Houghton Mifflin, 1975).

13. "Blue-Collar Robots," *Newsweek*, April 23, 1979, pp. 80–81.

2. The Reinvestment of Human Drives

1. *The Levinson Letter*, July 15, 1977, p. 2.

2. Sigmund Freud, "The Ego and the Id," *The Standard Edition of the Complete Psychological Works of Sigmund Freud*, vol. 19 (London: Hogarth Press, 1961); Charles Brenner, *An Elementary Textbook of Psychoanalysis* (New York: International Universities Press, 1955); Fritz Redlich and June Bingham, *The Inside Story* (New York: Alfred A. Knopf, 1953); William C. Menninger and Munro Leaf, *You and Psychiatry* (New York: Charles Scribner's Sons, 1948); Calvin Hall, *A Primer of Freudian Psychology* (New York: World Book Co., 1954).

This discussion of psychoanalytic theory is deliberately brief because an adequate discussion would take several chapters, if not a book. For a more complete short discussion, the reader is referred to the first four chapters of Harry Levinson, *Emotional Health: In the World of Work* (New York: Harper & Row, 1964). A good single-volume discussion is Charles Brenner, *An Elementary Textbook of Psychoanalysis* (New York: International Universities Press, 1955).

3. Samuel L. Clemens, *What Is Man?* and other philosophical writings, ed. Paul Baender, Mark Twain papers series, vol. 1 (Stanford: University of California Press, 1973), ch. 6.

4. Erik H. Erikson, *Childhood and Society*, 2nd ed. (New York: Norton, 1963), ch. 7.

5. Harry Stack Sullivan, *The Interpersonal Theory of Psychiatry*, ed. Helen Swick Perry and Mary Ladd Gawel (New York: W. W. Norton, 1953).

6. Carl Jung, *Psychology and Education*, trans. R. F. D. Hull (Princeton, N.J.: Princeton University Press, 1969).

7. Margaret Hennig and Anne Jardim, *The Managerial Woman* (Garden City, N.Y.: Anchor Press/Doubleday, 1977), p. xii.

8. Robert L. Dipboye, Richard D. Arvey, and David E. Terpstra, "Sex and Physical Attractiveness of Raters and Applicants as Determinants of Résumé Evaluations," *Journal of Applied Psychology* 62.3 (June 1977): 288–294.

9. Eleanor Maccoby and Carol N. Jacklin, *The Psychology of Sex Differences* (Stanford: Stanford University Press, 1974).

10. Matina S. Horner, "Femininity and Successful Achievement: Basic Inconsistency," in J. M. Bardwick, E. Douvan, M. S. Horner, and D. Gutman, *Feminine Personality and Conflict* (Bemont, Calif.: Brooks Cole Publishing Company, 1970), pp. 45–76.

11. Hennig and Jardim, *Managerial Woman.*

12. Lois Ann Koff and Joseph Handlon, "Women in Management: Keys to Success and Failure," *Personnel Administrator* 20 (April 1975): 2, 24–28.

13. Jean A. Briggs, "How You Going to Get 'Em Back in the Kitchen? (You Aren't.)" (interview with Eli Ginzberg), *Forbes*, June 15, 1977, pp. 177–184.

14. Nancy C. Morse and Robert S. Weiss, "The Function and Meaning of Work and the Job," *American Sociological Review* 20.2 (April 1955): 192.

15. George F. Will, "The Cold War among Women," *Newsweek*, June 26, 1978, p. 100.

16. U.S. Department of Health, Education, and Welfare, Feature Services, in *The Levinson Letter*, July 15, 1977.

17. Diana Trilling, "Daughters of the Middle Class," *Harper's*, April 1977, pp. 31–36, 92.

18. Morris S. Viteles, *Motivation and Morale in Industry* (New York: W.W. Norton, 1953); Victor H. Vroom, *Work and Motivation* (New York: John Wiley & Sons, 1964).

19. Edward E. Lawler and Lyman W. Porter, "Perceptions Regarding Management Compensation," *Industrial Relations* 3.1 (October 1963): 41–49; Edward E. Lawler, *Pay and Organizational Effectiveness* (New York: McGraw-Hill, 1971).

20. Eli Ginzberg, *The Unemployed* (New York: Harper & Bros., 1943).

21. J. Stacy Adams, "Wage Inequities, Productivity and Work Quality," *Industrial Relations* 3.1 (October 1963): 9–16.

22. Walter Toman, *Family Constellation* (New York: Springer, 1976).

23. Rebecca Oxford Manley, "Parental Warmth and Hostility as Related to Sex Differences in Children's Achievement Orientation," *Psychology of Women Quarterly* 1.3 (Spring 1977): 229–246.

24. Ivan Boszormenyi-Nagy and Geraldine M. Spark, *Invisible Loyalties* (New York: Harper & Row, 1973).

3. The Purposes Served by Organizations

1. Raymond Hill, "Interpersonal Needs in Functional Area of Management," *Journal of Vocational Behavior* 4.1 (1974): 15–24.

2. Harry Levinson et al., *Men, Management, and Mental Health* (Cambridge, Mass.: Harvard University Press, 1962).

3. Karl Menninger, *Theory of Psychoanalytic Technique* (New York: Basic Books, 1958).

4. Claude Fischer et al., *Network and Places: Social Relations in the Urban Setting* (Berkeley: Free Press, 1977).

5. J. Bernstein, "Volunteering—A Way of Life," *Council Women*, National Council of Jewish Women, October/December, 1977, p. 8.

6. Daniel Yankelovich, "The New Psychological Contracts at Work," *Psychology Today*, May 1978, pp. 46–50.

7. Elliot Jaques, "Social Systems as a Defense against Persecutory and Depressive Anxiety," in Melanie Klein, ed., *New Directions in Psychoanalysis* (New York: Basic Books, 1955).

8. Melanie Klein, "A Contribution to the Psychogenesis of Manic-Depressive States," in Klein, ed., *Contributions to Psychoanalysis, 1921–1945* (London: Hogarth Press, 1948).

9. Philip Selznick, *Leadership in Administration* (Evanston, Ill.: Row, Peterson, 1957).

10. Norman Reider, "Transference to Institutions," *Bulletin of the Menninger Clinic* 17.2 (March 1953): 60. Italics added.

11. H. A. Wilmer, "Transference to a Medical Center," *California Medicine* 96.3 (March 1962): 173.

12. Frederick Herzberg, Bernard Mausner, and Barbara Snyderman, *The Motivation to Work* (New York: John Wiley & Sons, 1959).

4. Reflections of the Culture

1. Paul M. Insel and Rudolph Moos, "Psychological Environments: Expanding the Scope of Human Ecology, *American Psychologist* 29.3 (March 1974): 179–188.

2. Robert S. Weiss, "A Structure-Function Approach to Organizations," *Journal of Social Issues* 12.2 (1956): 61–67.

3. Eleanor Wintour, "Bringing up Children: The American Way vs. the British Way," *Harper's* 229.1371 (August 1964): 58–63; Henry Fairlie, "American Kids?" *New York Times Magazine*, November 14, 1965, pp. 116ff.; Sheffield White, "The Underdeveloped British Businessman," *Atlantic* 217.3 (January 1966): 75–78; Howard R. Wolf, "British Fathers and Sons, 1773–1913: From Filial Submissiveness to Creativity," *Psychoanalytic Review* 52.2 (Summer 1965): 53–70.

4. "The Halfhearted Economy," *Time*, December 25, 1964, pp. 60–61.

5. George Vassilou and Vasso G. Vassilou, "Variations of the Group Process across Cultures," *International Journal of Group Psychotherapy* 24.1 (January 1974): 55–65.

6. Norman Bradburn, "Interpersonal Relations within Formal Organizations in Turkey," *Journal of Social Issues* 19.1 (January 1963): 61–67.

7. Luigi Barzini, *The Italians* (New York: Atheneum, 1964); John Fischer, "The Japanese Intellectuals: Cliques, Soft Edges, and the Dread of Power," *Harper's* 229.1372 (September 1964): 14–15ff.

8. Takeo Doi, *The Anatomy of Dependence* (Kodansha International, Ltd., distrib. Harper & Row, 1973).

9. Some classical examples of such studies are: Daniel Katz, Nathan Maccoby, and Nancy C. Morse, *Productivity, Supervision and Morale in an Office Situation* (Ann Arbor: University of Michigan Institute for Social Research, 1950); Daniel Katz et al., *Productivity, Supervision, and Morale among Railroad Workers* (Ann Arbor: University of Michigan Institute for Social Research, 1951); E. A. Fleishman, E. F. Harris, and Harold Burtt, *Leadership and Supervision in Industry* (Columbus: Ohio State University Press, 1955). Summaries of such studies may be found in the following, among others: Rensis Likert, *New Patterns of Management* (New York: John Wiley & Sons, 1961); Morris S. Viteles, *Motivation and Morale in Industry* (New York: W. W. Norton, 1953); Victor H. Vroom, *Work and Motivation* (New York: John Wiley & Sons, 1964).

10. Kenneth Boulding, *The Organizational Revolution* (New York: Harper & Row, 1963).

11. Curtis Gans, "The Politics of Selfishness: The Cause—The Empty Voting Booths," *Washington Monthly*, October 1978, pp. 27–30.

12. Ferenc Merli, "Group Leadership and Institutionalization," *Human Relations* 2.1 (January 1949): 23–29.

13. Luigi Barzini, "The Next Pope," *Harper's* 213.1277 (October 1956): 27–34.

14. James Worsham and Susan Trausch, "The 'Now' Generation Is Thinking 'Me First'," *Boston Globe*, October 15, 1978, p. 10.

15. Ibid.

16. Ibid.

17. Ibid.

18. U.S. Department of Commerce, *Social Indicators 1976: Selected Data on Social Conditions and Trends in the U.S.* (Washington, D.C.: U.S. Government Printing Office, 1976), p. 354.

19. Daniel Yankelovich, "The New Psychological Contracts at Work," *Psychology Today*, May 1978, p. 47.

20. Eric Hoffer, "A Time of Juveniles," *Harper's* 230.1381 (June 1965): 17–24.

21. Alvin W. Gouldner, "Cosmopolitans and Locals: Toward an Analysis of Latent Social Roles, I," *Administrative Science Quarterly* 2.3 (December 1957): 281–306.

22. U.S. Department of Commerce, *Social Indicators 1976*, p. 400.

23. Ibid., p. 336.

24. "Name of Prescription Should be on Label, AMA Council Asserts," *Wall Street Journal*, July 29, 1963.

25. Eli Ginzberg, "Man and His Work," *California Management Review* 5.2 (Winter 1962): 22.

26. Daniel Bell, "The Invisible Unemployed," in Sigmund Nosow and William H. Forms, eds., *Man, Work, and Society* (New York: Basic Books, 1962).

27. "Unwelcome News," *Saturday Review*, November 25, 1978, pp. 7–8.

28. Harold Leavitt and Thomas L. Whisler, "Management in the 1980's," *Harvard Business Review* 36.6 (November–December 1958): 41–48.

29. "GM's Spruce-up Plan for Detroit," *Newsweek*, September 25, 1978, p. 25. See also Iver Peterson, "States Seeking to Curb Impact of Closing Industrial Plants," *New York Times*, March 16, 1980, p. 26.

30. Irving S. Shapiro (interviewed), "Today's Executive: Private Steward and Public Servant," *Harvard Business Review* 56.2 (March–April 1978): 94–101.

31. Nicholas A. Ashford, *Crisis in the Workplace: Occupational Disease and Injury* (Cambridge, Mass: MIT Press, 1975).

32. "France: A Threat of Jail for Plant Managers," *Business Week*, March 29, 1976, pp. 48–49.

33. Archie Carroll, *Atlanta Gazette*, July 23, 1975.

34. George Cabot Lodge, *The New American Ideology* (New York: Knopf, 1975).

5. What the Executive Doesn't See

1. The role of unconscious motivation is given some attention in works such as: Abraham Zaleznik and Manfred Kets de Vries, *Power and the Corporate Mind* (Boston: Houghton Mifflin, 1975); Orvis F. Collins, David G. Moore, and Darab B. Unwalla, *The Enterprising Man* (East Lansing: Michigan State University Bureau of Business Research, 1964); Otto Kernberg, "Re-

gression in Organizational Leadership," *Psychiatry* 1.42 (February 1979): 24–39; Chris Argyris and Donald A. Schon, *Organizational Learning: A Theory of Action Perspective* (Reading, Mass.: Addison-Wesley, 1978); Chris Argyris and Donald A. Schon, *Theory in Practice: Increasing Professional Effectiveness* (San Francisco: Jossey Bass, 1974); and Richard C. Hodgson, Daniel J. Levinson, and Abraham Zaleznik, *The Executive Role Constellation* (Boston: Harvard Graduate School of Business Administration, 1965).

2. Morris West, *The Shoes of the Fisherman* (New York: Dell, 1964), p. 53.

3. "Cardinals Tried Polish, Quit," *Boston Globe*, October 19, 1978, p. 12.

4. Harry Levinson, *The Great Jackass Fallacy* (Boston: Harvard Graduate School of Business Administration, 1973).

5. Philip Selznick, *Leadership in Administration* (Evanston, Ill.: Row, Peterson, 1957), p. 5.

6. Chris Argyris, *Personality and Organization* (New York: Harper & Bros., 1958).

7. Lester Coch and John R. P. French, Jr., "Overcoming Resistance to Change," *Human Relations* 1.4 (August 1948): 512–532.

8. Ralph Hirschowitz, "Psychological Cost Accounting?" *The Levinson Letter*, Addendum, 1975.

9. Charles M. Solley and Gardner Murphy, *Development of the Perceptual World* (New York: Basic Books, 1960).

10. E. A. Fleischman, E. F. Harris, and Harold Burtt, *Leadership and Supervision in Industry* (Columbus, Ohio: Ohio State University Press, 1955), pp. 93–100.

11. Harry Levinson, "A Psychologist Looks at Executive Development," *Harvard Business Review* 40.5 (September–October 1962): 69–75.

12. Douglas McGregor, *Leadership and Motivation* (Cambridge, Mass.: MIT Press, 1966), p. 29.

13. Otto F. Kernberg, "Regression in Organizational Leadership," *Psychiatry* 1.42 (February, 1979): 24–39.

14. Henry Fairlie, "Too Rich for Heroes," *Harper's*, November 1978, pp. 33–98.

15. Peter F. Drucker, "Our Emerging Industrial Society," *Social Progress* 53.6 (April 1963): 28–40.

16. August B. Hollingshead and Frederick C. Redlich, *Social Class and Mental Illness* (New York: John Wiley & Sons, 1958); and Arthur Kornhauser, *Mental Health of the Industrial Worker* (New York: John Wiley & Sons, 1965).

17. Harry Levinson, et al., *Men, Management, and Mental Health* (Cambridge, Mass.: Harvard University Press, 1962).

18. Victor F. Zonana, "Battle of the Bulge," *Wall Street Journal*, August 18, 1975, pp. 1, 21.

19. John B. Miner, "Student Attitudes toward Bureaucratic Role Prescriptions and Prospects for Managerial Talent Shortages," *Personal Psychology* 27.4 (Winter, 1974): 605–613.

20. Roy Schafer, "The Loving and Beloved Superego in Freud's Structural Theory," *The Psychoanalytic Study of the Child*, vol. 15, (New York: International Universities Press, 1960), pp. 163–188.

21. Donald McDonald, *An Interview with Hans Bethe* (Santa Barbara, Calif: Center for the Study of Democratic Institutions, 1962), p. 6; Thomas A. Cowan, "Decision Theory in Law, Science and Technology," *Science,* June 7, 1963, pp. 1067–1068.

22. Donald L. Johnson and Arthur L. Kobler, "The Man-Computer Relationship," *Science,* November 23, 1962, p. 873.

23. Ibid., p. 879.

24. See Stanley A. Rudin, "The Personal Price of National Glory," *Transaction* 2.6 (September–October 1965): 4–9.

25. Phillip M. Boffey, "American Science Policy: OECD Publishes a Massive Critique," *Science,* January 12, 1968, pp. 176–178.

26. "More of Today's Executives Speak the Language of Science," *Personnel* 42.4 (July–August 1965): 7.

6. The Tasks of Top Management

1. Thomas J. Watson, Jr., *A Business and Its Beliefs* (New York: McGraw-Hill, 1963), p. 4.

2. Victor L. Burford and Allison J. Esposito, "Today's Executive: Private Steward and Public Servant: An Interview with Irving S. Shapiro," *Harvard Business Review* 56.2 (March–April 1978): 94.

3. "Business Must Be Socially Responsible as Well as Profitable, Ullrich Argues," *Harvard University Gazette,* May 14, 1976, p. 5.

4. Peter Drucker, "Our Emerging Industrial Society," *Social Progress* 53.6 (April 1963): 31.

5. Frederick Pollock, *Automation* (New York: Praeger, 1957).

6. Pehr G. Gyllenhammar, "How Volvo Adapts Work to People," *Harvard Business Review* 55.4 (July–August 1977): 102–113.

7. See Aaron Levenstein, *Why People Work* (New York: Crowell-Collier, 1962).

8. Bernard J. Muller-Thym, "Practices in General Management: New Directions for Organizational Management," American Society of Mechanical Engineers, paper no. 60-WA-59 (1960).

9. Ithiel de Sola Pool, "The Head of the Company: Conceptions of Role and Identity," *Behavioral Science* 9.2 (April 1964): 147–155.

10. Harold J. Leavitt and Thomas L. Whisler, "Management in the 1980's," *Harvard Business Review* 36.6 (November–December 1958): 41–48.

11. William F. Dowling, "Conversation with Fletcher Byrom," *Organizational Dynamics* 7.1 (Summer 1978): 43.

12. Seymour M. Lipset and Reinhard Bendix, *Social Mobility in Industrial Society* (Berkeley: University of California Press, 1959), p. 138.

13. Vance Packard, *The Pyramind Climbers* (New York: McGraw-Hill, 1962).

14. Andrew Hacker, "The Elected and the Anointed: Two American Elites," *American Political Science Review* 55.3 (September 1961): 539–549; "Fathers and Sons," *Wall Street Journal,* December 14, 1966.

15. Andrew Hacker, *The End of the American Era* (New York: Atheneum, 1970), pp. 60–61.

16. Frederick D. Sturdivant and Ray D. Adler, "Executive Origins: Still a Gray Flannel World?" *Harvard Business Review* 54.6 (November–December 1976): 125–132.

17. Lynn Langway, "Organization Men Still Run the Show," *Newsweek*, June 18, 1979, p. 75.

18. Margaret Hennig and Anne Jardim, *The Managerial Woman* (Garden City, N.Y.: Anchor Press/Doubleday, 1977)

19. Harold J. Leavitt and Thomas L. Whisler, "Management in the 1980's," *Harvard Business Review* 36.6 (November–December 1958): 41–48.

20. Muriel Cohen, "The Divided Trustees at B.U.," *Boston Globe*, April 16, 1979, p. 26.

21. Pollock, *Automation*, p. 83.

22. Donald N. Michael, *Cybernation: The Silent Conquest* (Santa Barbara, Calif.: Center for the Study of Democratic Institutions, 1962), p. 35.

23. Dowling, "Fletcher Byrom," pp. 42–43.

24. Wilfred Brown, *Organization* (London: Heinemann, 1971).

25. Leonard Sayles, *Individualism and Big Business* (New York: McGraw-Hill, 1963). Thomas J. Murray, "More Power for the Middle Manager," *Dun's Review*, June 1978, pp. 60–62.

26. Charles W. Stevens, "One Producer Finds Recall Is Bad Policy for a Hazardous Toy," *Wall Street Journal*, March 2, 1979, p. 32.

27. "When Businessmen Confess Their Social Sins," *Business Week*, November 6, 1978, pp. 175–178.

7. The Business as an Educational Institution

1. A. H. Raskin, "Automation: Key to Lifetime Jobs," *Saturday Review*, November 28, 1976, pp. 14–16; Allan Wood, "USW Draft Novel Agreement on Security for Workers," *Wall Street Journal*, January 11, 1965.

2. A. Harvey Belitsky, *Productivity and Job Security: Retraining to Adapt to Technological Change* (Washington, D.C.: National Center for Productivity and Quality of Working Life, 1977), p. 98.

3. Charles A. Myers, *The Role of the Private Sector in Manpower Development* (Baltimore: John Hopkins Press, 1971), p. 26.

4. "Why Retraining Results Are So Often Disappointing," and "Displaced Workers Who Stay That Way," *Personnel* 40.4 (July–August 1963): 5, and 40.2 (March–April 1963): 21; A. R. Weber, *Retraining the Unemployed* (Chicago: University of Chicago, Graduate School of Business, 1963), and "When Job Retraining Helps," *Business Week*, November 16, 1963, p. 50; "Scoreboard for Legislated Training Effort," *Industrial Relations News*, February 5, 1966, p. 2; "Technology's Impact: Du Pont Eases It by Locating New Plants Near Those It Closes, Pushing Retraining," *Wall Street Journal*, December 18, 1962.

5. Allen R. Dodd, Jr., *The Job Hunter* (New York: McGraw-Hill, 1965), p. 193.

6. Tom Collins, "Retirement Results in Void," *Topeka State Journal*, May 4, 1965.

7. Harold G. Wolff, "What Hope Does for Man," *Saturday Review,* January 5, 1957, pp. 42-45.

8. S. P. Goodwin, *Experience in Group Hiring, Training, and Adaptation* (Clifton, N.J.: Goerlick, 1963).

9. "Morality Play," *Forbes,* August 15, 1966, pp. 30-31.

10. "Industrial Program to Curtail High School Dropouts," and "Disadvantaged Youth Have a Friend at Chase Manhattan," *Industrial Relations News,* October 9, 1965, pp. 1-2, and May 7, 1966, p. 1

11. "Can Today's Unemployables Become Tomorrow's Salesmen?" *Merchandising Week,* March 29, 1965; "Peace Corps Stresses On-the-Scene Training over Classroom Work," *Wall Street Journal,* August 24, 1966.

12. "When Europe Tailor-Makes Programs for Millions Out of Work." *U.S. News and World Report,* February 21, 1977, pp. 61-62.

13. "Fight Unemployment—Six Experts Tell What's Needed," *U.S. News and World Report,* February 21, 1977, pp. 56-60.

14. Ibid.

15. "Find a Boss Who'll Pay for Your Education," *Changing Times,* May 1979, pp. 15-16.

16. Ibid.

17. "Wanted: A Manager to Fit Each Strategy ," *Business Week,* February 25, 1980, pp. 166-170.

18. "Following the Corporate Legend," *Business Week,* February 11, 1980, pp. 62-71.

19. "Manpower Shortages Predicted for Top and Bottom Echelons," *Industrial Relations News,* May 18, 1963, pp. 1-2.

20. Reed M. Powell and Charles S. David, "Do University Executive Development Programs Pay Off?" *Business Horizons,* 16.4 (August 1973): pp. 81-87.

21. George J. Odiorne, "Managerial Narcissism—the Great Self-Development Binge," *Management of Personnel Quarterly* 1.3 (Spring 1962): 21-25.

22. Raymond A. Bauer, "Social Psychology and the Study of Policy Formation," *American Psychologist* 21.10 (October 1966): 933-942.

23. Daniel P. Moynihan, "The United States in Opposition," *Commentary* 59.3 (March 1975): 31.

8. The Role and the Learners

1. "The Changing American Executive," *Dun's Review* 83.1 (January 1964): 38-41ff.

2. Henry Brandon, "Schlesinger at the White House," *Harper's* 229.1370 (July 1964): 56.

3. John Fischer, "The Editor's Trade," *Harper's* 231.1382 (July 1965): 20-23.

4. "Gut Feelings Are Still the Basis for Executive Decisions," *The Levinson Letter,* July 15, 1977.

5. Douglas McGregor, *The Human Side of Enterprise* (New York: McGraw-Hill, 1960).

6. Abraham Zaleznik, "Managers and Leaders, Are They Different?"

Harvard Business Review, 55.3 (May-June 1977): 67-78; Abraham Zaleznik and Manfred Kets de Vries, *Power and the Corporate Mind* (Boston: Houghton Mifflin, 1975).

7. Crawford H. Greenewalt, "Sensing Who Can Command," *Nation's Business* 53.10 (October 1965): 40ff; William D. Patterson, "David Rockefeller, Creative Banker, Champion of Change," *Saturday Review,* January 9, 1965, pp. 39-40ff.; "Looking Backward," *Time,* February 7, 1964, p. 52.

8. Henry A. Kissinger, "The Illusionist: Why We Misread deGaulle," *Harper's* 230.1378 (March 1965): 70.

9. Edith Jacobson, *The Self and the Object World* (New York: International Universities Press, 1964), p. 54.

10. Eugene Jennings, "The Emergence of New Managerial Style," paper presented to the Upper Midwest Hospital Conference, May 14, 1964.

11. John W. Gardner, *Self-Renewal* (New York: Harper & Row, 1963), p. 10.

12. Edgar H. Schein, "How to Break-In the College Graduate," *Harvard Business Review* 42.6 (November-December 1964): 68-76.

13. Arthur Letcher, "Understanding Today's Students," *Journal for College Placement* 26.3 (February-March 1966): 91-92; Duncan Norton-Taylor, "The Private World of the Class of '66," *Fortune* 73.2 (February 1966): 128-132; "Xerox Chairman Emphasizes Social Objectives of the Corporation as a Way of Attracting Bright New Leadership," *Industrial Relations News,* April 23, 1966, p. 1. See also Robert M. Hutchins, "Why They Don't Want Business Careers," *Think* 32.5 (September-October 1966): 2-5; "Notable and Quotable," *Wall Street Journal,* February 28, 1967; Elinor Langer, "The Berkeley Scene, 1966 (II): Educational Reform," *Science,* May 27, 1966, pp. 1220-1223.

14. "Lack of Purpose in Business Careers," *Industrial Relations News,* January 1, 1966, p. 4.

15. Jean Seligmann, "The Golden Passport," *Newsweek,* May 14, 1979, p. 110.

16. Ibid.

17. Ibid., p. 112.

18. See also Abraham Zaleznik and Manfred Kets de Vries, *Power and the Corporate Mind* (Boston: Houghton Mifflin, 1975); James McGregor Burns, *Leadership* (New York: Harper & Row, 1978); Fred Fiedler, et al., *Improving Leadership Effectiveness: The Leadership Match Concept* (New York: John Wiley & Sons, 1976); Victor H. Vroom and Philip W. Yetton, *Leadership and Decision-Making* (Pittsburgh: University of Pittsburgh Press, 1976); David C. McClelland and David H. Burnham, "Power is the Great Motivator," *Harvard Business Review,* March-April 1976, pp. 100-110.

9. The Executive as Teacher

1. Joseph Adelson, "The Teacher as a Model," *American Scholar* 30.3 (Summer 1961): 394-404.

2. Kenneth R. Mitchell, "Clinical Relevance of the Boundary Func-

tions of Language," *Bulletin of the Menninger Clinic* 40.1 (November 1976): 641–654.

3. Aaron Wildavsky, "Was Nixon Tough: Dilemma of American State Craft," *Social Science and Modern Society* 16.1 (November–December 1978): 25–35.

4. "On Criticism," *Royal Bank of Canada Monthly Letter* 57.11 (November 1976): 1–4.

5. Margery Jean Gross Doehrman, "Parallel Processes in Supervision and Psychotherapy," *Bulletin of the Menninger Clinic* 40.1 (January 1976): 9–104.

6. Philip H. Abelson, "What Are Professors For?" *Science*, June 18, 1965, p. 1546.

7. Abraham Zaleznik, "Managers and Leaders: Are They Different?" *Harvard Business Review* 55.3 (May–June 1977): 67–68.

8. "Everyone Who Makes It Has a Mentor" (interviews with F. J. Lunding, G. L. Clements, and D. S. Perkins) *Harvard Business Review* 56.4 (July–August 1978): 89–101.

9. Margaret Hennig and Barbara Hackman Franklin, "Men and Women at Harvard Business School," unpublished M.B.A. research paper; see Margaret Hennig and Anne Jardim, *The Managerial Woman* (Garden City, N.Y.: Anchor Press/Doubleday, 1977).

10. Anne Alonso, "Cross-Sex Supervision for Cross-Sex Therapy," *American Journal of Psychiatry* 135 (August 1978): 928–931.

11. Sigmund Freud, "Group Psychology and the Analysis of the Ego," *Standard Edition of the Complete Psychological Works of Sigmund Freud*, vol. 18 (London: Hogarth Press, 1955), p. 105.

12. Edith Jacobson, *The Self and the Object World* (New York: International Universities Press, 1964), p. 66.

13. Ruth Mack Brunswick, "The Preoedipal Phase of Libido Development," *Psychoanalytic Quarterly* 9.2. (April 1940): 293–319.

14. Joost A. M. Meerloo, "Plagiarism and Identification," *Archives of General Psychiatry* 11.4 (October 1964): 421–424.

15. Irving Knickerbocker, "Leadership: A Conception and Some Implications," *Journal of Social Issues* 4.3 (Summer 1948): 23–40.

16. Freud, "Group Psychology and the Analysis of the Ego," p. 108.

17. Suzanne H. Rudolph, "Self-Control and Political Potency: Gandhi's Asceticism," *American Scholar* 35.1 (Winter 1965–66): 79–97.

18. Freud, "Group Psychology and the Analysis of the Ego," p. 116.

19. Robert Waelder, "Conflict and Violence," *Bulletin of the Menninger Clinic* 30.5 (September 1966): 272.

20. William M. Easson, "The Ego Ideal in the Treatment of Children and Adolescents," *Archives of General Psychiatry* 15.3 (September 1966): 288–292.

21. W. Schindler, "The Role of the Doctor in Group Therapy," *International Journal of Group Psychotherapy* 16.2 (April 1966): 198–202; Joseph C. Bailey, "Clues for Success in the President's Job," *Harvard Business Review* 45.3 (May–June 1967): 97–104.

22. Ralph Waldo Emerson, "Self-Reliance," in Edward Waldo Emer-

son, ed., *The Complete Works of Ralph Waldo Emerson* (Boston: Houghton Mifflin, 1903/1904).

23. Anna Freud, *The Ego and the Mechanisms of Defense* (New York: International Universities Press, 1946), p. 121.

24. See James Mann, "Psychoanalytic Observations Regarding Conformity in Groups," *International Journal of Group Psychotherapy* 12.1 (January 1962): 8–10.

25. Selwyn W. Becker, "Personality and Effective Communication in the Organization," *Personnel Administration* 27.4 (July–August 1964): 28–30.

26. David G. Bowers, "Self-Esteem and Supervision," *Personnel Administration* 27.4 (July–August 1964): 23–26.

27. Karl Menninger, "Human Needs in Urban Society," *Menninger Quarterly* 13.3 (Fall 1959): 1–8.

28. Knickerbocker, "Leadership: A Conception and Some Implications."

29. Warren G. Bennis, *Changing Organizations* (New York: McGraw-Hill, 1966).

10. Ministration Needs

1. William C. Schultz, *FIRO; A Three-Dimensional Theory of Interpersonal Behavior* (New York: Henry Holt, 1958).

2. Harry Levinson et al., *Men, Management, and Mental Health* (Cambridge, Mass.: Harvard University Press, 1962).

3. John W. Gardner, *Self-Renewal* (New York: Harper & Row, 1963), p. 16.

4. Frederick Herzberg, Bernard Mausner, and Barbara Snyderman, *The Motivation to Work* (New York: John Wiley & Sons, 1959).

5. James L. Price, *The Study of Turnover* (Ames, Iowa: Iowa State University Press, 1977), pp. 73–74.

6. Edgar H. Schein, "How to Break-In the College Graduate," *Harvard Business Review* 42.6 (November–December 1964): 68–76.

7. S. R. Parker, "Type of Work, Friendship Patterns, and Leisure," *Human Relations* 17.3 (August 1964): 215–219.

8. Harold Lasswell and Abraham Kaplan, *Power and Society* (New Haven, Conn.: Yale University Press, 1963).

9. Selwyn W. Becker, "Personality and Effective Communication in the Organization," *Personnel Administration* 27.4 (July–August 1964): 28–30.

10. Levinson et al., *Men, Management, and Mental Health*, p. 63.

11. Michael Aiken and Jerold Hage, "Organizational Alienation: A Comparative Analysis," *American Sociological Review* 31.4 (August 1966): 497–507; Elliott Jaques, "Too Many Management Levels," *California Management Review* 8.1 (Fall 1965): 13–20; Rensis Likert, *Applying Modern Management Principles to Sales Organizations* (Ann Arbor, Mich.: Foundation for Research on Human Behavior, 1963).

12. Douglas McGregor, *Leadership and Motivation* (Cambridge, Mass.: MIT Press, 1966), p. 51.

13. Norman Reider, "Psychodynamics of Authority with Relation to

Some Psychiatric Problems in Offices," *Bulletin of the Menninger Clinic* 8.2 (March 1944): 55–58.

14. Stephen M. Holloway and Harvey A. Hornstein, "How Good News Makes Us Good," *Psychology Today* 10.7 (December 1976): 76–78, 106–108.

15. Rensis Likert, *New Patterns of Management* (New York: McGraw-Hill, 1961).

16. Norman R. F. Maier and L. Richard Hoffman, "Financial Incentives and Group Decision in Motivating Change," *Journal of Social Psychology* 64.2 (October 1964): 369–378.

17. "When the Boss Isn't Handling His Job" (an interview with Alfred J. Marrow), *U.S. News and World Report*, February 13, 1978, pp. 75–76.

18. David G. Bowers, "Self-Esteem and Supervision," *Personnel Administration*, 27.4 (July–August 1964), 23–26.

19. Berkely Rice, "Midlife Encounters: The Menninger Seminars for Businessmen," *Psychology Today* 12.11 (April 1979): 74.

20. Floyd C. Mann, "Toward an Understanding of the Leadership Role in Formal Organization," in Robert Dubin et al., eds., *Leadership and Productivity* (San Francisco: Chandler Publishing Co., 1965).

21. David T. A. Vernon, "Modeling and Birth Order in Responses to Painful Stimuli," *Journal of Personality and Social Psychology* 29.6 (1974): 794–799.

22. Likert, *New Patterns of Management*, p. 103.

23. Eric L. Trist et al., *Organizational Choice* (London: Tavistock Institute, 1963).

24. Salomon Rettig, "Group Discussion and Predicted Ethical Risk Taking," *Journal of Personality and Social Psychology* 3.6 (June 1966): 629–633.

25. Robert Dubin, "Supervision and Productivity: Empirical Findings and Theoretical Considerations," in Dubin et al., *Leadership and Productivity*, p. 30.

26. Leonard R. Sayles, "Managing Organizations: What We Know Now That We Didn't Know Before," *Management Review* 56.1 (January 1967): 50–53.

27. Abraham H. Maslow, *Motivation and Personality* (New York: Harper & Bros., 1954).

28. Martin Patchen, "Supervisory Methods and Group Performance Norms," *Administrative Science Quarterly* 7.3 (December 1962): 275–294.

29. Lyndall F. Urwick, "The Line/Staff Impasse—A Footnote," *Management Review* 56.1 (January 1967): 50–53.

30. Gardner, *Self-Renewal*, p. 73.

31. F. Reif, "The Competitive World of the Pure Scientist," *Science*, December 15, 1961, pp. 1957–1962.

32. Ralph Cordiner, "The Nature of the Work of the Chief Executive," address, General Electric Co., Schenectady, N.Y., September 16, 1963.

33. Eugene E. Jennings, "Two Schools of Thought about Executive Development," *Personnel Journal* 37.10 (March 1959): 370–372.

34. Raymond A. Katzell, "Reflections on Educating Executives," *Public Administrative Review* 19.1 (Winter 1959): 4–6.

35. McGregor, *Leadership and Motivation*, p. 25.

36. M. Gene Newport, "Problems of Middle Management Development," *Personnel Administration* 28.2 (March–April 1965): 17–20; Warren C. McGovney, "Start at the Top," *Advanced Management* 1.2 (February 1962): 11–12.

37. Mortimer R. Feinberg, quoted by Harwood F. Merrill in "The Listening Post," *Management News* 38.2 (February 1965): 1.

38. Walter R. Mahler, "Improving Coaching Skills," *Personnel Administration* 27.1 (January–February 1964): 28–33.

39. Robert L. Sutherland, "Can an Adult Change?" *Advanced Management* 17.3 (March 1952): 2–6.

40. Joseph F. Follmann, *Helping the Troubled Employee* (New York: AMACOM, 1978); Arthur X. Deegan, *Coaching: A Management Skill for Improving Individual Performance* (Reading, Mass.: Addison-Wesley, 1979); Theodore P. Peck, *Employee Counseling in Industry and Government: A Guide to Information Sources* (Detroit: Gale Research Co., 1979); Earl M. Bowler and Frances T. Dawson, *Counseling Employees* (Englewood Cliffs, N.J.: Prentice-Hall, 1948); Nathaniel Cantor, *Employee Counseling* (New York: McGraw-Hill, 1945); Benjamin Balinsky and Ruth Berger, *The Executive Interview: A Bridge to People* (New York: Harper & Bros., 1959); William J. Dickson and F. J. Roethlisberger, *Counseling in an Organization: A Sequel to the Hawthorne Researches* (Boston: Harvard University Graduate School of Business Administration, 1966); Felix M. Lopez, Jr., *Personnel Interviewing: Theory and Practice* (New York: McGraw-Hill, 1965).

41. Gertrude R. Ticho, "On Self-Analysis," *International Journal of Psychoanalysis* 48.2 (April 1967): 308–318.

42. Edwin Thomas, Norman Polansky, and Jacob Kounin, "The Expected Behavior of a Potentially Helpful Person," *Human Relations* 8.2 (May 1955): 165–174.

43. Lawrence L. Ferguson, "Better Management of Managers' Careers," *Harvard Business Review* 44.2 (March–April 1966): 139–153.

11. Maturation Needs

1. *Science* 202.4365 (October 1978): 295.

2. Dava Sobel, "Findings," *Harvard Magazine* 81.3 (January–February 1979): 15.

3. John W. Gardner, *Self-Renewal* (New York: Harper & Row, 1963): 35.

4. Abraham H. Maslow, "The Need for Creative People," *Personnel Administration* 28.3 (May–June 1965): 3–5ff.

5. Richard Crutchfield, "The Creative Process," in M. Bloomberg, ed., *Creativity* (New Haven, Conn.: College and University Press, 1973).

6. Arthur Koestler, *The Act of Creation* (New York: Macmillan, 1964), p. 96.

7. Rene Dubos, "Humanistic Biology," *American Scholar* 34.2 (Spring 1965): 179–198.

8. Alex F. Osborn, *Applied Imagination: Principles and Procedures of Creative Thinking* (New York: Charles Scribner's Sons, 1953).

9. Gardner, *Self-Renewal*, p. 71.

10. Donald W. MacKinnon, "The Nature and Nurture of Creative Talent," *American Psychologist* 17.7 (July 1962): 485, 488.

11. Gardner Murphy, *Human Potentialities* (New York: Basic Books, 1958), pp. 129–131.

12. Jacob W. Getzels and Mihaly Csikszentmihalyi, "Portrait of the Artist as an Explorer," *Trans-action* 3.6 (September–October 1966): 34.

13. Silvano Arieti, *Creativity: The Magic Synthesis* (New York: Basic Books, 1976).

14. "Why the Creative Student Is Out of Step in School," *National Observer*, January 13, 1964.

15. Robert Presthus, "University Bosses: The Executive Conquest of Academe," *New Republic*, February 20, 1965, pp. 20–24.

16. Murphy, *Human Potentialities*, p. 141.

17. Rensis Likert, "Conditions for Creativity," *Management Review* 51.9 (September 1962): 70.

18. Donald C. Pelz and Frank M. Andrews, *Scientists in Organizations* (New York: John Wiley & Sons, 1966).

19. Albert E. Meyers, "Performance Factors Contributing to the Acquisition of a Psychological Advantage in Competition," *Human Relations* 19.3 (August 1966): 283–295.

20. *Business Week*, July 28, 1975.

21. Raymond E. Miles, "The Affluent Organization," *Harvard Business Review* 44.3 (May–June 1966): 106–114.

22. Seymour Levy and D. Miriam Stene, "Construct Revalidation of a Forced-Choice Rating Form," *Journal of Applied Psychology* 49.2 (April 1965): 122–125.

23. Crawford H. Greenewalt, "Notable and Quotable," *Wall Street Journal*, November 15, 1965.

24. Daniel M. Colyer, "The Good Foreman—As His Men See Him," *Personnel* 28.2 (September 1951): 140–147.

25. "How You Look to the Man under You," *Management Methods* 14.5 (August 1958): 22–28.

26. Eugene H. Fram and Herbert J. Mossien, "High Scores on the Discourtesy Scale," *Harvard Business Review* 54.1 (January 1976): 12, 146.

27. Lyman W. Porter and Edwin E. Ghiselli, "The Self Perceptions of Top and Middle Management Personnel," *Personnel Psychology* 10.4 (Winter 1957): 400, 402.

28. Ralph M. Stogdill and Ellis L. Scott, "How Does Top Management's Conception of Its Own Responsibility and Authority Influence Behavior down the Line?" *Industrial Relations News*, June 8, 1957, pp. 1–2.

29. Lawrence K. Williams, William F. Whyte, and Charles S. Green, "Do Cultural Differences Affect Workers' Attitudes?" *Industrial Relations* 5.3 (May 1966): 105–117.

30. Hjalmar Rosen, "Managers Predict Their Futures," *Personnel Administration* 25.3 (May–June 1962): 49–52.

31. Dero Saunders, "Executive Discontent," *Fortune* 54.4 (October 1956): 155.

32. John Howard, "Ambition and the Manager," *Management Today*, March 1978, p. 84.

33. Robert W. White, "Ego and Reality in Psychoanalytic Theory," *Psychological Issues* 3.3, Monograph 11 (1963): 35.

34. Harry Press, "A Painting Must Die before It Can Live," *Stanford Observer* 12.6 (April 1978): 2.

35. Douglas McGregor, *Leadership and Motivation* (Cambridge, Mass.: MIT Press, 1966), p. 29.

36. John W. Gardner, "Notable and Quotable," *Wall Street Journal*, December 15, 1965.

37. Robert Dubin, "Supervision and Productivity: Empirical Findings and Theoretical Considerations," in Robert Dubin et al., eds., *Leadership and Productivity* (San Francisco: Chandler Publishing Co., 1965), p. vii.

38. Jerald G. Bachman, Claggett C. Smith, and Jonathan A. Slesinger, "Control, Performance, and Satisfaction: An Analysis of Structural and Individual Effects," paper presented to the American Psychological Association, 1965.

39. "Societal Narcissism Seen More Often in Patients," *Psychiatric News*, July 21, 1978.

40. Roy R. Grinker, Jr., "The Poor Rich: The Children of the Super-Rich," *American Journal of Psychiatry* 135.8 (August 1978): 913–916.

41. James W. Driscoll, Daniel J. Carroll, Jr., and Timothy A. Sprecher, "The First-Level Supervisor: Still 'the Man in the Middle,' " *Sloan Management Review* 19.2 (Winter 1978): 25–37.

42. Louis A. Allen, "Leaders Who Fail Their Companies," *Business Horizons* 8.2 (Summer 1965): 79–86.

43. Moss Hart, *Act One* (New York: Random House, 1959), pp. 107–108

44. Peter J. Burke, "Authority Relations and Disruptive Behavior in Small Discussion Groups," *Sociometry* 29.3 (September 1966): 237–250.

45. Edwin E. Ghiselli, "Psychological Properties of Groups and Group Learning," *Psychological Reports* 19.1 (July–December 1966): 17–18.

46. Abraham Zaleznik, "The Human Dilemmas of Leadership," *Harvard Business Review* 41.4 (July–August 1963): 49–55; Abraham Zaleznik and Manfred Kets de Vries, *Power and the Corporate Mind* (Boston: Houghton Mifflin, 1975).

47. Eric L. Trist et al., *Organizational Choice* (London: Tavistock Institute, 1963).

48. White, "Ego and Reality in Psychoanalytic Theory," p. 68.

49. T. H. Fitzgerald, "Appraisals: Personality, Performance, and Persons," *California Management Review* 8.2 (Winter 1965): 81–86.

50. Herbert H. Meyers, Emanuel Kay, and John R. P. French, Jr., "Split Roles in Performance Appraisal," *Harvard Business Review* 43.1 (January–February 1965): 123–129.

51. Harry Levinson, *Emotional Health: In the World of Work* (New York: Harper & Row, 1964), p. 268.

52. Personal communication.

53. "The Bookworm Turns: More Collegians Now Grade Their Teachers," *Wall Street Journal*, January 3, 1966.

54. Leopold W. Gruenfeld and Peter Weissenberg, "Supervisory Characteristics and Attitudes toward Performance Appraisals," *Personnel Psychology* 19.2 (Summer 1966): 143–151.

55. See Homans, "Effort, Supervision and Productivity" in Robert Dubin, *Leadership and Productivity: Some Facts of Industrial Life* (San Francisco: Chandler, 1965).

12. Mastery Needs

1. Edith Jacobson, *The Self and the Object World* (New York: International Universities Press, 1964).

2. Dero Saunders, "Executive Discontent," *Fortune* 54.4 (October 1956): 155.

3. H. Marshall McLuhan and Quentin Fiore, *The Medium is the Message* (New York: Random House, 1967).

4. Alvin Toffler, *Future Shock* (New York: Random House, 1970).

5. John Howard, "Ambition and the Manager," *Management Today* March 1978, p. 83.

6. Leo Cherne, "Mediocrity in the Future?" *Industrial Relations News*, July 17, 1965, p. 4.

7. John W. Gardner, *Self-Renewal* (New York: Harper & Row, 1963), p. 59.

8. David C. McClelland, "Power is a Great Motivator," *Harvard Business Review* 54.2 (March–April 1976): 100–110.

9. David C. McClelland, "That Urge to Achieve," *Think* 32.6 (November–December 1966): 19. See also Ralph D. Norman, "The Inter-personal Values of Parents of Achieving and Non-Achieving Gifted Children," *Journal of Psychology* 64.1 (September 1966): 49–57.

10. Paul E. McGhee and Richard C. Teevan, "The Childhood Development of Fear of Failure Motivation," paper presented to the American Psychological Association, September 4, 1965.

11. McClelland, "That Urge to Achieve."

12. Carol C. Nadelson, Malkah T. Notman, and Mona B. Bennett, "Success or Failure: Psychotherapeutic Considerations for Women in Conflict," *American Journal of Psychiatry* 135.9 (September 1978): 1092–1096.

13. Matina S. Horner, "Femininity and Successful Achievement: Basic Inconsistency;" in J. M. Bardwick, E. Douran, M. S. Horner, and D. Gutman, *Feminine Personality and Conflict* (Belmont, Calif.: Brooks Cole Publishing Co., 1970), pp. 45–76.

14. "Compulsive Gambler Diagnosed: A Success Type with a Disease," *New York Times*, December 10, 1978, p. 103.

15. David C. McClelland, "Toward a Theory of Motive Acquisition," *American Psychologist* 20.5 (May 1965): 321–333; Robert A. Stringer, "Achievement Motivation and Management Control," *Personnel Administration* 29.6 (November–December 1966): 3–5.

16. Douglas McGregor, *The Professional Manager*, ed. Warren G. Bennis (New York: McGraw-Hill, 1967) p. 129.

17. Virgil B. Day, address to the Congress of American Industry, Na-

tional Association of Manufacturers, New York City, December 5, 1963.

18. Richard Nason, "Harvardmen vs. Big Business," *Dun's Review* 83.1 (January 1964): 41-52ff.

19. Lyndall F. Urwick, "The Line/Staff Impasse—A Footnote," *Management Review* 56.1 (January 1967): 50-53. See also R. B. Zajonc and O. M. Wolfe, "Cognitive Consequences of a Person's Position in a Formal Organization," *Human Relations* 19.2 (May 1966): 139-150.

20. Roy W. Menninger, "What Values Are We Giving Our Children?" address to the Values Conference, Denver, Colorado, October 12, 1963.

21. Bernard J. Muller-Thym, "Practices in General Management: New Directions for Organizational Practices," American Society of Mechanical Engineers, paper no. 60-WA-59 (1960), p. 7.

22. Quoted in Henry Brandon, "Schlesinger at the White House," *Harper's* 229.1370 (July 1964): 56.

23. McClelland, "Toward a Theory of Motive Acquisition."

24. Gardner, *Self-Renewal*, p. 20.

25. Hudson Hoagland, "Notable and Quotable," *Wall Street Journal*, May 5, 1964.

26. Shirley Tuska and Benjamin Wright, "The Influence of a Teacher Model on Self-Conception during Teacher Training and Experience," *Proceedings of the 73rd Annual Convention of the American Psychological Association*, 1965, pp. 297-298.

27. Robert L. Swinth, "Certain Effects of Training Goals on Subsequent Task Performance," *Occupational Psychology* 40.3 (July 1966): 164.

28. David E. Berlew and Douglas T. Hall, "The Socialization of Managers: Effects of Expectations on Performance," *Administrative Science Quarterly* 11.2 (September 1966): 221.

29. Abram T. Collier, *Men, Management, and Values* (New York: Harper & Row, 1962); Louis W. Norris, "Moral Hazards of an Executive," *Harvard Business Review* 38.5 (September–October 1960): 72-79; Raymond C. Baumhart, "How Ethical Are Businessmen?" *Harvard Business Review* 39.4 (July–August 1961): 6-7ff.

30. William D. Guth and Renato Tagiuri, "Personal Values and Corporate Strategy," *Harvard Business Review* 43.5 (September–October 1965): 123-135.

31. Robert Waelder, "Conflict and Violence," *Bulletin of the Menninger Clinic* 30.5 (September 1966): 270, 274.

32. F. W. Richardson, *Conference Board Record*, July 1975.

33. Edwin A. Fleischman and James A. Salter, "Relations between the Leader's Behavior and His Empathy toward Subordinates," *Journal of Industrial Psychology* 1.3 (September 1963): 79-84.

34. Jeanne Lampl-de Groot, "Ego Ideal and Super Ego," *Psychoanalytic Study of the Child*, vol. 17 (New York: International Universities Press, 1962).

35. Ernest Jones, *Papers on Psychoanalysis*, 4th ed. (London: Balliere, 1938), p. 53.

36. Heinz Hartmann and Rudolph M. Lowenstein, "Notes on the Superego," *Psychoanalytic Study of the Child*, vol. 18.

37. Roy Schafer, "The Loving and Beloved Superego," ibid., vol. 15.

38. Kurt Goldstein, *The Organism* (New York: American Book Co., 1939), p. 88.

39. Abraham Maslow, *Personality and Motivation* (New York: Harper & Bros., 1954), p. 91.

40. See A. E. Hotchner, *Papa Hemingway* (New York: Random House, 1966); and A. A. Rogow, *James Forrestal: A Study of Personality, Politics, Policy* (New York: Macmillan, 1964).

41. Enid Nemy, "Professor Says Femininity May Block Career Success," *New York Times*, September 14, 1979, p. B6.

42. Sigmund Freud, "Group Psychology and the Analysis of the Ego," *The Standard Edition of the Complete Psychological Works of Sigmund Freud*, vol. 18 (London: Hogarth Press, 1961), p. 131. See also Joseph Sandler, "On the Concept of Superego," *Psychoanalytic Study of the Child*, vol. 15.

43. Karl Menninger, with Martin Mayman and Paul Pruyser, *The Vital Balance* (New York: Viking Press, 1963).

44. Erik H. Erikson, "Identity and the Life Cycle," *Psychological Issues* 1.1 (1959): 111.

45. Ibid., p. 98.

46. Lampl-de Groot, "Ego Ideal and Super Ego."

47. Schafer, "The Loving and Beloved Superego," p. 183.

13. Change: The One Constant

1. "And When You Just Plain Don't Know?" *The Levinson Letter*, March 3, 1975, p. 1.

2. SRI International Center for Research on Stress and Health, *New York Times*, December 31, 1978, sect. 4, p. 7.

3. Thomas H. Holmes and Richard H. Rahe, "The Social Readjustment Rating Scale," *Journal of Psychosomatic Research* 2 (1967): 216.

4. Nicholas Lemann, "Success in America," *Washington Monthly* 9.5. and 9.6 (July–August 1977): 48–53.

5. James Brian Quinn, "Strategic Change: 'Logical Incrementalism,'" *Sloan Management Review* 20.1 (Fall 1978): 7–21.

6. "Facing the Realities of Leaving," *The Levinson Letter*, July 1, 1977, p. 2.

7. Philip C. Shaak and Milton M. Schwartz, "Uniformity of Policy Interpretation among Managers in the Utility Industry," *Academy of Management Journal* 16.1 (March 1973): 77–83.

8. Charles Peters, "The Old Pro and the Comeback Kid," *Washington Monthly* 11.1 (March 1979): 32–35.

9. Douglas W. Bray and Ann Howard, "Keeping in Touch with Success: A Mid-Career Portrait at AT&T," *Wharton Magazine* 3.2 (Winter 1979): 28–33.

10. "Where Do I Go From Here?" *The Levinson Letter*, October 17, 1977, p. 2.

11. Seymour B. Sarason, *Work, Aging, and Social Change*, (New York: Free Press, 1977).

12. Interviews with Wheelock Whitney and William G. Damroth,

"Don't Call It 'Early Retirement,' " *Harvard Business Review* 53.5 (September–October 1975): 103–118.

13. David L. Krantz, "The Santa Fe Experience: In Search of a New Life: Radical Career Change in a Special Place," in *Work, Aging, and Social Change*, by Seymour B. Sarason (New York: Free Press, 1977).

14. Theodore Leavitt, "The Industrialization of Service," *Harvard Business Review* 54.5 (September–October 1976): 63–74.

15. Tobias Brocher, "Diagnosis of Organizations, Communities, and Political Units," *Bulletin of the Menninger Clinic* 40.5 (September 1976): 513–530.

16. Ronald N. Taylor, "Age and Experience as Determinants of Managerial Information Processing and Decision Making Performance," *Academy of Management Journal* 18.1 (March 1975): 74–81.

17. "A Decompression Tank for Xerox Executives," *Business Week*, May 16, 1977, p. 64.

18. "Who is Responsible for Psychological Injury?" *The Levinson Letter*, October 15, 1976, p. 2.

14. You Can't Win Them All

1. Karl Menninger, *Man against Himself* (New York: Harcourt, Brace, 1938).

2. Augustus Napier and Carl Whitaker, *The Family Crucible* (New York: Harper & Row, 1978).

3. Robert R. Blake and Jane S. Mouton, *The Managerial Grid* (Houston: Gulf Publishing Co., 1964), p. 19; Eugene E. Jennings, *The Executive: Autocrat, Bureaucrat, Democrat* (New York: Harper & Row, 1962), p. 114.

4. Harry Levinson, "The Abrasive Personality," 56.3 *Harvard Business Review* (May–June 1978): 86–94.

5. Robert F. Kahn et al., *Organizational Stress: Studies in Role Conflict and Ambiguity* (New York: John Wiley & Sons, 1964).

6. David Halberstam, *The Best and the Brightest* (New York: Random House, 1972).

7. Edgar H. Schein, *Organizational Psychology* (Englewood Cliffs, N.J.: Prentice-Hall, 1965).

8. Norman Dixon, *On the Psychology of Military Incompetence* (New York: Basic Books, 1976).

9. H. R. Trevor-Roper, review of *A Man Called Intrepid: The Secret War*, by William Stevenson, *New York Review of Books* 23.8 (May 13, 1976): 3.

10. "The Tragedy of Misemployment," *Futurist* 12.4 (August 1978): 213.

11. Charles L. Hughes, "Help Wanted. Present Employees Please Apply," *Personnel*, 51.4 (July–August 1974): 36–45.

12. Harry Levinson, "The Psychologist in Industry," *Harvard Business Review* 37.5 (September–October 1959): 93–100.

13. See Harry Levinson, *Executive Stress* (New York: New American Library, 1975); *Psychological Man* (Cambridge, Mass.: The Levinson Institute, 1976).

14. Ralph G. Hirschowitz, "Managing Termination: I," Addendum: *The Levinson Letter*, 1977, 1–6.

15. William A. Greene, Sidney Goldstein, and Arthur J. Moss, "Psychosocial Aspects of Sudden Death," *Archives of Internal Medicine* 129.5 (May 1972): 725–731.

16. William R. Cunnick, Jr., and Norbert J. Smith, "Occupationally Related Emotional Problems," *New York State Journal of Medicine* 77.11 (September 1977): 1737–1741.

17. Thomas D. Taber, Jeffrey T. Walsh, and Robert A. Cooke, "Developing a Community-Based Program for Reducing the Social Impact of a Plant Closing," *Journal of Applied Behavioral Science* 15.2 (April–June 1979): 133–155.

18. Martin Abramson, "Recycling the Discarded Exec," *TWA Ambassador*, August 1978, pp. 38–54.

19. Winslow Hunt, "Sense of Effort Said to Reflect Sense of Guilt," *Psychiatric News*, February 18, 1977, p. 36.

15. Strengthening The Organization

1. Robert M. Guion, "The Hawthorne Type—among Others," in Eugene L. Cass and Frederick G. Zimmer, eds., *Man and Work in Society* (New York: Van Nostrand Reinhold, 1975), pp. 3–18.

2. James Robbins, "Firms Try Newer Way to Slash Absenteeism as Carrot and Stick Fail," *Wall Street Journal*, March 14, 1979, pp. 1–35.

3. Kathleen R. Garrison and Paul M. Muchinsky, "Evaluating the Concept of Absentee-Proneness with Two Measures of Absence," *Personnel Psychology* 30.3 (Autumn 1977): 389–393.

4. Jean R. Renshaw, "He Can't Even Manage His Own Family," *Wharton Magazine* 1 (Winter 1977): 42–47.

5. Rene Dubos, "The Despairing Optimist," *American Scholar* 45.1 (Winter 1976/77): 10.

6. Richard H. Franke and James D. Kaul, "The Hawthorne Experiments: First Statistical Interpretation," *American Sociological Review* 43.5 (October 1978): 623–642.

7. Agis Salpukas, "Work Democracy Tested at Scandinavian Plants," *New York Times*, November 11, 1974, p. 1.

8. Richard E. Walton, "Work Innovations in the United States," *Harvard Business Review* 57.4 (July–August 1979): 88–98.

9. Fred Best, "Recycling People: Work Sharing through Life Scheduling," *Futurist* 7.1 (February 1978): 5.

10. Karen Winkler, "Two Who Share One Academic Job Say the Pro's Outweigh the Con's," *Chronicle of Higher Education* 19.14 (December 3, 1979): 3–4.

11. Richard Walton, "Work Innovations."

12. Irmtraud S. Seeborg, "The Influence of Employee Participation in Job Redesign," *Journal of Applied Behavioral Science* 14.1 (January–March 1978): 87.

13. J. Kenneth White, "Individual Differences and the Job Quality—

Worker Response Relationship: Review, Integration, and Comments," *Academy of Management Review* 3.2 (April 1978): 267–280.

14. Don R. Lipsett, "The Doctor as Patient," *Psychiatric Opinion* 12.5 (May 1975): 20–25.

15. Richard Sennett, "The Boss's New Clothes," *New York Review of Books*, February 22, 1979, p. 42.

16. "Democracy in Minneapolis," *Time*, April 23, 1979, p. 49.

17. James O'Toole, "The Uneven Record of Employee Ownership," *Harvard Business Review* 57.6 (November–December 1979): 185–197.

18. "Strategy in Working with People," *Royal Bank of Canada Monthly Letter* 58.2 (February 1977): 1.

19. Michael R. Cooper, Brian S. Morgan, Patricia Mortenson Foley, and Leon B. Kaplan, "Changing Employee Values: Deepening Discontent?" *Harvard Business Review* 57.1 (January–February 1979): 117–125.

20. James Gavin, *On to Berlin* (New York: Viking, 1978).

21. Harry Levinson, "How to Speak Up to the Boss," Addendum, *The Levinson Letter*, 1978.

Index